American Tariff Policy towards The Philippines

American Tariff Policy towards The Philippines

1898-1946

PEDRO E. ABELARDE, PH.D.
Formerly of the
DEPARTMENT OF POLITICAL SCIENCE
UNIVERSITY OF THE PHILIPPINES

King's Crown Press
Morningside Heights, New York
1947

Printed in the United States of America
The Vermont Printing Company

KING'S CROWN PRESS
is a division of Columbia University Press organized for the purpose of making certain scholarly material available at minimum cost. Toward that end, the publishers have adopted every reasonable economy except such as would interfere with a legible format. The work is presented substantially as submitted by the author, without the usual editorial attention of Columbia University Press.

HMS

TO JOSEPH P. CHAMBERLAIN

Foreword

THE PURPOSE of this study has been to show the role of the Congress of the United States in handling tariff legislation for the Philippines. Over the course of years, since that day when Admiral Dewey's fleet of light cruisers so changed the destiny of the Filipino people, the Philippines have been the subject of much legislation the effects of which have entered so deeply into the economic life of the inhabitants of those Islands that, with the dawn of independence, they find that the patterns so formed cannot easily be changed. Their ultimate effect on the social life of the Filipinos under an independent government is still to be determined.

A detailed examination of the making of tariff laws, even if they determine the welfare of millions of people, is on the surface a tedious as well as a dry and uninteresting enterprise. But implied throughout this account of the development of American tariff policy in the Philippines is the tug of war between conflicting interests, between idealism and a considerably narrower policy—between immediate advantage and ultimate benefit.

The author is not one of those who feel that Philippine dependence for nearly fifty years upon the United States has been bad for the Islands; quite the contrary. But wherever the Philippines may eventually arrive, and whatever the form and philosophy of government which might be instituted there, it is certain that the laws the development of which is here described will have in large measure prescribed the result. That the result will not be of disadvantage to the United States has, I feel, already been demonstrated by the loyalty of the overwhelming majority of the Filipino people to their common ideals with the American people during the war. It is essential, however, that this close relation between them should not be allowed to deteriorate for want of continued sympathy and understanding and be permitted to bog down in the slough of postwar inertia and indifference.

This study was undertaken during the Fall of 1933, and results from a suggestion made by the late Professor Parker T. Moon. But a series of events ultimately topped by the war delayed its appearance. It is unfortunate, therefore, that this great scholar cannot read the result of his inspiration. From 1936 on, Professor Joseph P. Chamberlain has been my guide and friend. It is not too much to say that without his help this work would never have appeared.

To Professors Charles Cheney Hyde, Philip C. Jessup and Lindsay Rogers I am grateful for their friendly advice. To Professor James W. Angell I express my sincere appreciation for many valuable suggestions. I also wish to thank Miss Mariana Smith for helping me go over the proofs of this book. My thanks are also due to Mr. E. Llamas Rosario, Director of the Philippine Research Bureau, for extending to me ungrudgingly the clerical facilities of the Bureau, and to Mr. Manuel A. Adeva for permission to use part of my article which was published in *The Filipino Student Bulletin*. There remains one person who has not only shared with me the vicissitudes of preparing this study but who also has been the source of much-needed inspiration, "my silent partner." To her my profoundest thanks are due.

For all statements of fact and expressions of opinion in this work the author is solely responsible.

PEDRO E. ABELARDE

New York: December, 1946

Contents

Introduction

THE UNITED STATES came into possession of the Philippine Islands as an incident of the Spanish-American War.

While the manner of the Philippine acquisition had the appearance of accident, the industrial development of the United States, which was greatly accentuated after the Civil War, together with the increase in wealth and the "uncontainable expansive force" of the industrial genius of the American people compelled them to seek outlets for their ever-increasing capital[1] and to find new opportunities for their enterprise and to re-examine their most revered political maxims in the light of changed conditions.[2] Viewed in this light, therefore, the quarrel with Spain merely served as a definite taking-off place for the flight which had to be made.

Hence, notwithstanding the possible influence which the then prevailing conditions in the Far East might have had upon the final decision of President McKinley on the acquisition of the Philippines, commercial motives were among the primary causes for the ultimate insistence by the Administration on the cession of the entire Archipelago. Official declarations and statements by persons close to the Administration re-enforce this view.[3] On the other hand, to a good

[1] Mr. Charles A. Conant, who later became one of the tariff experts of the Philippine Commission, maintained that the increasing capital in the United States was one of the potent factors in America's adventure in the Philippines. *United States in the Orient,* 1900.

Professor Thurman W. Van Metre tells us that, having recovered from the worst effects of the depression of 1893-1894, "the United States entered upon a period of remarkable industrial development, which soon gave the country a leading place among the industrial nations of the world." *Economic History of the United States,* 1921, p. 541 *et seq.*

[2] See article of Frank A. Vanderlip, then Assistant Secretary of the Treasury, entitled "Facts about the Philippines, with a discussion of pending problems," *The Century Magazine,* August, 1898, Vol. LVI, p. 555 *et seq.*

[3] See copy of the wire of the Secretary of the Navy to Admiral Dewey of August 13, 1898 regarding the desire of the President for information about commercial advantages of the Islands and Dewey's reply in the *Cong. Record,* 56th Cong., 1st Sess., Part I, p. 895. See also Frank A. Vanderlip, *op. cit.* For a report of President McKinley's

many Americans the Philippine acquisition offered a fresh field for their missionary enthusiasm.[4]

Under the command of Major General Wesley Merritt the expeditionary forces effected the surrender of the city of Manila on August 13, 1898, after the signature of the Peace Protocol in Washington the day before.[5] Seven days later, the Manila custom house was re-opened, and the resumption of commercial relations between that city and the outside world took place.

Since, in general, trade and commerce motivated, to a large extent, the Philippine acquisition, it would seem logical to expect that at the outset the commercial policy of the American Government in the Philippine Islands as expressed in the laws enacted by the Congress should have been predicated upon the general prosperity of the Filipinos. The increase in the general purchasing power of the Filipino people which would accrue would be profitable not only to those Americans who might settle in the Islands but also to those who might engage in trade and commerce there. Not long after the ratification of the Treaty of Paris, however, certain American interests began to fear the possibility of being harmed by the competition of Philippine products.

The conflicting claims of these vested interests revolved around two major issues, the determination of protected industries to oppose concessions to foreign goods in the home market, and the desire of exporting industries to increase their markets abroad. In the famous "Insular Cases" the Supreme Court of the United States, by ruling that the American Constitution did not in its entirety follow the flag in the

---

speech at Hastings, Iowa, in the *New York Tribune*, October 14, 1898, his speech at Terre Haute, Indiana, two days later, *Ibid.*, October 16, 1898, and his speech at Chicago, *Ibid.*, October 19, 1898.

[4] See President McKinley's statement purported to have been made before a delegation of Methodist dignitaries, cited in Charles S. Olcott, *Life of William McKinley*, Vol. II, pp. 110-111.

[5] The pertinent provision of this Protocol relative to the Philippines was as follows: Article III—"The United States will occupy and hold the city, bay and harbor of Manila, pending the conclusion of the treaty of peace which shall determine the control, disposition and government of the Philippines." *Sen. Doc. No. 62*, Part II, pp. 828-830, 55th Cong., 3rd Sess.

Hostilities were not proclaimed suspended until M. Cambon had on the 12th received from Spain authority to sign the Protocol in her behalf; and he and Secretary of State Day were putting their pens to it at about the hour the American forces were preparing to enter Manila (about 5 P.M. on August 12 in Washington and about 6 A.M. on August 13 in Manila). See James A. Le Roy, *The Americans in the Philippines*, Vol. I, p. 356.

Philippines, paved the way to the reconciliation of these two major issues by Congressional action insofar as the Islands were concerned.

Inspired by Mr. Elihu Root, Secretary of War, the government of the Philippines (under the President through his power as Commander-in-Chief) laid down laws for the new dependency with paramount consideration of the needs of the situation in the Islands and their treasury, which under Congressional control were less strongly urged than the interests of the American producers and exporters.[6] An outline of Congressional policy was curtly expressed by the late Senator Henry Cabot Lodge in his keynote speech delivered on June 20, 1900 as the Permanent Chairman of the Republican National Convention held in Philadelphia. He said: "We make no hypocritical pretense of being interested in the Philippines solely on account of others. While we regard the welfare of these people as a sacred trust, we regard the welfare of the American people first."[7]

This study of the Congress acting as the body which determined the American economic policy in the Philippines is divided into five chronological periods, namely (1) August 20, 1898 to March 8, 1902 (2) March 8, 1902 to August 5, 1909 (3) August 5, 1909 to October 3, 1913 (4) October 3, 1913 to March 24, 1934 and (5) March 24, 1934 to March 1946.

[6] Secretary of War Root, in his report to the President under date of November 29, 1899, pointed out that the disturbed internal conditions of the Philippines "have greatly reduced the possibilities of revenue from internal taxation, and the principal source of revenue has been the customs duties. These have been levied under tariffs established . . . on the basis of the Spanish tariffs, with such modifications as seemed best adapted to the interests of the islands." *Report* of the Secretary of War for the fiscal year ended June 30, 1899, Vol. I, Part I, p. 19.

[7] Republican Party, *Official Proceedings of the Twelfth Republican National Convention held in the city of Philadelphia*, June 19-21, 1900, p. 88.

1: Customs Tariff under the Military Government

(August 20, 1898 to March 8, 1902)

On May 19, 1898, President McKinley, acting under his authority as Commander-in-Chief of the armed forces of the United States, instructed the Secretary of War that the occupation of any part of the Philippines would be that of a military occupation and that "the taxes and duties payable by the inhabitants to the former government become payable to the military occupant, unless he sees fit to substitute for them other rates or modes of contribution to the expenses of government."[1] Furthermore, President McKinley directed the opening of "all ports and places in the Philippines which may be in actual possession of our land and naval forces . . . while our military occupation may continue, to the commerce of all neutral nations, as well as our own, in articles not contraband of war, and upon payment of the prescribed rates of duty which may be in force at the time of importation."[2]

On August 14, 1898, following the occupation of the city of Manila the day before, General Wesley Merritt, as commanding general and military governor of that part of the Philippines under American control, issued a proclamation[3] to the people of the Philippines substantially in the language of President McKinley's instruction of May 19, 1898. General Merritt assured the Filipino people of the friendly intention of the American Government toward them and "that so long as they preserve the peace and perform their duties toward the representatives of the United States, they will not be disturbed in their persons and property, except in so far as may be found necessary for the good of the service of the United States and the benefit of the people of the Philippines."[4] He indicated also that the port of Manila and all other ports and places in the Islands under American control would

[1] *Messages and Papers of the Presidents*, Vol. X, 1897-1909, p. 346.

[2] *Ibid.*

[3] For a copy of General Merritt's proclamation, see William Cameron Forbes, *The Philippine Islands*, Vol. II, Appendix IV.

[4] W. C. Forbes, *op. cit.*, Vol. II, Appendix IV.

be opened to the commerce of all neutral nations as well as the commerce of the United States, in articles not contraband of war, upon payment of the prescribed rates of duty.[5]

When the Manila custom house was re-opened for business on August 20, 1898, General Merritt, under President McKinley's instruction of May 19, 1898, thought it advisable to continue the Spanish tariff then found in force without, of course, the extensive preferences granted to Spanish goods.[6] While no preference or tariff reductions were accorded to American products entering the Philippines and *vice versa*,[7] materials and supplies which were to be used by the United States Army and Navy and by the Insular government were to be admitted duty free in the Islands.[8]

Although General Merritt found it advisable to continue the modified Spanish tariff, the necessity for its revision was recognized at the outset. There were two primary reasons why revision was then necessary.

In the first place, the rates of duty on commodities of prime necessity for a great many Filipinos were high while luxuries consumed mostly by the rich were taxed at lower rates. For instance, according to the figures presented by the Philippine Commission for 1899,[9] cotton cloth and rice, the poor natives' dress and food, paid 25.6 percent and 18.2 percent respectively. On the other hand, silk and prepared foods paid only 20.8 percent and 9.4 percent respectively. Then, too, applying specific duties to classes containing both high and low priced com-

[5] W. C. Forbes, *op. cit.*, Vol. II, Appendix IV.

Note: From August 20, 1898 to February 1899, customs collection was confined to Manila only.

[6] Wallace McClure, *A New American Commercial Policy as Evidenced by Section 317 of the Tariff Act of 1922.*

[7] The collection of Philippine import duties on goods from the United States and *vice versa*, and of export duties on Philippine products shipped to the United States prior to March 8, 1902 was legalized under the Act of Congress of June 30, 1906—*United States Statutes at Large*, Vol. XXXI, Part I, Chapter 3912.

On March 4, 1903, President Theodore Roosevelt approved *H. R.* 15155 which was unanimously adopted by Congress refunding the amount of duties paid on merchandise brought into the United States from Puerto Rico between April 11, 1899, and May 1, 1900, and also on merchandise brought into the United States from the Philippine Islands between April 11, 1899, and March 8, 1902.

[8] See *Customs Tariff and Regulations for the Philippine Islands with Tariff Circulars Modifying same to November 28, 1899*, Paragraphs 19, 23, 363, in *Senate Document* (hereafter cited as *Sen. Doc.*) Vol. XXV, pp. 307-322, 56th Congress, 1st Session (hereafter cited as 56th Cong., 1st Sess.) 1899-1900.

[9] *Report of the Philippine Commission* (hereafter cited as *Report*, Philippine Commission), dated November 30, 1900, pp. 99-100.

modities would discriminate in favor of the rich. This was illustrated in the practice of applying the same rate of specific duty on boots and shoes of all kinds.

Finally, under the Spanish tariff each item of import, under the existing schedules, was subject to a fixed duty. In some instances, this duty consisted of as many as six component parts, separately expressed, each of which must be calculated before the total duty on each item of import could be ascertained.

Due to unsettled conditions resulting from the Philippine insurrection, it was deemed proper by the military authorities to disturb as little and to change as gradually[10] as possible the conditions affecting trade and commerce in the Archipelago.

As noted above, the Spanish tariff was the basis of the early American tariff laws in the Philippines. In spite of the fact that it was modified from time to time,[11] its essential features were continued until November 15, 1901, when the new tariff for the Philippines promulgated by the Philippine Commission on September 17, 1901 became effective. In view of this fact, further inquiry into the essential features of the Spanish tariff system is a permissible digression.

The Spanish tariff system[12] consisted of (1) specific duties on all imports (2) surtaxes for harbor improvements (3) taxes on imports (almojarifazgo) based on "official fixed values," termed *ad valorem* duties by the military authorities (4) consumption taxes on certain imports (5) miscellaneous charges and (6) export taxes.

Specific duties on all imports were the ten percent levy on the fixed official valuation on commodities made by the Tariff Board.[13] In some

[10] See Tariff Circulars No. 7, 9, 10, 14, 18, 26, 43, 48, 50, 53, 62, 65, 68, 81, 104, 111, and 112.—*Sen. Doc.* Vol. XXV, 56th Cong., 1st Sess., (1899-1900) pp. 307-322; see also José S. Reyes, *Legislative History of America's Economic Policy Toward the Philippines*, 1923, pp. 64-65; 89-91.

[11] See Tariff Circulars Nos. 7, 9, 10, 14, 18, 26, 43, 48, 50, 53, 62, 65, 68, 81, 104, 111 and 112, *Sen. Doc.* Vol. XXV 56th Cong., 1st Sess., 1899-1900, pp. 307-322.

[12] For an historical background of this system see Carl C. Plehn, "Taxation in the Philippines," *Political Science Quarterly*, Vols. XVI and XVII, pp. 680-711, 125-148 respectively. Also *Report of the Schurman Commission to the President*, Vol. I, 1900, pp. 75-82.

[13] The board was composed of the intendent general of finances, president; the assistant intendent, vice-president; the comptroller general of the state, the collector of customs (*administrador de la aduana*), the vice-president of the Economic Society of the Friends of the Country (*Sociedad economica de amigos del pais*), one of the alternate graduate members of the board of health, and the vice-president of the board of agriculture, industry and commerce (*junta de agricultura, industria y commercio*), as members ex-officio, and twelve merchants and tradesmen appointed by royal order at the request of the intendency-general of finances; one secretary chosen by the same

instances, the reason for this tax was to give protection to the industries of the Archipelago, but the main purpose, of course, was to favor the market for Spanish goods which were exempted from the payment of these duties.

The harbor improvement tax is self-explanatory. As originally constituted, this additional tax amounted to twenty percent of the regular duties on all merchandise entering the port of Manila. Goods originating in Spain, although exempt from the regular duties, paid this tax. However, as goods from other ports of the Philippines did not pay this tax, the way was open for fraud and it became necessary in 1891 to reduce this tax to ten percent and extend it to other ports of the Islands. Collections were thereafter made by the regular customs officials. This surtax was continued by the succeeding American administration.

The so-called *ad valorem* taxes came really as a result of an experiment with taxes for loading and unloading as a possible substitute for export taxes. The result of these experiments was the two percent *ad valorem* unloading tax on all goods coming into the Islands including those from Spain. The *ad valorem* taxes were based upon a table of fixed "official values," arbitrarily placed upon all articles enumerated in the tariff and had no relation to the real value of the merchandise. This table of values was prepared in Spain and given official recognition in the Archipelago in August, 1896.[14] A year later an extraordinary tax of six percent *ad valorem* was established. This appears to have been purely a war tax. Like the unloading tax, it was based on the table of official values, and covered Spanish goods as well as those of other countries.

The American customs authorities simply added these two *ad valorem* taxes together and levied eight percent *ad valorem* upon all imports, in addition to the specific duties according to the table of official values.[15]

The consumption taxes took the form of additional import duties on spirituous liquors, beer and cider, flour and salt, petroleum and

intendency from among the chiefs of bureaus (*jefes de negociado*), and officers of the custom house, besides the chief of the bureau of customs in the intendency, who acts as vice-secretary. For more details regarding the functions of this board see *Report, Philippine Commission*, Vol. I, 1900.

[14] See C. C. Plehn, *op. cit.*, p. 134.

[15] These "official values" were arbitrarily fixed by the Spanish Government without regard to the actual value of the goods imported into the Philippines. The last one in effect at the time of the American occupation was that set forth in the *Official Gazette* of Manila, No. 228, August 27, 1896.

other mineral oils. The tariff that was prepared by the War Department, to which reference will be made presently,[16] proposed the removal of these taxes on the last five products, substituting for them an internal revenue tax on cigars and cigarettes. This proposed change, however, was found to be unwise and as a result, consumption taxes were retained *in toto*.

To the above-mentioned taxes, which constituted the tariff proper, were added such miscellaneous charges as wharf charges and harbor dues of seventy-five cents per ton of 1,000 kilos which were imposed on all exported goods. All imported goods destined for transshipment to other ports of the Archipelago paid wharfage of twenty-five cents per ton of 1,000 kilos. Upon entry at any other port of the Islands, vessels carrying these goods paid also a tonnage tax or light-house dues of five cents per net ton and stamp taxes on the ship's papers: in all, the latter taxes amounted to $2.

In order to show how the additional taxes modified the original specific duties, Professor Carl C. Plehn[17] has graphically presented the case of 100 kilos of salt imported into the Islands. According to him the total duty on this quantity would be calculated as follows:[18]

a. Specific duty (*derecho de arancel*)	₱0.650
b. Surtax for Manila harbor (10 percent of the above duty)	₱0.065
c. 6 percent plus 2 percent *ad valorem* (on official value of ₱0.40)	₱0.032
d. Consumption tax	₱1.00
Total duty	₱1.747

(A peso (₱) equals $0.50 at par)

Another good example of the difficulty of arriving at the duty is represented in paragraph 174 under which oak staves are classified. The duty is forty cents (Mexican) per 1,000. Now to arrive at the total amount of duty to be collected upon 1,000 oak staves, there must be added together:[19]

a. The duty as per tariff	$ 0.40
b. Ten percent of the above duty	$ 0.04
c. Eight percent of the official value ($220)	$17.60
Total duty	$18.04

[16] *Infra*, p. 20.

[17] Professor Carl C. Plehn, by virtue of Act No. 7 of the Philippine Commission passed September 26, 1900, was appointed chief statistician of the Philippine Government. Together with Mr. Lyons, he assisted in the preparation of the tariff bill promulgated later by the Commission as Tariff Act No. 230.

[18] *Political Science Quarterly*, Vol. XVII, pp. 134-135.

[19] For the rates of duty of the Spanish tariff see *Sen. Doc. No. 134* (1901-1902) Exhibit D, 57th Cong., 1st Sess., pp. 69-81.

It was but natural that this method of taxation would cause much friction, annoyance and misunderstanding. American merchants, more especially, were prone to look up the specific duty and were greatly irritated by the additional taxes which they regarded as impositions.[20] "Yet, although the total duties on any article never varied per unit of weight or other measure, the Spanish system of a separate calculation of each of these duties was continued for two years by the American Administration."[21]

The principal exports of the Islands, namely, hemp, sugar, tobacco and coconuts, were each subject to a specific export duty, expressed in pesos, to wit:[22]

Hemp 100 kilos gross	₱0.75
Sugar 100 kilos gross	.10
Coconuts, fresh and dried copra, 100 kilos gross	.10
Tobacco, manufactured, of all kinds and whatever origin, 100 kilos gross	₱3.00
Tobacco, raw, grown in the provinces of Cagayan, Isabela and Nueva Biscaya, 100 kilos gross	₱3.00
Tobacco, raw, grown in the Visayas and Mindanao, 100 kilos gross	₱2.00
Tobacco, raw, grown in other provinces of the Archipelago, 100 kilos gross	₱3.00

Note:—Certificates of origin of raw tobacco may be required by the customs authorities when proof of the place of production is necessary.

Export duties were in operation for many years and a revenue of as high as $350,000 a year was collected. In the years 1891-1892 these duties were suspended, as already noted, and an effort was made to obtain an equal revenue in the form of taxes for loading and unloading. Export duties were restored, however, in 1893 and were continued in force until 1913. It may be observed in passing that, with the exception of Manila hemp, of which the Philippines had a natural monopoly, an export tax tends to increase cost and thereby lessen the competitive advantage of the Philippine product. The export tax on Manila hemp could be passed on to the consumer.

The above-stated apportionment of indirect taxation was, according to Governor Taft, in conformity with Spanish ideas as the most efficacious means of raising revenues.[23]

[20] Charles B. Elliott, *The Philippines to the End of the Military Regime,* p. 262.

[21] *Political Science Quarterly,* Vol. XVII, p. 134.

[22] See *Customs Tariff and Regulations for the Philippine Islands, in Sen. Doc.,* Vol. XXV (1899-1900), p. 286.

[23] See *Hearings before the Senate Committee on the Philippines,* 57th Cong., 1st Sess., 1901-1902, p. 151, Statement of Hon. William Howard Taft.

Philippine products were given preferential treatment in the Spanish market. The law of 1882 provided that, with the exception of tobacco, rum, sugar, cacao, chocolate and coffee, the products of the Archipelago were to be admitted free of duty. After 1892, with the exception of sugar—made subject to an internal tax, higher than that paid by the native Spanish products—products of the Islands were admitted free in Spain.

The preferential treatment given to the above-named products of the Archipelago in the Spanish market was used later[24] to support the arguments of both Americans and Filipinos for a more liberal treatment of Philippine products in American markets. A reduction of at least fifty percent of the Dingley rates on Philippine sugar and tobacco, it was pointed out, would tend to compensate the Filipinos for their loss of the Spanish market.[25] On the other hand, American sugar and tobacco interests found a strong argument in the survey made by the Department of Agriculture on Philippine trade during the Spanish rule in the Islands.[26] This study indicated that from 1887 to 1891 Spanish imports from the Philippines averaged only $3,819,426 while the averages of the United States and the United Kingdom for the same period were $8,785,988 and $8,729,072 respectively. For the years 1892 to 1896 the average of the Spanish importation from the Philippines was $3,855,165 against $6,053,232 for the United States and $8,844,026 for the United Kingdom. However, as we shall see presently, there were also other reasons which made it impracticable then to institute a more liberal trade policy in the Philippines.

In anticipation of the American occupation of the Philippines, President McKinley, acting under his authority as Commander-in-Chief of the armed forces of the United States, issued an order on July 12, 1898 which directed "that upon the occupation of any ports and places in the Philippine Islands by the forces of the United States the following tariff of duties and taxes, to be levied and collected as a military contribution and regulations for the administration thereof, shall take effect and be in force in the ports and places so occupied."[27]

On July 13, 1898[28] Secretary of War Russell A. Alger, after consultation with the United States Treasury Department, sent the President's

[24] See *Report, Philippine Commission* (1903) Part I, Exhibit M, p. 357; See also *Infra,* Chapter III.

[25] *Report, Philippine Commission* (1903) Part I, Exhibit M, p. 357.

[26] *Bulletin No. 14,* Department of Agriculture, 1898.

[27] *Sen. Doc.* Vol. XXV, 56th Cong., 1st Sess. (1899-1900), p. 269.

[28] *Correspondence Relating to the War with Spain,* from April 15, 1898 to July 30, 1902, Vol. I, p. 738. Also *Report, Philippine Commission,* November 30, 1900, pp. 94-95.

order to the Philippines with the tariff for the Islands, prepared by the War Department and entitled "Regulations for the Guidance of Officers Concerned in the Collection of Duties on Imports and Exports, Taxes, and Other Charges and Exactions to Be Levied and Collected as a Military Contribution at Ports and Places in the Possession of or under the Control of the Forces of the United States, in the Philippines."[29] These documents were received in the Archipelago early in September,[30] several weeks after the city of Manila was reopened to foreign trade. On September 24 a circular was issued by order of the military governor putting this new customs tariff into effect on October 1, 1898.[31]

Close on the heels of this announcement came many protests, petitions and requests from local merchants and persons doing business in Manila. It was claimed that more time was required for needed readjustments. Mention was also made of the fact that many merchants bought goods in Spain at high market rates for the purpose of securing the trade privileges on home products, but were unable to have delivery made in Manila on account of the War. It was fair, so it was claimed, that the *status quo ante* in respect to Spanish trade privileges be extended to these goods to avoid the great pecuniary loss which otherwise must be suffered.[32]

The strength of these claims, when backed with documentary evidence, can hardly be over-emphasized. Then, too, necessary re-adjustments would mean a longer period of time than was offered in the announcement. Judged on these two considerations alone, governmental leniency seemed justified.

Already, on September 24, General Otis had appointed a board of officers to consider the modification of the taxes on tobacco, cigars and cigarettes. An internal revenue tax, a feature unknown in the Spanish tariff, amounting to one dollar per thousand had been laid upon all cigars and cigarettes manufactured in the Islands or sold for consumption therein. As already indicated, this tax upon cigars and cigarettes was intended as a substitute for the consumption tax upon beer and cider, flour and salt, petroleum and other mineral oils.

[29] *Sen. Doc.* Vol. XXV, pp. 271-326; See also *Infra*, pp. 26-28.

[30] *Report, Military Governor of the Philippine Islands on Civil Affairs*, 1899, pp. 313-314; also H. Parker Willis, *Our Philippine Problem*, p. 272.

[31] *Report, Military Governor of the Philippine Islands on Civil Affairs*, 1899, pp. 313-314.

[32] *Report*, Major General E. S. Otis, 1899, pp. 14 *et seq.*, incorporated as a part of the *Annual Report of the War Department* for the fiscal year ended June 30, 1899, in three parts, Part II; also *Report, Philippine Commission*, 1901, pp. 95-101.

What the board of military officers thought would be the effect of this tax was set forth by Colonel Spurgin in the following language: "As the prices of manufactured cigars range from $9 to $100 per thousand, the tax of $1 would only slightly increase these prices; but as the prices of cigarettes manufactured in those Islands range from forty cents to $2.25 per thousand, the tax of $1 per thousand would, in this case, increase these prices about fifty percent for the higher grades, and the increase for the cheaper grades would be something over two hundred percent."[33] It was therefore apparent to both those officers and the Philippine tobacco dealers that the enforcement of this tax would mean the ultimate suppression of the manufacture of cigarettes, or "the removal of that branch of industry beyond the limits of the territory occupied by the United States in these Islands."[34]

On September 26, therefore, the board submitted its recommendation to the military governor for the suspension of the tax since nonsuspension might be prejudicial to American interests.[35]

Thus on September 29, an announcement was made that the enforcement of the modified customs tariff prepared by the War Department was to be postponed until November 10, 1898. This announcement was approved later by President McKinley, for on October 13 Secretary of War Alger communicated with General Otis ordering him to suspend the application of the Presidential order of July 12 and to continue "the Spanish tariff as now applied."[36] It was further announced that all goods leaving a Spanish port prior to April 1, 1898,[37] and arriving in Manila before November 10 were to be granted the trade privileges of the Spanish tariff.[38]

In passing, mention should be made of the fact that the administration of the customs tariff was carried out as best as might be by a customs force composed of soldier inspectors, soldier examiners, soldier bookkeepers, soldier cashiers, soldier chiefs of departments, and a few of the old Spanish contingent who had been induced to resume their duties by a higher salary and the promise of better things to come.

[33] *Report,* Lt. Col. William F. Spurgin, Collector of Customs, attached as Appendix "S" to the *Annual Report of the War Department* for the fiscal year ended June 30, 1899, Part II, pp. 313-314.

[34] *Ibid.*

[35] *Ibid.*

[36] See *Tariff Circular No. 18.*

[37] The United States Government officially declared war against Spain on April 25, 1898.

[38] *Report,* Major General E. S. Otis, 1899, p. 14. For his communications with the German Consul, dated Manila October 5 and December 21, 1898, see *Ibid.*, pp. 48-49.

That the customs administration in the Islands was not devoid of humor was shown in the fact that the majority of those who did business with the custom house did not speak English, while it was told on good authority that the only acquaintance of the majority of the customs personnel with the official language of the country was a very "expressive vocabulary" of *poco tempo vamose.*[39] It was even doubted by General James F. Smith, then collector of customs, whether "a single man responsible for the proper collection of the customs dues had ever before been placed in such relations to a customs machine as to obtain a comprehensive idea of its general operations, to say nothing of an intimate acquaintance with its complicated, delicate and difficult mechanism."[40] In view of these circumstances, the operations of the customs administration were "a trifle jerky for the first few months, and lacked the rhythm which results from perfect coördination."[41]

It was in recognition of these difficulties that a revenue expert in the person of Captain Joseph F. Evans of the volunteer subsistence department was detailed to Manila by the War Department to assist in revenue matters. On October 3, 1898, he was assigned to duty at the custom house to "make a careful consideration of trade conditions" and to "conduct an exhaustive study of the United States customs tariff prescribed for application with a view of suggesting amendments and modifications therein to render them as practical as possible to existing circumstances."[42] His report was submitted on October 24, and according to the military governor it "has given satisfaction to all parties concerned, and has worked smoothly, only a few minor amendments having been made since it became operative."[43]

To facilitate customs collection the American authorities in the Islands worked out every number of the tariff and published the con-

[39] In correct Spanish the above statement should be either, *en poco tiempo iremos* or, *iremos pronto.* Literally the above statement means "by and by we go." Quoted from *Report* of Brigadier General James F. Smith, collector of customs, attached as Appendix "P" to the *Annual Report of the War Department,* for the fiscal year ended June 30, 1901, Part II, pp. 282-308.

[40] *Ibid.*

[41] *Annual Report of the War Department* for the fiscal year ended June 30, 1901, Part II, Appendix "P."

[42] *Report,* Maj. Gen. E. S. Otis, 1899, Part II, p. 14 *et seq.*

[43] *Ibid.* See also Gen. Otis' cablegram which was received in Washington, December 3, 1898 in *Correspondence Relating to the War with Spain,* Vol. I, p. 843.

That this new tariff and regulations was expected to improve the customs administration in the Islands was admitted by Gen. J. F. Smith when he said that now. "it was possible for the American examiner to understand that the duty on 'gemelos' didn't mean a tax on twins, but on opera glasses." Quoted from his *Report,* attached as Appendix "P" to the *Annual Report of the War Department,* 1901, Part II, p. 283.

solidated duties "for the guidance of merchants and customs officers until the new tariff went into effect, November 15, 1901."[44] In many instances, as in the case of rice and the cheaper grades of cotton goods used by the poorer class of the Philippine people, the military authorities abolished the duties entirely. With the exception of commodities placed on the free list, the rates of the modified tariff on goods entering the Islands were substantially the same as the rates of the Spanish tariff.[45]

According to the Insular collector of customs, the modified tariff which took effect on November 10, 1898 and continued until November 15, 1901 was quite satisfactory both in the amount of customs revenue collected and in its general effects on the business conditions of the Islands.[46] For instance during 1893 and 1894, the last two normal years of Spanish rule, the total value of imports into the Philippines for 1893 was $25,916,734 and the total value of imports for 1894 was $28,529,777 (Mexican). The total value of exports of the Islands for 1893 was $33,137,984. The total customs revenue collected during 1893 was $4,238,814, and $4,702,951 was collected for 1894.[47]

During the first two years of the American regime, the total value of imports of the Philippines in 1899 was $40,972,472 and in 1900 it amounted to $55,544,366 (Mexican). The total customs revenue received during 1899 amounted to $9,155,598, while the total customs revenue for 1900 was $16,453,704.[48]

It might be noted that the American military authorities in the Philippines continued the two percent tax for loading and unloading and the six percent tax which was collected by the Spanish authorities in 1897 as a war tax. These two taxes were added together by the military authorities and formed the eight percent *ad valorem* duty which was based upon the "official values."[49] Although this *ad valorem* tax might have played an important role toward increasing the customs revenue in the Islands, the fact remains that, in spite of the free entry of a number of articles previously noted, the total customs revenue collected during 1899 and 1900 had increased.

[44] *Sen. Doc. No. 134*, p. 69 (57th Cong., 1st Sess.). Attached to this document as Exhibit D is an English translation of the Spanish tariff and that enforced by the military authorities upon the occupation of Manila.

[45] *Ibid.*

[46] *Report*, Brig. Gen. J. F. Smith, collector of customs, *op. cit.*, pp. 283-286.

[47] *Ibid.*

[48] *Ibid,*

[49] See *Supra*, pp. 6-7.

TARIFF REVISION

The Military authorities in the Philippines recognized at the outset the necessity of a general revision of the existing tariff. However, in view of the unsettled conditions then prevailing, the necessity of instituting gradual changes in the commerce and trade of the Islands and the desirability of allowing more time for "needed re-adjustment" made themselves apparent. Then, too, the Treaty of Paris was ultimately approved by the United States Senate, and it was subsequently promulgated by President McKinley.[50] This Treaty provided that for a period of ten years Spanish ships and merchandise entering the Philippines should be admitted on equal terms with ships and merchandise of the United States.[51] In view of these circumstances, therefore, a general revision of the existing tariff was not attempted.

The practice indulged in among European competitors during the Spanish regime was recalled. By importing competing goods in Spanish vessels by way of Barcelona and other ports of Spain, European products could claim equal treatment as promised in the Treaty.[52] This, it was pointed out, would militate not only against the revenue of the Islands but also against American trade there.[53] American business men engaged in Philippine trade and other American interests expecting to establish business or business connections in the Islands found cause for complaints.

On April 20, 1899, ten American commercial firms[54] in Manila sent a letter to the President of the San Francisco Chamber of Commerce urging that body "to use its efforts in order to obtain a reduction of

[50] The Treaty of Paris was signed December 10, 1898. Exchange of ratification was effected on April 11, 1899, and it was proclaimed by the President on the same day.

[51] See the provision of Article IV of the Treaty of Paris, quoted *Infra*, p. 243. See also the provisions of Articles XIII and XV. Article XIII provides that for a period of 10 years Spanish scientific, literary and artistic works not subversive of public order should continue to be admitted into the Philippine Islands free of duty. And Article XV provided that during the same period merchant vessels of each country not engaged in the coastwise trade should be given the same treatment "in respect of all charges, including entrance and clearance dues, light dues, and tonnage duties, as it accords to its own merchant vessels." *Sen. Doc. No. 62*, Part I, pp. 5-11, 55th Cong., 3rd Sess. (1899).

[52] See *Report, Military Governor of the Philippine Islands on Civil Affairs*, 1899, p. 314 *et seq.*

[53] *Ibid.*

[54] These commercial firms were: Henry D. Woolfe, William C. Kallin and Co., Pabst Brewing Co., The H. A. Williams Co., Macondray Co., American Commercial Co., Pacific Oriental Trading Co., Engenskjon and Woolfe, North American Trading Co., and American Philippine Co.

the customs duties now levied in these islands."[55] This letter, subsequently transmitted to the Secretary of War, pointed out that the prevailing "excessive duties" of the tariff were "continued on the plea that any diminution would militate against the interests of importers and dealers who had stocks of goods on hand or had ordered same."[56] It was maintained, however, that the reasons therefor no longer existed. These interests pointed out that "Americans and American goods labor to obtain a foothold"[57] in the Islands. Drillings and canned fruits were given as examples to illustrate how the Philippine modified tariff affected American products when imported into the Islands.[58]

A piece (40 yards) of American drillings costing, laid down in Manila with all charges, $3.18½ Mexican, had levied upon it the following duties:

Weight of piece, 6 kilos 8 grams	
1. Duty at 25 cents a kilo	$1.52
2. Ten percent additional on $1.52	.152
3. Eight percent *ad valorem* on Spanish valuation of $1.35 per kilo	.656
	$2.328

As a further illustration it was pointed out that the duty on a can of California fruit was thirty-two cents Mexican or about sixteen cents in United States currency. Under this rate it would be prohibitive to import canned fruits from the United States.[59]

They urged the reduction of at least one-half of the present rates upon articles of consumption, asked the imposition of a higher rate upon articles of luxury and a lower tariff upon productions special to the United States. Such changes, they maintained, would increase the Insular revenue by a large percentage and would enable the United States to "derive some benefits accruing from the victories gained by her soldiers and sailors, many of whom desire to settle in the Islands."[60]

With the reductions in the customs tariff they saw the opening of a new field for American "fictile[61] and textile manufacturers and the

[55] *Sen. Doc. No. 171*, 57th Cong., 1st Sess., 1901-1902, pp. 6-7.
[56] *Ibid.*
[57] *Ibid.*
[58] *Ibid.*, pp. 6-7.
[59] *Ibid.*, p. 7.
[60] *Ibid.*
[61] Fictile—relating to pottery or to molding in any soft material.

boundless productions of our agriculturists."[62] They saw no objection to the granting of a "reciprocal tariff" for all nations, for, "with a reduction in the tariff rates so arranged as to enable the people of these islands to purchase at as low a price as possible, American goods can and will compete with productions from any country in the world."[63]

Prior to the Spanish-American War, Messrs. Lanman and Kemp, New York perfume manufacturers, took advantage of the Spanish tariff in the Philippines by establishing a branch plant in Spain. Subsequent to the establishment of the American regime in the Islands and the enforcement therein of the modified tariff of November 10, 1898, the advantages their products had formerly enjoyed were done away with. In view of this fact, they addressed a letter to Honorable Russell A. Alger, Secretary of War, under date of June 29, 1899, asking for the amendment of the tariff rates on perfumery and propietary articles in order that these products might be allowed to enter the Islands "on at least as favorable conditions as those of Spain formerly did."[64]

The Chamber of Commerce of Portland, Oregon, found out that a hundred pounds of prunes costing five dollars in the United States when sent to Manila would cost, including all charges, $23.25, Mexican. On the other hand, it was figured out that, if the charge was only ten percent *ad valorem* on the same quantity of prunes laid down in Manila, the entire cost, including tariff duties and freight charges would be only $13.50 Mexican. "This," it was pointed out, "would place goods within the reach of many more people, and imports from the United States, in this respect alone, would be very much more extensive."[65] This body urged, therefore, the "revision of the customs duties as far as concerns American goods imported into Manila and the Philippine Islands."[66]

On November 22, 1899, Acting Secretary of War, George D. Meiklejohn, sent an inquiry to the Collector of Customs for the Philippines "as to the desirability of making a reduction of fifty percent in the present duties on flour, alimentary preserves, pork, butcher's products, sauces, garden produce, fruits, pork lard, bacon, newspaper, wrapping paper, butter, cheese, soaps, and pickles imported into the Philippines, as to *ad valorem* duties being based upon certified invoices at the point

[62] *Sen. Doc. No. 171*, p. 7.
[63] *Ibid.*
[64] *Ibid.*, pp. 9-11.
[65] *Ibid.*, pp. 12-13.
[66] *Ibid.*

of shipment,"[67] and as to the reduction of duty on flour, if the record showed that it was imported from other countries. He informed the Insular Collector of Customs that interested parties maintained that such changes in the tariff would be extremely desirable in order "to encourage the importation into those islands of American products."[68]

In his reply to this inquiry, Colonel Spurgin, the Insular Collector of Customs, informed the acting Secretary of War that flour imported into the Islands came chiefly from the United States. However, Australia and Japan furnished also a considerable quantity. He was of the opinion that reduction in the duties on flour at that time would neither increase the revenue nor the importation of flour from the United States. However, he urged the amendment of the tariff schedules (paragraphs 242 and 243) on canned fruits, vegetables, and other articles classified as alimentary preserves to include vegetables and fruits as preserved exclusively in their own juices, and put in cans or other receptacles. He pointed out that while large quantities of canned fruits, vegetables, and other articles classified as alimentary preserves were sent to the Islands from the United States on Government transports, these were only for the use of the troops and for sale by the United States Commissary Department to the civilian employees of the government. He pointed out that under the existing tariff, the finest grades of compound preserves such as French and Italian *pâté de foie grois,* Crosse & Blackwell's goods, and so forth, paid "no higher duty than the cheap 'pie fruits' and vegetables put up in the United States, and especially along the Pacific Coast."[69] He believed that the adoption of this amendment would increase not only the importation of that class of goods and the revenue derived therefrom, but also the amendment would be favorably received by the people in the Islands and probably would do away with the "just criticism which is now made upon the Philippine tariff by the fruit and vegetable producers and canners of the United States."[70]

The Insular Collector of Customs believed that a reduction of duties on canned meats, pork lard, bacon and cheese to an equivalent of two

[67] *Ibid*,. pp. 13-14.
Apparently what the Acting Secretary of War had in mind, was to base the *ad valorem* duties upon the certified invoices at the point of shipment rather than upon the arbitrary "Official figures" set forth in the *Official Gazette* of Manila, No. 228, August 29, 1896.

[68] *Ibid.*, pp. 13-14.

[69] *Ibid.*, pp. 14-15.

[70] *Ibid.*

dollars, gold, per hundred kilos would not affect the revenue. Neither would a reduction of fifty percent of the duties on "news prints." On the other hand, reduction would materially increase their consumption.

On the subject of butter, the Insular Collector of Customs pointed out that a reduction of the duty to an equivalent of three dollars, gold, per hundred pounds would increase its importation and revenue derived therefrom. However, the duty on "common soap," chiefly imported from the United States and England, should be allowed to remain. He recommended the reduction on the duty on perfumed soap (principally imported from France) to an equivalent of three dollars, gold, per hundred pounds, for such reduction would be beneficial to revenue.[71]

Although Colonel Spurgin admitted the complicated nature of the existing tariff and the advisability of revising the value as occasion demanded, he was of the opinion that "the present tariff will be much more easily applied by the use of fixed values (the present system) than if the *ad valorem* duties were based upon values taken from certified invoices at the port of shipment."[72]

In a cable to the War Department under date of April 13, 1900,[73] General Otis, then military governor of the Philippines, pointed out that, in view of the equality provision of Article IV of the Treaty of Paris, a general tariff reduction recommended by Colonel Spurgin was unwise. However, he emphasized the desirability of a fifty percent reduction on all canned or bottled fruits and vegetables or on all vegetables and fruits preserved exclusively in their own juices, and on canned meats, bacon, lard and butter, fresh meats and vegetables. On the whole, he wanted a low rate of duty on goods which Spain did not produce, but which could be imported from the United States, for the adoption of such reduction would be beneficial both to the Insular government and to the Filipino people. The next day, in a letter addressed to the Assistant Secretary of War, General Otis repeated his recommendations and maintained that "in the matter of canned fruits and vegetables the United States must be relied upon."[74]

In behalf of the fruit growers and canners of California, Represen-

[71] 2.2046 Lbs. = 1 Kilo.
Philippine Customs officials use kilos and pounds together frequently.

[72] *Sen. Doc. No. 171*, p. 17.

[73] *Ibid.*, p. 18.

[74] *Ibid.*

tative James C. Needham addressed a letter to the Secretary of War under date of April 7, 1900 urging the revision of the Philippine tariff schedules on all alimentary preserves to include the following provision:[75] "Vegetables and fruits preserved in any manner, except in brandy, in tins or otherwise, two cents per kilogram." He figured out that under the rate of twenty cents, Mexican, per kilogram charged on all alimentary preserves, the rate of duty "on a can of tomatoes is about twenty cents, or several times the cost price in California."[76] It was essential, therefore, that the above provision be adopted. However, if the above amendment could not be adopted, Mr. Needham thought it equitable that the California fruit growers and canners should be charged in the Philippines the same *ad valorem* rate of fifteen percent "enjoyed by the Eastern fruit growers and canners in shipping into Puerto Rico."[77] It was pointed out that the Puerto Rican rate was lower than the above rate of two cents per kilogram.

Congressman Thomas H. Tongue of Oregon emphasized the interest of the Pacific Coast States in establishing a market for flour in Eastern Asia. One of the necessary steps in this direction, he believed, would be to teach the Filipinos "to use flour, make and eat bread." He thought it essential, therefore, that "the Government, as much as possible" should "lend encouragement to this enterprise."[78]

Representative George P. Lawrence, in the interest of the Chemical Paper Company of Holyoke, Massachusetts, claimed that the rates of the Philippine tariff raised the cost of paper boxes for tobacco, cigarettes, medicine bottles, ice cream and other similar articles to the purchaser in Manila, and thereabouts, to one hundred and fifty percent. As a result of these increased rates, it was impossible to do business in Manila. On the other hand, "the same material when delivered to foreigners in Japan or China or adjacent countries pays only about fifteen percent duty."[79]

The Keystone Watch Case Company of Philadelphia urged the adoption of *ad valorem* instead of specific rates on watches. By way of illustration, it was pointed out that under the specific rates, the duty on watches would be a very inequitable one. For instance, under the Philippine modified tariff, the specific duty on watches ranged as follows:

[75] *Ibid.*, p. 21.
[76] *Ibid.*
[77] *Ibid.*
[78] *Ibid.*, p. 23.
[79] *Ibid.*, p. 24.

Gold watches	$4 each
Silver watches	$2 each
Watches of other metals	$2 each

The practice of customs officials in the Philippines had always been to include "gold filled watches" under the heading of "gold watches." Due to competition, lower grades of "gold filled watches" ranging in price from about three dollars up to forty dollars were brought into the market. It would be quite apparent that "a specific duty of four dollars each, which applies to a gold filled watch running from three dollars to forty dollars also to a gold watch which may run up as high as one hundred dollars is a very unjust one."[80] The same thing, so it was pointed out, would apply also to silver and base metal watches. The Company was of the opinion that a fifteen percent *ad valorem* rate on watches would be a maximum amount that Filipinos could stand. On the other hand, a ten percent *ad valorem* would facilitate the entry of American watches into the Islands and placed them "within the limit and reach of a large class of people."[81]

Representative John H. Ketcham, in behalf of the Borden's Condensed Milk Company of Dover Plains, New York, urged the reduction of the duty on condensed milk, for under the high rates of the existing tariff, only the cheapest known brands of milk, usually adulterated and skimmed milk, manufactured in Europe, more especially in Holland, could be sent to the Philippines. In the United States, on the other hand, "it is not permissible for any manufacturer to put up skimmed condensed milk"[82] therefore American products "can not successfully enter into competition with that which has been deprived of its butter fats."[83] If, however, the Cuban rate of duty of ten percent *ad valorem* on pure unadulterated condensed milk were to be enforced in the Philippines, American products would be placed "within the reach of the people as to prices, and the United States on a fair footing can secure the bulk of the business in this line."[84] Mr. Ketcham pointed out also that should the above recommendation be adopted, there would result a "larger income of revenue for the islands."[85]

The Cotton Export and Import Company of New York asked the

[80] *Sen. Doc. No. 171*, pp. 25-26; also pp. 27-29.
[81] *Ibid.*
[82] *Ibid.*, pp. 36-37.
[83] *Ibid.*
[84] *Ibid.*
[85] *Ibid.*

reduction of duties on toilet and laundry soaps and on canned goods in order to increase a demand for them in the Philippines. It was pointed out that on cotton cloths of both good and poor qualities, up to twenty-five threads per square millimeter there was a charge of twenty cents, Mexican, per kilo; and on cotton cloths of both good and poor qualities up to thirty-five threads per square millimeter the duty was thirty-two cents, Mexican, per kilo. In addition to these duties, there was a surtax of twenty percent on the duty, ten percent of the duty and eight percent *ad valorem.* Due to the fact that American mills did not turn out "the very cheapest fabrics so largely manufactured by the Manchester and Barcelona mills," it would be very difficult to sell American products of the same number of threads, but of better quality, in the Philippines. Therefore, tariff reduction was asked on the medium and better classes of cotton cloths of the same number of threads, as "a large business is possible in American goods."[86]

Armour and Company of Chicago, Illinois, wanted the reduction of duties on leaf lard, ham or bacon, and roast beef in order to place these products within the "reach of the average consumer," thereby making it possible to enlarge the present trade of the Company with the Philippines.[87]

Eventually these interests succeeded in convincing the Administration that tariff revision was of vital importance, and a cablegram dated June 7, 1900, was sent to General MacArthur, military governor of the Philippines, ordering him to appoint a board of officers[88] to undertake the task of revising the existing customs tariff of the Islands.

Pursuant to General Orders, No. 80, of the military governor under date of June 9, 1900, this board of military officers convened at ten o'clock in the morning of June 18, 1900 at the office of the collector of customs of Manila. The board, however, deemed it advisable to await instructions from Washington. Before they adjourned, the recorder was asked to notify in writing the three Chambers of Commerce in Manila—the American, the Manila, and the Spanish—informing them of the existence of the board, and its purpose, and to request from them and the merchants which they represented, written criticisms of the customs tariff. And to facilitate the improvement of the said tariff,

[86] *Sen. Doc. No. 171,* pp. 38-39. With reference to these *ad valorem* duties see *supra;* pp. 7, note 4.

[87] *Ibid.,* pp. 39-40.

[88] This board was composed of the following officers: Lt. Col. W. F. Spurgin, Capt. W. Wotherspoon, and Capt. Charles H. Marple.

the board asked these bodies for "specific and detailed suggestions concerning all changes, substitutions or amendments."[89]

In the meantime, Colonel Edwards, chief of the Bureau of Insular Affairs, transmitted to General MacArthur on June 15, 1900, the complaints and suggestions regarding the Philippine tariff, which had been received by the War Department for the consideration of the military officers recently appointed to revise the Philippine tariff.[90]

When the board reconvened on July 13, notices were immediately sent to the above-named commercial bodies again inviting their opinions on all matters affecting the customs tariff of the Islands either by writing or by oral statement before the board. In a number of instances individual members of the board even called in person upon merchants and importers to request of them data which would be of assistance in the framing of a "just and equitable schedule of charges."[91] Although there were numerous criticisms as to the general nature of the tariff, definite and tangible suggestions for its general improvement were sadly lacking, as indicated in the following extract from the board's letter of transmittal:[92]

> It is felt that whenever the system of charges and imposts submitted with this report, may upon actual application or upon special or particular analysis of the different sections, prove unequal or inadequate, the apathy shown by the merchants and importers in the matter directly affecting their own interests will be largely to blame therefor.

The military board, in considering the subject of American products and the duties to be levied thereon, was in doubt whether other nations—especially those in whose commercial agreements with the United States the "most favored-nation" clause occurred—could not rightfully claim the benefit of any privileges that Spain might acquire, especially under Article IV of the Treaty of Paris. This Article has the

[89] Proceedings of the board of officers to revise the United States customs tariff and regulations in the Philippine Islands, convened at Manila, June 18, 1900. Attached as Appendix "EE" to the *Annual Report of the War Department* for the fiscal year ended June 30, 1900, p. 80. Also *Sen. Doc. No. 134*, p. 4.

[90] For the information of these officers in their deliberations the following documents were also sent to the Islands, namely, copies of the latest Cuban Tariff, the Dingley Tariff and Tariff's of Foreign Countries, a copy of the report of Honorable R. P. Porter in connection with the revision of the Cuban Tariff and a copy of Bulletin No. 14, Department of Agriculture, published November 5, 1898. See *Sen. Doc. No. 171*, pp. 44-45.

[91] *Annual Report of the War Department* for the fiscal year ended June 30, 1900, Appendix "EE," pp. 83-84.

[92] *Ibid.*

following provision:[93] "That the United States will, for the term of ten years from the date of the exchange of the ratifications of the present treaty, admit Spanish ships and merchandise to the ports of the Philippine Islands on the same terms as ships and merchandise of the United States."

The board remembered the statement made by the American negotiators regarding the policy of the United States "to maintain in the Philippines an open door to the world's commerce."[94] As an answer to the request by the Spanish commissioners for an explicit statement regarding the "open door" policy of the United States in the Philippines, the American negotiators[95] replied:[96]

> The declaration that the policy of the United States in the Philippines will be that of an open door to the world's commerce necessarily implies that the offer to place Spanish vessels and merchandise on the same footing as American is not intended to be exclusive. But the offer to give Spain that privilege for a term of years, is intended to secure it to her for a certain period by special treaty stipulation, whatever might be at any time the general policy of the United States.

In view of these circumstances, the board recognized the desirability of instituting only "guarded changes" on the tariff rates. It was felt that a system of taxation which would give a maximum revenue with the least injury and greatest encouragement to the industries of the Islands ought to be adopted. Consequently, the rates of the proposed tariff were arranged so as to allow the free entry of all agricultural apparatus and machinery and lower the cost of the staple food of the inhabitants. It was expected that, on such a basis, prosperity would eventually come and that the farming and marketing of the Philippine crops would bring such increase of wealth in the near future as to augment greatly the revenue.

The fact that the Islands then were wholly without suitable roadways and that the small coasting-trade vessels were charging high freights for carrying the produce from the points of production to the ports of exportation made the marketing of crops exceedingly costly. Hence, the board recommended the admission of railway and tram-

[93] *Sen. Doc. No. 62*, Part I, p. 6.

[94] *Annual Report of the War Department* for the fiscal year ended June 30, 1900, Appendix "EE," p. 84. Also *Sen. Doc. No. 62*, Part II, p. 210.

[95] The American negotiators were William R. Day, Cushman K. Davis, William P. Frye, George Gray, and Whitelaw Reid. John Bassett Moore acted as Secretary and Counsel of the Commission, Mr. Ferguson acted as interpreter.

[96] *Annual Reports of the War Department* for the fiscal year ending June 30, 1900, Appendix "EE," p. 84. See also *Sen. Doc. No. 62*, Part II, p. 218.

way materials free of duty for a period of six years, and reduced the duties on such furnishings for ships as canvas, metal sheathing, and rope, in the expectation that by cheapening the cost of maintaining vessels and stimulating the construction of railways and tramways the freight charges would be greatly reduced.

The board believed that the existing high charges on petroleum were responsible for its small consumption. It was expected, on the other hand, that the lowering of the duties would increase consumption and so increase the revenue. Therefore, the board reduced the duties upon petroleum crude and refined, twenty-five and fifty percent respectively.[97]

The duties on husked and unhusked rice were reduced from $1.257 and $1.177 (Mexican) per hundred kilos to $0.75 and $0.70 (Mexican) respectively. The duties on cotton, raw, in yarns, and in tissues were retained. So were the duties on table oils, liquors, and wines, while the duty on champagnes was increased two hundred percent. A reduction of thirty-three percent of the existing duty was made on still wine in order to "benefit alike the consumer in the islands and the producers of California."[98]

Large reduction was made on the duties on canned meats, vegetables, and fruits, and fruits and vegetables preserved exclusively in their own juices.

Export duties in the existing tariff were maintained. The board pointed out that although export duties had added considerably to the Insular revenue these duties were so "slight as to occasion no hardship to anyone."[99] While it was apparent to the board that export duties, on the whole, would tend to restrict production, that body was of the opinion nevertheless that the retention of export duties would "be more than offset by the encouragement that is afforded the agricultural industries of the islands."[100] This was expected to follow the free entry, provided for in the proposed measure, of "machinery and apparatus that must largely increase production, and at a reduced cost."[101]

Anticipating an end of the rebellion in the Philippines, President

[97] *Annual Report of the War Department* for the fiscal year ending June 30, 1900, Appendix "EE".
[98] *Ibid.*
[99] *Ibid.*
[100] *Ibid.*
[101] *Ibid.*

McKinley, exercising his power as Commander-in-Chief of the Army and the Navy, created on April 12, 1900, a second Commission commonly known as the Taft Commission. As set forth in the instructions to this Commission (drafted by Secretary of War Root)[102] President McKinley desired to create "a quasi civil government," to exercise "quasi civil powers" that a military commander must have in a conquered country, and to offer to the Filipino people an actual demonstration of the character of government which, should tranquility follow, they would have under the sovereignty of the United States.[103] The Commission was instructed, therefore, that beginning September 1, 1900, the legislative function of the government in the Philippines should be transferred from the military governor to the Philipine Commission "under such rules and regulations as the Secretary of War shall prescribe"[104] until civil government has been established in the Islands. Congress, by the Spooner Amendment which became law on March 2, 1901, expressly authorized the President to vest the powers of government in the Islands in "such person and persons" to be exercised in such manner as he shall direct.[105] Under the Act of Congress of July 1, 1902, civil government was established in the Philippines on July 4, 1902.[106]

The military board's work of tariff revision having been completed, General Arthur MacArthur was instructed by the Secretary of War to

[102] Honorable William Howard Taft, in an address before the Brooklyn Institute of Arts and Sciences on November 19, 1913 tells us that "Mr. Root, who more than any other man initiated our Philippine policy, and is responsible for its success from the standpoint of statesmanship and far-sightedness, drafted the instructions which President McKinley issued to Mr. Root as Secretary of War to guide our course of government in the Philippines. That letter has had a conspicuous place in the history of our relations to the Philippines. . . ." Quotation taken from W. C. Forbes,*op. cit.*, Vol. II, Appendix XXIV; see also *Ibid*,. Vol. I, p. 130, note 2 for Mr. Forbes' note during his interview with President Taft in the Summer of 1912.

[103] Professor H. Parker Willis tells us that the desire to establish civil government in the Philippines was based on the following reasons: (a) It was considered discreditable to the Administration that it had so long maintained military rule in the Philippines; (b) It was believed that the severities inflicted by the military would be mitigated if even a portion of the authority of government were to be transferred to a civil authority, which could act as a check on the army; (c) These facts and a natural desire to go before the country in the campaign of 1900 as having taken distinct steps toward terminating the period of war and securing the establishment of civil order led President McKinley in April 1900 to appoint a Commission consisting of William H. Taft, chairman, Henry C. Ide, Bernard Moses, Luke E. Wright and Dean C. Worcester—See H. Parker Willis, *Our Philippine Problem*, p. 29.

[104] See President McKinley's instructions to the Taft Commission in Elihu Root, *The Military and Colonial Policy of the United States*, pp. 287-294.

[105] *United States Statutes at Large*, Vol. XXXI, p. 910.

[106] *Ibid.*, Vol. XXXII, Part I, chapter 1369.

turn over to the Philippine Commission the board's recommendation together with the pertinent documents received from the War Department[107] and bearing on the board's work of revision. This was done on August 25, 1900, and the Philippine Commission immediately took up the work of further revision.[108] With the assistance of George W. Lyon, who "had large experience as surveyor of the Port of New York,"[109] the Commission completed its work on December 29, and its recommendation was transmitted to the War Department on the same day.[110]

In its letter of transmittal the Philippine Commission pointed out that public sessions were held in the Philippines and local merchants and consumers were given the opportunity to present their views on the various schedules of the proposed measure, but admitted that due to the "limited facilities of the newspapers" in the Islands only the first nine classes of the proposed tariff were printed and that very imperfectly. For this reason "the public generally had not the opportunity which has been afforded it heretofore in all important legislation."[111] It was maintained, however, that "the fullest publication would have caused small increased attention as the disposition of the business interests here is to accept any tariff which the commission proposes,"[112] provided that "duties are specific and not *ad valorem*."[113]

After the receipt on February 9, 1901, of the Commission's proposed tariff for the Philippines, the War Department sent it immediately to the government printer with an order for five hundred copies bearing the following title:[114]

PROPOSED CUSTOMS TARIFF
FOR PORTS IN THE PHILIPPINE ARCHIPELAGO
AS RECOMMENDED BY THE PHILIPPINE COMMISSION.

Suggestions and recommendations invited by the War Department until April 15, 1901, to be considered with a view to amendments before promulgation. Insular Division, Office of the Secretary, War Department, Washington, D. C.

These were sent to various newspapers, trade journals, boards of trade,

[107] See *Supra*, p. 33, note 90.
[108] *Report, Philippine Commission,* from December 1, 1900 to October 15, 1901, p. 191.
[109] *Ibid.*
[110] See Letter of Transmittal of the Proposed Tariff for the Philippine Islands, in *Sen. Doc. No. 171*, pp. 51-54.
[111] *Ibid.*
[112] *Ibid.*
[113] *Ibid.*
[114] *Ibid.*, p. 49.

commercial bodies, chambers of commerce, exporters and manufacturers in all parts of the United States. In point of fact this proposed legislation was given the greatest possible publicity. As a result, therefore, there was a generous response from a variety of sources.[115] A résumé of the most important of these responses may be undertaken since they bring to light the factors that played leading parts in the formulation of the revised tariff law for the Philippines enacted on September 17, 1901.

The Hercules Gas Engine Works of San Francisco pointed out that the proposed duty of two dollars per hundred kilos on gasoline, which would be about six cents a gallon, would work to the entire exclusion of American-made engines in the Philippine market. On the other hand, if gasoline were allowed free entry into the Islands, or, if a material reduction in the proposed rate should be made a "large trade can soon be established" with the Archipelago "not only for gasoline engines but stoves as well."[116]

The Keystone Watch Case Company of Philadelphia again[117] urged the adoption of *ad valorem* rather than specific rates on watches. At this time it was joined by the Elgin Watch Company of Elgin, Illinois. Both companies urged a levy of only fifteen percent *ad valorem,* for "we believe that that rate will encourage importation, remove incentive for smuggling, and [would] thus produce the greatest amount of revenue."[118] for the Insular treasury.

Exporters of precious and semi-precious stones pointed out that a specific duty on these products would always discriminate against cheaper goods. However, should a ten percent *ad valorem* or some classification of duty as is paid on imports into the United States be adopted, "this would allow the importation of this general class of American goods into the Philippines."[119]

Manufacturers of typewriters joined hands with the manufacturers of printing paper in urging a nominal rate on their prospective products on the ground of the educational results that might be expected to follow.[120]

[115] *Sen. Doc. No. 171* contains a good many communications from these groups bearing suggestions and recommendations regarding some particular item or items of the proposed tariff.

[116] *Ibid.,* pp. 223-224.

[117] *Ibid.,* pp. 176-178.

[118] *Ibid.*

[119] *Ibid.,* pp. 217-223.

[120] *Ibid.,* pp. 250-254.

[121] *Ibid.,* pp. 267-270.

The American harness and saddlery interests of Cincinnati, endorsed by Senator J. B. Foraker and Representative J. H. Bromwell, objected to the Philippine Commission's proposed rate of duty on:[121]

(a) Light harness .... $0.60 per kilogram
(b) Heavy harness .... $0.30 per kilogram
(c) All other goods in the saddlery line including riding saddles .... $0.75 per kilogram

It was pointed out that the above rates would make the duty equal to about forty percent *ad valorem*, and would be practically prohibitory. A reduction of thirty cents and fifteen cents respectively on the first two, and forty-five cents on the last would allow the importation of American products into the Islands. It was claimed that should the above recommendation be adopted, American made harness would eventually "control the market on such class of goods as against Spain, England and Germany."[122]

Certain industries merely contented themselves in asking for more favorable rates for their manufactured articles,[123] while Eastern and Middle Western interests raised serious objections regarding the cotton schedules and the provisions requiring that samples be washed and dried before being appraised for duty. It was pointed out that in the interest of American textile manufacturers the washing and drying provisions of the proposed tariff should be done away with and that the weight of eight kilos be substituted for ten kilos. This amendment was urged in order to enable the entry of American calicoes desired by the Philippine market.[124]

The War Department carefully considered these suggestions and recommendations, together with those received from General Tasker Bliss,[125] in the light of Cuban experience. In the meantime, the Philippine Commission in Manila was informed of these suggestions by the Department. After April 15, 1901, the War Department, aided by W. Morgan Shuster and Charles A. Conant,[126] took up the work of revision in view of previous information received. In respect to some schedules of the tariff, the Department asked the assistance of the De-

[122] *Ibid.*
[123] *Ibid.*, p. 319 *et seq.*
[124] *Ibid.*, pp. 194-195; 197-203.
[125] General Bliss was then collector of customs of Cuba.
[126] Mr. Shuster had been a special deputy collector of customs of Havana, Cuba, and was recommended to the Philippine Commission for Collector of Customs for the Philippines. Mr. Conant was appointed special Commissioner in the Philippines.

partment of Agriculture and the Treasury Department. The United States appraiser of merchandise for the port of New York was requested to suggest changes in the language of the customs tariff as revised by the War Department in order to avoid as far as possible all ambiguous and contradictory statements.[127]

After all these changes had been made and approved, two hundred copies of the tariff, now called the "Customs Tariff for the Philippine Archipelago," were printed. Messrs. Shuster and Conant were instructed to proceed to Manila with one hundred copies of the tariff via San Francisco to explain "the changes that had been made, with the reasons therefor."[128] The Philippine Commission was instructed to approve or modify the revised tariff by cable, and authorized to enact, promulgate, and enforce the same.[129]

About the time the final revisions were made by the War Department there were received from the Manufacturers and Producers' Association of San Francisco communications both by mail and by wire urging a change in the rates prescribed on canned fish and fruit.[130] Messrs. Shuster and Conant were instructed that, while in San Francisco, they were to meet the representatives of the commercial bodies of that city and discuss with those bodies their representations. As a result some changes in the rates on canned fish and fruit were recommended. These changes were approved later both by the Secretary of War and the Philippine Commission and became a part of the tariff as finally enacted.

When Messrs. Shuster and Conant reached Manila on September 6, 1901, the Philippine Commission immediately considered the tariff as amended by the War Department. Minor changes regarding borax, canvas, firearms, shoes, string frames and so forth were recommended by the Commission.[131] On September 17, 1901, the Commission enacted the "Customs Tariff for the Philippine Archipelago" as Act Number 230. This Act became effective on November 15, 1901 with the important proviso "that during the first sixty days after the law becomes effective importers of goods en route to Manila at the time the law becomes effective might elect to pay under the new tariff or the old."[132]

[127] See *Sen. Doc. No. 171*, pp. 225-227; 273-279; 289-303.

[128] *Sen. Doc. No. 134*, p. 9.

[129] *Ibid.*

[130] See *Sen. Doc. No. 171*, pp. 228-239. For changes recommended by Shuster and Conant and those by interested parties of California see *Ibid.*, pp. 240-243; 318-319.

[131] *Sen. Doc. No. 134*, Appendix B, p. 11.

[132] *Report, Philippine Commission,* from December 1, 1900 to October 15, 1901, p. 122.

The Revised Tariff

The customs tariff for the Islands as finally enacted by the Philippine Commission had adopted, on the whole, the recommendations and suggestions given by American interests. Although aiming to retain a "competitive market" in the Islands and the realization thereby of a maximum revenue, these suggestions and recommendations were motivated by the desire to facilitate as much as possible the importation of American products in the Philippines.

Colonel Edwards, Chief of the Bureau of Insular Affairs, in a letter to Mr. Taft, then President of the Philippine Commission, dated March 21, 1901, admitted that the cases of Cuba and the Philippines were "entirely different." And that while the Cuban tariff under preparation in Havana was for the "protection and furtherance of Cuban interests and not for the benefit of the United States as against the interests of that island, the tariff for the Philippines will be based upon what is considered best for those islands as well as for this country."[133]

In a letter under date of July 24, 1901 addressed to William R. Corwine of the Merchants' Association of New York, Colonel Edwards informed the former of the adoption of the following classification as a part of Paragraph 117 of the final act:[134]

Textiles plain and without figures, not stamped or printed, whatever be their width, weighing 8 kilograms per 100 square meters, having:

(a) Up to 18 threads, n. w. kilogram	$0.10
(b) From 19 to 30 threads, n. w. kilogram	0.14
(c) From 31 to 38 threads, n. w. kilogram	0.18
(d) 39 threads or more, n. w. kilogram	0.28

He believed that the above provisions "would admit American unprinted cottons under the most favorable classification, as we were given to understand that they were usually more than 65 centimeters in width."[135]

On the insistence of Everett, Heany and Company, of New York, and the Cincinnati Board of Trade, the provisions in Rule 2 of the proposed tariff of the Philippine Commission regarding washing and drying of samples before the imposition of duties on textiles were done away with. They pointed out that the provisions in Rule 2 were

[133] *Sen. Doc. No. 171,* p. 286.
[134] *Ibid.* Also *Sen. Doc. No. 134,* Exhibit C, pp. 44-45.
[135] *Sen. Doc. No. 171,* p. 214.

decidedly opposed to the interests of American manufacturers of cotton fabrics. Since the American manufacturers do not size or weight goods while the foreign manufacturers do, why not assess the goods for duty by weight without any attempt to remove the weighting of materials? Thus the suspension of the above-noted provisions in Rule 2 in the final tariff act, meant a discrimination in favor of the American manufacturers of cotton prints. In the language of Tasker Bliss, "wherever tariff classifies tissues by weight and number of threads, the trade is bound to remain in the hands of those who manufacture to meet those conditions."[136] In other words, since the suggestions given by American cotton interests in respect to cotton schedules were adopted, Philippine trade in cotton would tend to be in American hands sooner or later.

The Crown Distilleries Company of San Francisco, California, in a letter to Colonel Edwards dated March 22, 1901 wrote:[137]

> We recognize that the treaty relations prevent the securing of preferential duty rates for the American over the foreign article, but we feel from our experience that the products above referred to (whisky, rum, gin) would be advantaged if cocktails, blackberry, and ginger brandies, and therefore, all other articles under that heading, would be given the same duty in glass as in wood, which more strongly applies to whiskey, rum, gin, etc.

The same Company, speaking through Mr. Lilienthal, after the War Department had adopted practically all of its suggestions in Paragraph 308 of the final draft of the tariff law, thanked Colonel Edwards[138]

> for the patriotic impulse which prompted the consideration manifestly given American export interests in the framing of the Philippine tariff.
>
> It is a matter of general recognition that our officials in their desire to prefer American interests have been hampered by the treaty of Spain[139] but all admit that as the tariff is now framed a decided advantage has been gained and will be realized.

The suggestions by the American harness and saddlery interests of Cincinnati were adopted in their entirety[140] in Paragraph 228 of the final draft of the Philippine tariff.

In compliance with the suggestions by Armour and Company, the classifications regarding canned or potted meats were amended to ex-

[136] *Ibid.*, pp. 196-197.
[137] *Ibid.*, pp. 254-255.
[138] *Sen. Doc. No. 171*, pp. 260-261.
[139] What was meant apparently was the Treaty of Paris.
[140] See *Supra*, p. 29.

clude the words "not spiced or highly seasoned" and the following words substituted:[141]

When not exceeding in value $1 per dozen cans of the weight of one-eighth of a kilogram for each can and not exceeding in value $1.75 per dozen cans of the weight of one-quarter (subsequently lowered to one-fifth in the final draft, Paragraph 315) kilogram for each can.

As a result of the interviews of Messrs. Shuster and Conant while in San Francisco[142] it was discovered that the interests of the fruit and fish canning industries of the entire Pacific Coast coincided with the revenue interests of the Philippine government. Therefore, they wrote to the Department and suggested a modification of the tariff on canned fish and fruits.[143] In order to see at a glance how the original rates were modified attention is invited to the following:[144]

As drafted by the Philippine Commission

Paragraph 329. Canned or potted fish, and sea food, such as cod, salmon, herring, sardines, oysters, clams, and generally all sea products preserved in cans, or jars, not highly spiced or seasoned, n. w. kilogram $0.05.

As revised by the War Department

Paragraph 317. Canned or potted fish, and sea food, such as cod, salmon, herring, sardines, oysters, clams, and generally all sea products preserved in cans or jars, n. w. kilo $0.05.

Modification recommended by Shuster and Conant in their letter to the Department

Paragraph 317. Salmon, cod and herring in cans or jars, n. w. kilo $0.035.

(a) Other canned or potted fish, and sea food, such as sardines, oysters, clams and generally all sea products preserved in cans or jars, n. w. kilo $0.06.

By dividing the Paragraph (317) into two parts and taking cod, herring and salmon out of the general class and giving them a rate of three and a half cents, a reduction of one and a half cents per kilo, Messrs. Shuster and Conant, in recommending this change were actuated by the desire to facilitate the entry into the Philippines of lower grades of cod, herring and salmon and thereby increasing the revenue

[141] *Sen. Doc. No. 171*, pp. 245-246. Also *Sen. Doc. No. 134*, Exhibit C, p. 61.

[142] See *Supra*, p. 30.

[143] For their letter to Colonel Edwards under date of July 31, 1901, suggesting modifications on the rates on canned fish and fruits, see *Sen. Doc. No. 171*, pp. 239-243.

[144] *Sen. Doc. No. 171*, pp. 318-319.

of the Insular treasury. It was pointed out that only for the cheaper grades can a market in the Islands be created.

On the subject of canned fruits attention is invited to the following:[145]

As drafted by the Philippine Commission

Paragraph 334. Canned or preserved fruits:

(a) With just sufficient sugar to preserve the fruit, belonging to the class known as pie fruits, in wood, g. w. 100 kilos $3.50

(b) With more sugar than in the foregoing paragraph, but not belonging to the class of preserves, whether put in tin or glass, such as pears, apples, peaches, and the like, n. w. kilo $0.05.

Paragraph 335. Canned or bottled preserves and jams, with high percentage of sugar, whether put up in tin or glass, n. w. kilo $0.09.

As revised by the War Department

Paragraph 322. Canned or preserved fruits:

(a) In wood, g. w. 100 kilos $3.50.

(b) In tin or glass, n. w. kilo $0.06.

Modification recommended by Shuster and Conant in their letter to the Department

Paragraph 322. Canned or preserved fruits:

(a) In wood, and those belonging to the class known as "pie fruits," packed in water, in tins or glass, n. w. kilo $0.02.

(b) Others, in tins or glass, including those packed in sirups, known as "table fruits," n. w. kilo $0.04.

It will be noted that the paragraph as revised by the War Department was simplified in its classification, and no change was made in the lower rate in articles preserved in wood, but (b) under Paragraph 334 and Paragraph 335 were placed together under (b) of Paragraph 322 and the two rates of five and nine cents were combined into a single rate of six cents per kilo.

According to representations made by interested parties in California the above rates of $3.50 per 100 kilos, gross weight, levied on "pie fruits" would amount to about sixty-five percent, since the average value of pie fruits was $2.25 per dozen and the duty would be $1.44 per dozen. It was pointed out that the five cents per kilo levied on canned fruits preserved in sugar would amount to a duty of four and one tenth cents per can or forty-eight cents per dozen. The average value of what were termed two and a half pound tins was $1.20 per dozen or ten cents per tin. Therefore, Messrs. Shuster and Conant rec-

[145] *Sen. Doc. No. 171*, p. 319.

ommended in their joint letter the reduction of duties to two and four cents respectively in order to build a market in the Philippines for these products of California.[146]

The duties on gasoline and printing paper were reduced to $1.25 and one dollar per hundred kilos respectively. The duties on watches and precious and semi-precious stones were made *ad valorem* and the rates of twenty and fifteen percent were placed on them respectively. The duties on beer as provided for in paragraph 312 were so arranged as to give preference to American products shipped in barrels. As a matter of fact, every effort was made in this tariff to favor the American and hamper the foreign shipper.[147]

In a number of cases[148] "provisos" were inserted in order to raise the duty on the more expensive article in a particular classification.

Section 13 of the revised tariff retained the export duties on the principal exports of the Islands, namely, hemp, sugar, copra and tobacco. With the exception of the increase in the rates on hemp and copra which were levied at seventy-five and ten cents respectively, the duties on sugar and tobacco remained the same as in the old Spanish tariff.[149]

The reason given for the one hundred percent increase in the duties levied on hemp was that, as hemp was not "capable of production elsewhere, the revenues therefrom will be doubled without being burdensome here."[150] On the other hand, the one hundred percent increase on the export tax on copra was justified on the anticipation of an increased demand for it. It was pointed out that a similar increase in revenue would result "without appreciably affecting the producer or burdening his power of competition."[151]

The following broad principles were the guiding motives in all the steps taken by the board of officers, by the Philippine Commission and by the Bureau of Insular Affairs in formulating the new customs tariff for the Philippines. It was desired, in the first place, that this tariff should raise revenue sufficient to cover the expenses of the government of the Islands. Secondly, it was aimed to foster the agricultural, commercial and industrial development of the Philippines. Thirdly, it was

[146] *Sen. Doc. No. 171,* pp. 235-237.

[147] H. Parker Willis, *op. cit.,* p. 276.

[148] See Paragraphs 13-16; 21; 46; 51-54; 69; 73; 97-99; 105; 197-200; 266-271; 330-332, in *Sen. Doc. No. 134,* pp. 33-68, Exhibit C.

[149] *Ibid.,* p. 35; also *Supra,* p. 9.

[150] See Philippine Commission letter of Transmittal in *Sen. Doc. No. 171,* p. 53.

[151] *Ibid.*

felt that articles of prime necessity and imported articles consumed by the poor should bear but a light burden of taxation while articles of luxury consumed by the well-to-do should lend material aid to the expenses of the Government. And finally, this tariff was designed also to encourage Philippine importation of American goods.

When the control over the tariff legislations of the Philippines fell into the hands of Congress the attitude which it would take was foreshadowed by the late Senator Henry Cabot Lodge. In his keynote speech as chairman of the Republican National Convention delivered on June 20, 1900 in Philadelphia he amplified his remarks, already given on page 3, as follows:[152]

> We see our duty to ourselves as well as to others. We believe in trade expansion. By every legitimate means within the province of government and legislation we mean to stimulate the expansion of our trade and to open new markets. Greatest of all markets is China. Our trade there is growing by leaps and bounds. Manila, the prize of war, gives us inestimable advantages in developing that trade. . . . Manila is the corner-stone of our Eastern policy, and the brilliant diplomacy of John Hay in securing from all nations a guarantee of our treaty rights and of the open door in China rests upon it.

The Insular Cases

Hardly a month after the enactment by the Philippine Commission of the Tariff Act of September 1901 the Supreme Court of the United States, in the Fourteen Diamond Rings case,[153] was called upon to determine whether Philippine goods imported into the United States had not come from a foreign country and, therefore, were subject to the regular rates of duty imposed by the Dingley law. This question came up when Emil J. Pepke, an American citizen, enlisted in the Army at the outbreak of the Spanish-American War, was sent with his regiment to the island of Luzon in the Philippines. While there, and subsequent to the ratification of the Treaty of Paris, he acquired possession of fourteen diamond rings. Later he was ordered back to the United States and took the rings with him on an Army Transport on July 31, 1899. On September 25 of the same year he obtained his discharge from the Army and later proceeded to Chicago where the rings were seized by the customs officers as having been brought unlawfully into the United States. The Court ruled, however, that the Philippines, like Puerto Rico,[154] is not a "foreign country" within the meaning of the

[152] *Official Proceedings of the Twelfth Republican National Convention held in the City of Philadelphia,* June 19-21, 1900, pp. 88-89.

[153] *183 U. S.* pp. 176 *et seq.* (Decision rendered on December 2, 1901).

[154] *182 U. S.* pp. 1 *et seq.* (Decision rendered on May 27, 1901).

Dingley law. Consequently, goods imported into the United States from the Philippines, and *vice versa,* should be duty free.

This ruling not only invalidated the application of the Philippine Tariff Act of September 1901 (Philippine Commission Act No. 230) which provided for the collection of duties on commodities coming from the United States, and the application of the Dingley law to Philippine products, but also made the former act itself subject to question regarding its constitutionality. There was no doubt as to the power of Congress to enact laws determining what trade relationship should exist between the United States and the Philippines. In view of the equality provisions of the Treaty of Paris,[155] free trade between the Philippines and the United States might be disastrous to American products in their own home markets. For, might it not be possible that as a consequence of this commercial relationship the Philippines might be converted into a backdoor for competing low-priced European products in American markets?[156]

On April 12, 1900, Congress enacted the Foraker Act for Puerto Rico.[157] This legislation served later as the basis for the passage of the Philippine Tariff Act of March 8, 1902.[158] In both these Acts, Congress adopted the principle of preferential treatment.

The law of April 12, 1900, granting an eighty-five percent preferential on Puerto Rican products imported into the United States, immediately raised the question of its legality since Article 1, section 8, of the Constitution of the United States specifically provides for the uniformity of "all duties, imposts and excises throughout the United States." This question came up in Downes v. Bidwell,[159] when Downes and Company sought to recover the duties paid by it under the Foraker Act to the New York Collector of Customs on a shipment of oranges from Puerto Rico. The highest court of the land decreed, however, that Puerto Rico (and inferentially the Philippines also) although not a foreign territory within the meaning of the Dingley law, was merely "appurtenant to" and not a part of the United States within the meaning of the revenue clauses of the Constitution. In

[155] See the provisions of Article IV of the Treaty of Paris; also those of Articles XIII and XV.

[156] *Insular Cases,* comprising the records, briefs and arguments of counsel in the insular cases, of the October term, 1900, in the Supreme Court of the United States, including appendices thereto, pp. 693-695.

[157] *United States Statutes at Large,* Vol. XXXI, 71.

[158] *Ibid.,* Vol. XXXII, Part I, p. 54; See also *Supra,* chapter II.

[159] *182 U. S.* p. 244.

other words, and borrowing the language of Chief Justice Fuller in his dissenting opinion, Congress has the power to keep these newly acquired territories "in an intermediate state of ambiguous existence for an indefinite period," and commerce with them, in the meantime, would be "absolutely subject to the will of Congress irrespective of constitutional provisions."[160] Thus Congress has the power to throw around certain American industries the mantle of protection even against similar products of territories under American sovereignty. The novelty of this ruling hinges on the reconciliation of imperialism and protection.

In arguing the case of the government the Attorney General reminded the court[161]

> that at the bottom of these acquisitions of territory, at the bottom of that clause of the Constitution which authorized the acquisition, authorized the Government of the acquisition, lay the material, the commercial, the expansive idea of the thrifty, progressive, active American, the pioneer spirit that, pressing onward from frontier to frontier, went out to reduce and conquer territory for their own use and benefit . . . that when our forefathers made the Consttiution they made it as states, or as people of the states.

And reaching the height of his oratory the chief legal adviser of the government concluded by saying:[162]

> We have not sought a doctrine which by subtle disputation would entangle and embarrass. We have remembered that a great world power, extending its domain from the frozen seas of the North to where the encircling palm trees grow in the Pacific islands, must not be bound by rules too strict or too confining; that what might tend toward progress and development in one place might only hamper in another. Therefore we have sought an interpretation which should continue in the legislative body which represents the American people that wise and sound discretion which it would be a slander and an imputation upon our country for a moment to believe that they would not always exercise. . . .

The late Professor John W. Burgess saw in the Supreme Court's judgment in the Downes case nothing but "an arbitrary bit of patch-

[160] *182 U. S.* p. 372. There is one provision of the Constitution which limits the powers of Congress in dealing with territories. The thirteenth amendment prohibits slavery not only "within the United States" but also within "any place subject to their jurisdiction." But with this exception the power granted to Congress by the Constitution "to dispose of and make all needful rules and regulations respecting the territory or other property belonging to the United States," is unlimited. See G. A. Malcolm, *The Government of the Philippine Islands, its development and fundamentals,* pp. 319-333.

[161] *Insular Cases,* comprising the records, briefs, etc., p. 282.

[162] *Ibid.,* p. 338.

work," the purpose of which was "to satisfy a certain demand of fancied political expediency in the work of imperial expansion."[163]

It cannot be denied that an influential portion, if not a "powerful portion," of the American people had already made up its mind not to extend to these newly acquired possessions, as far as their commercial and political status was concerned, the privilege of being incorporated into the United States. This idea was entertained in spite of its apparent inconsistency. When the Supreme Court was called upon to pass judgment on the constitutional questions involved in the acquisition of these territories, it gave a constitutional sanction to the popular theory. "Consequently," in the language of Latané, they had to "bow their heads before *un fait accompli*."[164] By placing in Congress that "wise and sound discretion" in regard to the governance of the newly acquired territories, that policy-making body of the American Government was enabled to separate the bitter portion of imperialism and retain only the sweet.

How far Congress in its wise and sound discretion utilized this power to reconcile the current divergent interests in the United States, namely, those that reflect the agricultural interests on the one hand and the manufacturing interests on the other hand, will be the subject of succeeding chapters.

[163] *Political Science Quarterly* A Review devoted to the Historical, Statistical and Comparative Study of Politics, Economics and Public Law, 1901, Vol. XVI, p. 504.

[164] J. H. Latané, *America as a World Power*, pp. 151-152; also Charles A. Beard, *Contemporary American History*, pp. 213, 218-220.

2: *The Act of March 8, 1902*

MARCH 8, 1902 TO AUGUST 5, 1909

THE ADMINISTRATION felt that there was doubt whether the Puerto Rican case[1] applied to the Philippines, so that the Islands continued to be governed under the war powers of the President.[2] But after the decision in the Fourteen Diamond Rings case[3] it was apparent that Congress must act to authorize the tariff and fiscal legislation of the Islands.

As already indicated[4] Congress had enacted the Foraker Act for Puerto Rico which the Supreme Court found to be constitutional. On December 13, 1901, the House Committee on Ways and Means acted favorably on H. R. 5833 entitled "An Act Temporarily to Provide Revenue for the Philippine Islands and for Other Purposes," as a substitute for H. R. 4325;[5] and five days later the House of Representatives passed this bill and it was immediately sent to the Senate which referred it to the Senate Committee on the Philippines.[6]

This proposed measure (H. R. 5833) contained the following important provisions for:[7]

1. The incorporation of the tariff act of September 17, 1901, of the Philippine Commission as a part of the proposed measure.
2. The levying of the full rates of the Dingley law on Philippine products.
3. The collection of tonnage taxes on vessels plying between the ports of the United States and the Philippine Islands.
4. The remission to the Insular treasury of the duties and taxes collected in the United States upon articles coming from the Philippines

[1] *182 U. S.* 1.

[2] This fact was stated by Secretary of War Root in his letter of June 5, 1901 to Senator John T. Morgan of Alabama. For a copy of this letter I am indebted to Professor Philip C. Jessup.

[3] *183 U. S.* 176.

[4] *Supra*, pp. 36-37.

[5] *Cong. Record*, 57th Cong., 1st Sess. (1901-1902) Part 1, pp. 281-286.

[6] *Ibid.*, p. 438. For the debate on the bill in the House, see *Ibid.*, pp. 328, 409, 425.

[7] For a copy of the bill (*H. R. 5833*) see *Ibid.*, p. 750.

and upon foreign vessels coming therefrom "to be used and expended for the government and benefit of said islands."[8]

5. The levying of duties according to the weights of merchandise at the time of entry. The exemption from internal revenue tax of the Islands of articles containing imported materials upon which the internal-revenue tax of the United States was collected, manufactured in bonded manufacturing warehouses intended for shipment to the Philippines. These articles should be subject only to the rates of the Philippine tariff levied on similar products imported therein. Where duties have been collected on materials used in the manufacture of articles manufactured or produced in the United States, such articles when shipped to the Philippines should be allowed a draw-back equal to the duties paid on materials used less one percent of such duties.

In favorably reporting H. R. 5833 to the Senate on January 20, 1902 with the various amendments[9] proposed by the Senate Committee on the Philippines, chairman Henry C. Lodge agreed with Representative Sereno E. Payne, chairman of the House Committee on Ways and Means, regarding the desirability of immediate legislation. To Senator Lodge's mind the decisions of the Supreme Court not only rendered doubtful the legality itself of the Tariff Act of September 17, 1901, enacted by the Philippine Commission in view of the provisions of the Spooner Amendment of March 2, 1901, but also voided the applicability of the Dingley law to Philippine goods imported into the United States. Consequently, unless Congress would legislate otherwise, the following would logically follow: (a) the establishment of free trade between the Philippines and the United States (b) the extension of the operation of the Dingley law to foreign goods entering the Philippines and (c) the application of the American coastwise shipping laws to commerce between the Islands and the United States.

The establishment of free trade between the Philippines and the United States could hardly be thought of then. Aside from the objections by the American agricultural interests[10]—notably sugar and tobacco—there were other reasons why free trade then was not advisable. In the first place, the Philippines had been accustomed for many years to raising the bulk of their revenue by import duties.[11] Then, too, free

[8] Section IV, *H. R. 5833*.

[9] See *Sen. Report* No. 181, Part I, 57th Cong., 1st Sess., p. 39. Also *Cong. Record*, 57th Cong., 1st Sess., Part I, p. 750.

[10] See *Hearings* before the Senate Committee on the Philippines in Relation to Affairs in the Philippine Islands, 1901-1902, Part I, pp. 149, 156, 329-330.

[11] *Cong. Record*, 57th Cong., 1st Sess., Part I, p. 284.

trade between the United States and the Philippines would mean also free trade between Spain and the Archipelago in view of Article IV of the Treaty of Paris. Consequently, this would tend to decrease materially the revenue of the Islands. While direct taxation might be resorted to, Senator Lodge agreed with Governor Taft[12] that such an experiment ought not to be entered upon—certainly not at that time—since the Insular government could not be supported then by direct taxation.[13] Finally, it was shown that to maintain the "open door" which the United States advocated in China, it would be necessary to continue "the tariff as it now stands" in the Philippines, and its operation there should be extended "to all nations of the earth including ourselves."[14]

The establishment of a uniform tariff between the Philippines and the United States would be impractical due to the existing chasm between the economic and social conditions of the two countries. Under these conditions it would be very hard, if not practically impossible, to devise a uniform dutiable list of revenue-producing commodities. Again, uniformity of protective tariffs under such conditions could hardly be equitable.[15] It was also feared that the equality provisions of the Treaty of Paris might transform the Philippines into a backdoor for competing European products in American markets.

On the other hand, it was not deemed wise to extend immediately the application of the American coastwise shipping laws to commerce between the Philippines and the United States.[16] Since there was a "small number of American ships engaged in Philippine trade" the extension of the American coastwise shipping laws to the Islands, would eventually "drive the commerce of the Archipelago to foreign countries whose vessels could trade between the Philippines and foreign ports, but not between the Philippines and American ports."[17]

In view of these circumstances, therefore, immediate legislation was deemed to be a very "pressing emergncy."

It was obvious, however, to both the Senate Committee on the Philippines and the House Committee on Ways and Means that they could not hope to improve upon the Act of September 17, 1901 enacted by

[12] See *Hearings* before the Senate Committee on the Philippines, 1901-1902, Part I, statement by Governor Taft, p. 149.

[13] *Ibid.* See also *Cong. Record,* 57th Cong., 1st Sess., Part I, p. 824.

[14] *Cong. Record,* 57th Cong., 1st Sess., Part I, p. 284.

[15] *Report,* Philippine Commission, Jan. 31, 1900, Vol. I, pp. 116-117.

[16] *Cong. Record,* 57th Cong., 1st Sess., Part III, pp. 2112-2113, 2123.

[17] U. S. Tariff Commission, *Colonial Tariff Policies,* p. 592.

the Philippine Commission, or enter upon its revision, without involving a very long delay. It was recognized that a delay would be "extremely prejudicial" both to American sugar and tobacco interests, for, in the meantime, there would be the free entry into the United States of similar products from the Philippines, and delay would occasion loss of revenue for the Philippine treasury.[18] Due to this consideration and because of the necessity of immediate legislation, the House Committee acceded to the amendments of the Senate Committee, the most important of which will be discussed presently.

Senator Joseph L. Rawlins of Utah, in the course of his remarks, maintained that the proposed measure would in reality "impose a discriminating tax upon the trade between the people of the islands and the people of the United States."[19] Continuing a little later, he pointed out that the Republican Party had concluded that it would be dangerous to the welfare of the people of the United States to treat the Philippines Islands as a part of the American territory and to deal with their inhabitants upon the same footing as American citizens. "The Supreme Court having decided that in the normal operations of government there should be free trade between the islands and the people of the United States, this bill is an urgent bill for the purpose of precluding the possibility of that."[20] In behalf of the minority members of the Senate Committee on the Philippines he had offered a substitute for H. R. 5833 entitled "A bill to Promote the Prosperity and Establish the Independence of the Philippine Islands." This substitute measure provided for the relinquishment of American sovereignty in the Philippines when a stable government had been establishd therein and sufficient guarantees had been obtained for the fulfilment of American contractual obligations with Spain, and that until the complete withdrawal of American sovereignty in the Islands there should be free trade between the Philippines and the United States.[21]

This substitute bill offered by the minority member of the Senate Committee on the Philippines was not adopted, of course, and hence H. R. 5833 as amended and passed by Congress became law when President Theodore Roosevelt approved it on March 8, 1902.[22]

[18] *Cong. Record,* 57th Cong., 1st Sess., Part I, pp. 329, 823.

[19] *Ibid.,* Part II, p. 1060.

[20] *Ibid.,* p. 1061.

[21] *Senate Report No. 181,* Part 1, p. 45. For the views of the minority see *Ibid.,* Part II, pp. 1-5. For an interesting comment regarding the "plausibility" of this amendment see *Hearings* before the Senate Committee on the Philippines in Relation to Affairs in the Philippine Islands (1901-1902), Part I, pp. 326-327; 329-330.

[22] *Public No. 28, United States Statutes at Large,* Vol. XXXII, Part I, p. 54.

An inquiry into the most important of the Senate amendments which are pertinent to the present study, and finally acceded to by the House of Representatives and incorporated into the Act of Congress of March 8, 1902,[23] may be attempted now.

Both the Senate Committee on the Philippines and the House Committee on Ways and Means were agreed on Section 1, incorporating the Philippine Tariff Act enacted by the Philippine Commission of September 17, 1901 as a part of the Act of Congress of March 8, 1902, thereby maintaining the rate of import duties imposed by the Philippine Act.[24]

Section 2 of the House bill (H. R. 5833) which merely provided for the levying of the full Dingley rates on Philippine goods imported into the United States, was amended to include the following provisions:[25]

Provided, that upon all articles the growth and product of the Philippine Archipelago coming into the United States from the Philippine Archipelago there shall be levied, collected, and paid only 75 per cent of the rates of duty aforesaid: And provided further that the rates of duty which are required hereby to be levied, collected, and paid upon products of the Philippine Archipelago coming into the United States shall be less any duty or taxes levied, collected, and paid thereon upon the shipment thereof from the Philippine Archipelago, as provided by the act of the United States Philippine Commission referred to in section 1 of this act under such rules and regulations as the Secretary of the Treasury may prescribe, but all articles the growth and product of the Philippine Islands admitted into the ports of the United States free of duty and coming directly from said islands to the United States for use and consumption therein shall be hereafter exempt from any export duties imposed in the Philippine Islands.

In the meantime, the Philippine Commission had recommended a reduction of from fifty percent to seventy-five percent of the Dingley rates on Philippine products imported into the United States.[26] On January 28, 1902, the Senate which was then considering H. R. 5833, passed a resolution empowering the Senate Committee on the Philippines to hold a public hearing during the sessions of the Senate in relation to affairs in the Philippines.[27] Governor Taft, who was then in the United States on a leave of absence, in his testimony before the

[23] For these amendments and debates see *Cong., Record,* 56th Cong., 1st Sess., Part I, p. 750; Part III, pp. 2123, 2186-2192, 2287, 2331-2333, 2358.

[24] *Supra,* pp. 40-42.

[25] *Cong., Record,* 57th Cong., 1st Sess., Part I, p. 750.

[26] *Hearings* before the Senate Committee on the Philippines (1901-1902), Part I, p. 156.

[27] *Cong. Record,* 57th Cong., 1st Sess., Part II, p. 1047.

Senate Committee maintained that a reduction of at least fifty percent of the Dingley rates on Philippine products imported into the United States would not be large. In the case of Philippine tobacco, a seventy-five percent reduction would be necessary in order to place that product in American markets. This reduction was also necessary in order that the Philippine tobacco manufacturers would be able to import Connecticut wrappers. Governor Taft pointed out that this recommendation was made also for "sentimental reason" since this reduction could be shown as a tangible indication "that the American people are friendly to them and are anxious to show that friendliness by something substantial."[28] However, on being asked by Senator Thomas M. Patterson of Colorado, one of the greatest defenders of the home sugar industry, whether he would knowingly advocate any policy that would injure the industries of the United States, his own country, Mr. Taft answered that he did not think he would. The Governor pointed out, however, that the Philippine Commission did not approach it from the standpoint of those interests.[29]

None the less, the original reduction of twenty-five percent of the Dingley rates was allowed to remain on the ground that the measure, by its title, was temporary and could always be amended when it was found necessary to do so.[30]

Section 3 was also amended to extend to foreign vessels engaged in interisland commerce the House provision for raising tonnage dues on foreign vessels trading between the Philippines and the United States. However, in view of the small number of American vessels engaged in Philippine trade it was thought wise to suspend the application of these provisions until July 1, 1904.[31]

Section 4 of the House bill providing for the return into the Insular treasury of duties and taxes collected in the United States upon Philippine articles and upon foreign vessels coming therefrom was retained in its entirety. Commenting on the provision of this Section, Governor Taft maintained that the return of the duties collected in the United States on goods from the Philippines and foreign vessels coming therefrom would have no "material influence on the trade between the two

[28] *Hearings* before the Senate Committee on the Philippines (1901-1902), Part I, p. 156.

[29] *Ibid.*

[30] See *Senate Report No. 181,* Part I, p. 39.

[31] *Ibid.,* see also *Infra,* p. 51.

countries."[32] What the Islands needed most, aside from capital and labor, was a market for their produce.[33]

On the whole, the original House provision regarding the collection of duties according to the weights of merchandise at the time of entry and the internal-revenue tax exemption and drawbacks as provided for in Sections 5 and 6 respectively were retained and a new section, 7, was added. This section provided that

merchandise in bonded warehouses or otherwise in the custody and control of the officers of the customs, upon which duties have been paid, shall be entitled on the shipment to the Philippine Islands within three years from the date of the original arrival, to a return of the duties paid less 1 per centum, and the merchandise upon which duties have not been paid may be shipped without the payment of duties to the Philippine Islands within said period, under such rules and regulations as may be prescribed by the Secretary of the Treasury.

While Section 7 aimed at encouraging, within certain limitations and subject to certain regulations, the re-exportation to the Philippines of merchandise held in bonded warehouses of the United States or otherwise in the custody and control of the customs authorities without the payment of duty, section 6 provided in general that a drawback of ninety-nine percent on the duties paid on materials used, whether in whole or in part, in the manufacture of articles manufactured or produced in the United States when such articles were to be sent to the Islands, was designed to open up a favorable market in the Philippines for American manufactured goods of this class. Hence American cigars using Havana or Sumatra wrappers, as the case might be, or other manufactured tobacco using imported fillers, or other manufactured products using foreign materials were entitled, under this provision, to a drawback "equal in amount to the duties paid on the materials used less one percent of such duties."[34]

Remitting the internal-revenue tax on American manufactured articles, when intended for shipment to the Philippines, would further encourage and stimulate the importation of American beer, wine and whiskey in the Islands. The tariff act of the Philippine Commission which was re-enacted by Congress as a part of the law under review imposed a duty on whiskey of only thirty-five cents a liter (about equal to a quart), while the Dingley rate was $2.50 a gallon or about sixty-two cents a quart. The Philippine tariff rates on beer ranged

[32] *Hearings* before the Senate Committee on the Philippines (1901-1902), Part I, pp. 276, 279.

[33] *Ibid.*, p. 276.

[34] *Public No. 28, United States Statutes at Large*, Vol. XXXII, p. 56.

from thirteen cents to eighteen cents per gallon, while the rates charged on it by the Dingley tariff ranged from twenty cents to forty cents per gallon. In other words, the duty on beer in the Archipelago was about one-half what it was in the United States. There was no wonder then, according to Representative Thayer of Massachusetts, "that most of our brewers and distillers are expansionists and imperialists."[35]

In plain language Section 2 provided that (a) seventy-five percent of the Dingley rates should be levied on Philippine products imported into the United States (b) Philippine products on which export duties were collected when imported into the United States should be given a further reduction equivalent to their respective export duties and (c) finally, products of the Archipelago, admitted free of duty by the Dingley law, should be relieved of their export duties when sent directly to the United States for use and consumption therein.

The application of the provisions of Section 3 relating to the extension of the American coastwise shipping laws to commerce between the Philippines and the United States was suspended.[36]

Section 4 of this Act (March 8, 1902) provided that

> all duties and taxes collected in the United States upon all articles coming from the Philippine Archipelago and upon foreign vessels coming therefrom . . . shall be held as a separate fund and be paid into the treasury of the Philippine Islands to be used and expended for the government and benefit of said islands.

Under the tariff act of the Philippine Commission (Act No. 230), re-enacted as a part of the Act of Congress of March 8, 1902, export duties were levied on the following important products of the Islands: hemp, rice, sugar, copra and tobacco. Expressed in United States currency, an export duty of $0.75 was levied on one hundred kilograms of hemp; $0.25 on one hundred kilograms of rice; $0.05 on one hundred kilograms of sugar and $0.10 on one hundred kilograms of copra. On the other hand, the export duties on tobacco were arranged according to its place of origin in the Islands. The rates were as follows:[37]

$1.50 per 100 kilograms (Raw, grown in the provinces of Cagayan, Isabela, and Nueva Vizcaya).
$1.00 per 100 kilograms (Raw, grown in Visayas and Mindanao).
$0.75 per 100 kilograms (Raw, grown in other provinces of the Archipelago).

[35] *Cong. Record,* 57th Cong., 1st Sess., Part I, p. 335.
[36] *Infra,* p. 51.
[37] See Section 13, *Public No. 28, United States Statutes at Large,* Vol. XXXII, p. 57.

$1.50 per 100 kilograms (Manufactured, of all kinds of whatever origin).
Note: Certificates of origin of raw tobacco may be required by the customs authorities when proof of the place of production is necessary.

In view of the fact that the best quality of Philippine tobacco was produced—and is still being produced—only in the provinces of Cagayan, Isabela and Nueva Vizcaya, it is obvious that under the above rates only the low grade unmanufactured tobacco of the Islands could be imported and placed in the American markets. This, according to Professor Willis, would tend to give "the Manila output a bad reputation, which it would take some time to overcome."[38]

Under the Dingley tariff, on the other hand, copra and hemp were admitted free of duty into the United States, thus leaving Philippine rice, sugar and tobacco to receive an additional reduction in the Dingley rates equal to the export duties of these products respectively whenever they were imported into the United States, as provided for in Section 2 of the Act of March 8, 1902.

The Philippines, however, do not export rice. On the contrary, large quantities of rice have been continuously imported to meet the home demands. As a matter of fact, from 1899 to 1912, the percentage of rice imported into the Philippines from neighboring countries averaged eighteen percent of the total imports for the same period, but since 1918, however, this importation had decreased to eight percent and in 1933 to one percent of the total imports.[39]

This provision of Section 2 of the Act of Congress of March 8, 1902, therefore, was to be applied only to the two remaining important products of the Philippines, namely, sugar and tobacco.

From 1899 to 1902, sugar production in the Philippines under the American régime did not increase materially.[40] This was due, in the first place, to the general depression of 1897 occasioned by the competition of beet sugar in the great centers of consumption,[41] and secondly, the years of rebellion against Spain followed later by the Filipino insurrection against the United States coupled with the ravages of cholera and other diseases[42] with their consequent diminution of the labor supply of the Archipelago, imposing a great hardship upon

[38] H. Parker Willis, *op. cit.*, p. 292.
[39] *Annual Report,* Insular Collector of Customs, 1933, p. 90.
[40] See *Appendix II* Table No. 1.
[41] Frank W. Taussig, *Some Aspects of the Tariff Question,* chapter XII.
[42] See *Report,* Philippine Commission, 1902, Part II, pp. 309-445; also *Ibid.,* 1903, Part II, pp. 105-112, 224-228, 239-245; Part III, pp. 122 *et seq.*, and in *Ibid.,* 1904, Part II, pp. 83-327.

the industry.[43] Again, the considerable destruction of work animals occasioned by rinderpest and other cattle diseases and the need for capital greatly affected the sugar industry of the Philippines. Finally, the fall in the price of silver[44] brought about a financial crisis which in turn caused continual fluctuations in the price of sugar, resulting in the failure of many sugar planters. There is no wondering, then, why the industry languished for a great number of years.[45]

In view of the high rates on tobacco provided in the Dingley law[46] the twenty-five percent reduction extended to Philippine tobacco and the additional reduction equivalent to the export duty levied on them in the Archipelago as provided for in Section 2 of the Act of Congress of March 8, 1902,[47] were not sufficient to place this particular product of the Islands on the American markets. As a matter of fact, from 1899 to 1908 only a very negligible quantity of Philippine tobacco was imported into the United States.[48]

In view of this fact, it was clear that there must be a more substantial reduction of the Dingley rates if a large quantity of Philippine tobacco was to enter the American market. The Tobacco Workers' Guild of the Philippines, in its petition under date of October 22, 1903 addressed to President Theodore Roosevelt, urged the reduction of the Dingley rates on Philippine tobacco to fifteen percent *ad valorem* or even its admittance into the United States free of duty. It was pointed out that "the precarious state of our agriculture and primitive methods here followed in tobacco culture" would tend to show that under "such conditions Philippine tobacco cannot really compete with the American products."[49]

The Guild maintained that while the wages of the Filipino operatives in the tobacco factories were decreased, "necessary articles of food and raiment have, on the other hand, increased in value to an extraordinary degree, staples without which the workingman cannot get along costing three times as much as they formerly did."[50]

On December 17, 1903, in an address before the Union Reading

[43] *Report,* Philippine Commission, 1903, Part II, pp. 112-114, 216-228.
[44] For an interesting and detailed account of the fluctuation of the currency and its immediate effects, see *Report,* Philippine Commission, 1904, Part III, pp. 546-547.
[45] *Report,* Philippine Commission, 1902, Part II, pp. 712 *et seq.*
[46] *The Dingley Tariff,* pp. 13-14, 73.
[47] *Supra,* pp. 44-45.
[48] See *Appendix* II, Tables No. 2 and 5.
[49] See Petition of Tobacco Workers' Guild of the Philippines respecting the tariff on tobacco and cigars, published as *House Document No. 571,* 58th Cong., 2nd Sess., p. 2.
[50] *Ibid.,* p. 2. See also *Report,* Philippine Commission, 1904, Part III, pp. 546, 547.

College, Manila, Governor Taft expressed the hope that the Congress of the United States might reduce the Dingley rates on sugar and tobacco to twenty-five percent. He pointed out that should such a reduction be made, it would result in "a counter trade in American products" in the Philippines. "The discrimination in favor of these islands by a reduction of the Dingley tariff," continued Mr. Taft, "must operate to turn a great proportion of the trade of these islands toward the United States, and the material development of the people must increase that trade."[51]

An interesting sidelight on America's Philippine policy as expressed in the law under consideration, is reflected in a provision of Section 2 to the effect that products of the Islands admitted free of duty into the United States should be relieved of their export duties when sent directly to the United States for use and consumption therein. Hemp and copra, being allowed free entry by the Dingley law, fall under this provision. Hence, no export duties were levied on them when sent directly to the United States.

According to the report of the Insular Collector of Customs, from 1899 to 1901, there was a negligible amount of Philippine copra exported to the United States.[52] From 1902 to 1905 the percentage of American import of Philippine copra to the total value of copra imported by other countries was also negligible.[53]

A public hearing was held in Washington on January 21, 1904 on Senator William P. Frye's bill (S. 2259) "to regulate shipping in trade between the ports or places in the Philippine Archipelago, and for other purposes,"[54] providing for the extension of the American shipping laws to the Philippines. This would mean that only American vessels could carry on business between the Philippines and the United States. It was shown how both the American and foreign cordage interests had been solely dependent for their essential raw material on the Philippine hemp supply. It was admitted also that for years hemp had been the most important item of the American importation from the Philippines. In view of the fact that hemp was then the most important raw material in the manufacture of cordage, ropes, twines, and so forth, which were in demand the world over, hemp—the natural mo-

[51] See *Senate Document No. 191*, 58th Cong., 2nd Sess., pp. 1-17 for a copy of Governor Taft's address.

[52] *Annual Report*, Insular Collector of Customs, 1905, p. 18.

[53] *Ibid.;* See also *Appendix II*, Table 3.

[54] *Hearings* before the Senate Committee on the Philippines on the bill (S. 2259) published as *Senate Document No. 124*, 58th Cong., 2nd Sess.

nopoly of the Philippines—would always be in demand not only in the United States but also in England and in other foreign countries.

One of the most important reasons presented by the American cordage interests against the passage of the Frye bill was that it would create a monopoly for American shipping and that, unless properly safeguarded, the American shipping interests would charge very high freight rates. This, so it was maintained, would practically eliminate the American advantage derived from the non-imposition of export duty on hemp when imported into the United States, because the added cost of freight in American ships would more than compensate for the export duty. The trade would return to London.[55]

In buying their hemp in London, the American cordage manufacturers would have to pay the freight rate of around $0.46 on a hundred pounds of hemp from Manila to London plus the rate of $0.20 on the same quantity from London to the Atlantic seaboard and in addition the $0.35 rebate or thereabout on a hundred pounds of hemp—or a total cost of around $1.05. Under the Frye bill the freight rate on a hundred pounds of hemp direct from Manila either via the Pacific coast thence to the Atlantic seaboard or through the strait of Magellan or the Suez Canal would be at least $1.46.[56] Thus, the advantage to American manufacturers of the rebate of $7.50 a ton would be lost.

While this bill was ultimately passed and approved on April 15, 1904,[57] its operation was suspended until July 1, 1906. The extension of the American coastwise shipping laws to the Philippines was suspended again by virtue of the Acts of Congress of April 30, 1906[58] and April 29, 1908.[59] Finally, on June 5, 1920 the Merchant Marine Act was passed. This law provided that the American coastwise shipping laws should apply to all the island territories and possessions of the United States on February 1, 1922. There was attached however, a proviso to the effect that the extension of the law should not cover the Philippines "until the President of the United States after a full investigation of the local needs and conditions shall by proclamation, declare that an adequate shipping service has been established . . . and have fixed a date for the going into effect of the same."[60]

[55] *Hearings* before the Senate Committee on the Philippines on the bill (S. 2259) published as *Senate Document No. 124*, 58 Cong., 2nd Sess., p. 12. See also statement of Mr. G. F. Holmes, in *Ibid.*, pp. 32-38.

[56] *Ibid.*, p. 12.

[57] *Public No. 114, United States Statutes at Large*, Vol. XXXIII, Part I, p. 181.

[58] *Public No. 136, United States Statutes at Large*, Vol. XXXIV, Part I, p. 154.

[59] *Public No. 103, United States Statutes at Large*, Vol. XXXV, Part I, p. 70.

[60] Section 21, *Public No. 261, United States Statutes at Large*, Vol. XLI, Part I, p. 997.

Since hemp was then—and to a great extent is now—a Philippine natural monopoly, an export duty on this commodity would operate to increase its cost by practically the amount of the duty. The withdrawal of the export duty on American importation as provided for in Section 2 of the law under review, would tend to mean a differential advantage by practically the amount of the duty to be derived by the American cordage manufacturers, consequently, increasing their profits by the same amount, or giving them the American market exclusively. It was pointed out, however, that the $7.50 a ton rebate was for the benefit of the merchant and the farmer in the form of lower prices for binding twine, and other manufactures of hemp which the farmer uses.[61] On being reminded by Senator Lodge that early in 1902 the American cordage manufacturers urged the removal of the Philippine export duty on hemp imported directly into the United States as beneficial to the cordage manufacturers, Mr. Loring, President of the Plymouth Cordage Company, maintained that the American cordage manufacturers, being exporters did not need the rebate. He even expressed a willingness to return the rebate to the Filipinos.[62]

It should be noted that, notwithstanding the general economic distress in the Islands which characterized the period from 1897 to the early part of 1905, the only industry which actually flourished in spite of this distress, was hemp.[63] This is so, because hemp, a fiber of a banana-like plant thrives regardless of the labor expended. For instance, from 1899 to 1905 inclusive the total value of Philippine exports to all countries was listed at $184,015,232, while the total value of hemp was $121,325,877, or more than one-half of the total value. During the same period, from 1899 to 1905 inclusive, the total value of Philippine exports to the United States was $62,985,147. Of this amount $56,155,566 represented the total value of hemp exported to the United States.[64]

In view of the above figures the importance of hemp as the money

[61] See *Hearings* Before the Senate Committee on the Philippines on S. 2259, statement of Mr. A. P. Loring, pp. 1 *et seq*. See also statement of Mr. E. D. Metcalf, pp. 30-31.

[62] *Ibid.*, p. 11.

[63] While copra exports to the United States were negligible from 1899 to 1905, the entire value of copra exported to all countries steadily increased from $726,652 in 1899 to $3,244,703 in 1905, or from 5 per cent of the total exports in 1899 to 10 per cent in 1905. Notwithstanding fluctuations in value, the figures show an unmistakable and steady growth of the industry. See also *Annual Report*, Insular Collector of Customs, 1927, p. 75.

[64] *Annual Report*, Insular Collector of Customs, 1927, p. 73.

crop of the Filipinos and as one of the primary sources of revenue for the Philippine government can hardly be over emphasized. However, to compensate for the loss of revenue which would result from the $7.50 a ton rebate of the export duty extended to American importers of hemp, it was provided in Section 4 of the law under review that

> all duties and taxes collected in the United States upon all articles coming from the Philippine Archipelago and upon foreign vessels coming therefrom . . . shall be held as a separate fund and be paid into the treasury of the Philippine Islands to be used and expended for the government and benefit of said islands.

The extent of this compensation can be appreciated upon examination of the following figures showing United States customs collections and transfers to the Philippine treasury for the four fiscal years ending June 30:[65]

United States Customs Collections and Transfers to the Philippine Insular Treasury Under the Act of March 8, 1902 (1902-1905)

Fiscal Years	Import Duties	Tonnage Duties	Fines	Total by Years
1902	$ 72,045	$ 1,173	——	$ 73,218
1903	619,988	3,070	——	622,068
1904	472,496	1,252	$ 92	473,480
1905	248,992	2,603	36	251,631

Thus, from June 30, 1902 to June 30, 1905 the Insular treasury received $1,421,397 in consequence of the provision of Section 4. On the other hand, from 1902 to 1905 inclusive, the total American importation of Philippine hemp was 248,444 tons.[66] Since the export duty of $0.75 per 100 kilograms, or $7.50 per ton, was not collected on hemp imported directly into the United States, the American importers received a benefit of $1,863,330, and the Philippine government suffered diminution of revenue to the amount of $441,933.

In view of the fact that hemp was the only industry that did not suffer from the general economic distress that was characteristic of the period from 1897 to the early part of 1905, and was practically a monopoly, an export duty would not bear hardly on the producers.[67] It

[65] U. S. Tariff Commission, *United States Philippine Tariff and Trade Relations, Report* No. 18, Second Series, Table No. 36, p. 121.

[66] *Report,* Philippine Commission, 1908, Part II, pp. 590-592.

[67] *Annual Report,* Insular Collector of Customs, 1927, p. 73.

was in recognition of this fact that the Philippine Commission raised the export duty on hemp to $0.75 per one hundred kilograms.[68]

It should be recalled, in passing, that the rates of duty and the classification of goods in the tariff act of the Philippine Commission of September 17, 1901, and incorporated as a part of the law under review, were arranged so as to favor the Philippine market for American products. On the other hand, Congress did not give a sufficient advantage really to help Philippine sugar and tobacco.

The Act of March 3, 1905

Hardly had a year elapsed after the passage of the Act of March 8, 1902 when the economic distress in the Philippines had reached such an acute stage that it was deemed necessary to lower the duties on Philippine products. The Islands, be it recalled, had just emerged from a devastating warfare of almost six years with its attendant destruction of lives and property and the dislocation of the habits of peaceful industry. To make matters worse, the Philippines had undergone a frightful calamity. Aside from the ravages of cholera and other diseases, the Filipinos lost nearly ninety percent of their carabaos, cattle and horses through rinderpest, anthrax and surrax. And to increase their sufferings almost seventy-five percent of their rice crop was destroyed by locusts.[69]

Bearing in mind the general dependence of the Filipinos then—and even to a great extent at the present time—upon their draft animals to till the soil, aid in some ordinary work in the farm and farm life and transportation, the effects of their loss can be readily seen. Again, the damage done by locusts to their rice crops would raise the price of rice, their chief article of diet.

So serious did this situation appear to be that on December 5, 1902, Representative Henry A. Cooper of Wisconsin introduced a bill (H. R. 15702) to amend the Act of Congress of March 8, 1902. On December 17, the House Committee on Ways and Means, to which this bill was referred, reported the proposed measure favorably without amendment to the House of Representatives.[70] The purpose of this bill was merely to amend Section 2 of the Act of March 8, 1902 by lowering the rates charged on Philippine products imported into the

[68] See letter of transmittal of the proposed tariff for the Philippine Islands in *Senate Document No. 171*, p. 53.

[69] See, *Report*, Philippine Commission, 1903, Part II, pp. 114-115; Part III, pp. 123, *et seq.*

[70] *H. R. Report No. 2907*, p. 1.

United States from seventy-five percent to twenty-five percent of the Dingley rates.

In presenting the bill to the House of Representatives on December 18, Chairman Payne of the Ways and Means Committee informed the House of the calamity that had befallen the Filipinos. He indicated also that, from June 30 to September 30, the total revenue collected on Philippine products imported into the United States was only $15,-183.07, a very small sum compared with $12,000,000 of revenue which was received from other sources in the Islands.[71]

In recommending the immediate passage of the proposed measure, the House Committee on Ways and Means through its chairman concurred with the opinions of the Secretary of War and of the Philippine Commission that the reduction of the duty on Philippine products imported into the United States to twenty-five percent of the Dingley rates would not effect the market of commodities in the United States especially sugar and tobacco.[72] On the other hand, it was maintained that, should the proposed measure be adopted, while it would enable the Filipinos to place their sugar and tobacco in the United States, it would result also in a corresponding increase of Philippine importation of American products, hence, increasing the revenues of the Insular treasury. It would be reasonable to conclude according to Mr. Payne, that the benefits resulting from this tariff reduction would go directly to the Filipino people.[73] Not only that, but this tariff reduction also would tend to "help out and promote the agricultural and commercial interests of the islands."[74] The retention of the twenty-five percent levy of the Dingley tariff on Philippine goods imported into the United States was necessary for Philippine revenue purposes.[75]

Representative McClellan of New York, in expressing the views of the minority, deplored the "unusual haste" with which the proposed legislation had been reported to the House without awaiting the publication of the opinion of the Honorable Luke E. Wright, vice-governor of the Philippines, heard by the Ways and Means Committee upon the question involved in this bill.[76] The members of the House

[71] *Ibid.*, p. 2. Also *Cong. Record*, 57th Cong., 2nd Sess., Part I, p. 425. For the debate on this bill in the House see *Ibid.*, pp. 424-432.

[72] The recommendation of the Secretary of War incorporating the recommendation of the Philippine Commission is quoted on pp. 1-2 of the *H. R. Report No. 2907*.

[73] *H. R. Report No. 2907*, p. 2.

[74] *Cong., Record*, 57th Cong., 2nd Sess., Part I, p. 425.

[75] *H. R. Report, No. 2907* p. 2.

[76] *Ibid.*, p. 4.

should have been given the opportunity to look into the opinion of the vice-governor before casting their votes upon this proposed legislation. They were entitled to know, continued Mr. McClellan, that the interests of the Filipinos would be better served by allowing the free entry of their products into the United States rather than by the provision of the bill under review.[77]

In view of the fact that Congress would be in recess from December 2, 1902 to January 5, 1903, Mr. McClellan thought that it would scarcely be possible that this bill should be considered by the Senate until after the recess. However, if the Republican party was really solicitous to improve the conditions of the Filipinos, it should be courageous enough to adopt the amendment of the minority by repealing the Act of March 8, 1902, "to permit goods to come from the Philippines to the United States free of duty."[78] Of course, time must be given the country to forget the "extravagant expressions" used by members of the majority when the Act of March 8, 1902 was before the House, in which they insisted that the American workingmen and American interests must be protected from a flood of cheap Philippine products. In view of this, therefore, the barriers must not be let down as yet.

Mr. McClellan pointed out, however, that under the rules of the House it would be impossible for the minority to amend or radically alter the terms of a bill, and that the minority was powerless to relieve the Philippines from a system that it considered unconstitutional. On the other hand, a vote against the bill would be to maintain the existing rates of seventy-five percent of the Dingley law imposed upon Philippine products imported into the United States. A vote for the bill, however, would be a vote in favor of reducing the present rates to twenty-five percent of the Dingley law. Therefore, "as a choice between two evils, we shall vote for the bill."[79]

With reference to the establishment of free trade between the Philippines and the United States which was urged by the Democratic members of the House, Mr. Payne maintained that its adoption at that time was most unwise, for, it would mean the taking of about one-fifth of the revenue from the customs duty representing the duties collected on American and Spanish products entering the Philippines.[80]

This proposed measure (H. R. 15702) to amend the Act of March

[77] *Cong. Record*, 57th Cong., 2nd Sess., Part I, pp. 426-427.
[78] *H. R. Report No. 2907*, p. 5.
[79] *Ibid.*
[80] *Cong. Record*, 57th Cong., 2nd Sess., Part I, p. 430.

8, 1902, was passed by the House of Representatives on the same day (December 18) it was presented to the House by Mr. Payne, and it was immediately sent to the Senate.[81]

So convinced was the Administration of the seriousness of the universal economic distress in the Archipelago and the necessity for immediate action, that President Theodore Roosevelt on February 27, 1903 sent a special message to the Senate which was then considering the Cooper bill (H. R. 15702) the purpose of which was to reduce the existing rates on Philippine products to twenty-five percent of the Dingley rates. The President, after quoting Governor Taft's cablegram regarding the conditions in the Archipelago, asked the Senate to act favorably on the bill

> not merely from the standpoint of wise governmental policy, but as a measure of humanity in response to an appeal to which this great people should not close its ears. We have assumed responsibility toward the Philippine Islands which we are in honor bound to fulfil. We have the specific duty of taking every measure in our power to see to their prosperity. The first and most important step in this direction has been accomplished by the joint action of the military and civil authorities in securing peace and civil government. The wisdom of Congress at the present session has provided for them a stable currency and its spirit of humane liberality and justice toward them will be shown in the appropriation now substantially agreed upon of $3,000,000 to meet the pressing immediate necessities; but there remains a vital need that one thing further shall be done. The calamities which have befallen them . . . could have been averted by no human wisdom. They cannot be completely repaired; but the suffering can be greatly alleviated and a permanent basis of future prosperity assured if the economic relations of the islands with the United States are put upon a satisfactory basis.[82]

On January 22, 1903, the Senate Committee on the Philippines favorably reported to the Senate the Cooper bill (H. R. 15702) with two amendments.[83] The first amendment provided for the free admission for five years of all materials to be used in the construction and equipment of railroads in the Islands. It was pointed out that the Philippine Commission was wholly in favor of this provision in order to encourage the investment of American capital in such enterprises in the Archipelago.[84] The second amendment, and by far the most important,

[81] *Ibid.*, p. 468.

[82] *Messages and Papers of the Presidents*, Vol. XV, p. 6737.

[83] *Senate Report No. 2586*, p. 1. For the debate on this bill in the Senate, see *Cong. Record*, 57th Cong., 2nd Sess., Part III, pp. 2186-2188; 2977-2985; 2987-2988; 2991-3003; 3005-3006; 3008; 3066-3070.

[84] See *Senate Report No. 2586*, p. 1, for the letter of Hon. Elihu Root, Secretary of War, to Senator Henry Cabot Lodge under date of January 16, 1906.

was the reduction of the rates of duty levied on Philippine sugar and tobacco to fifty percent of the Dingley law while other products were to be allowed free entry into United States. The House bill, be it recalled, reduced the existing rates on all Philippine products to twenty-five percent of the Dingley law.[85]

Senator Lodge, chairman of the Senate Committee on the Philippines, in his reply to Senator Foraker's argument for the original House provision, admitted his preference for the larger reduction provided for in the House bill. The learned Senator was willing enough, however, to take the compromise rate of fifty percent of the Dingley law to be levied on Philippine sugar and tobacco and the provision allowing the free entry into the United States of all other products from the Islands rather than lose the bill for that session.[86]

It was a "notorious fact," according to Senator Carmack of Tennessee that the Senate was permitted to pass the bill (H. R. 15702) as amended by the Senate Committee on the Philippines "only after the sugar and tobacco interests realized that the fifty percent reduction of the Dingley rates on Philippine sugar and tobacco would not do them any harm or do the Filipinos any good."[87] While this statement was obviously an expression of the Senator's opinion on the matter, nevertheless, it showed even then the reluctance of domestic interests to give concessions on similar products from the Philippines imported into the United States.

Senator Patterson of Colorado, one of the strongest defenders of the home sugar industry, while cognizant of the economic distress in the Philippines, was opposed nevertheless to the passage of the bill. To his mind, the passage of the bill would furnish the necessary incentive for the great exploiting corporations to get possession of the eight million acres of Philippine lands adapted to the raising of sugar. He said that should the bill become a law, within less than ten years after its enactment "the local industry of the United States will be practically wiped out; that the sugar cane industry of Louisiana and the beet industry of Michigan, Colorado and other beet-sugar raising States, in ten years will be wiped out on account of the immense area of the Philippine territory that may be used for the cultivation of sugar."[88]

On being asked by Senator Beveridge of Indiana whether he was in favor of a tariff for revenue only, Mr. Patterson replied that "as long

[85] *Ibid.*
[86] *Cong. Record,* 57th Cong., 2nd Sess., Part III, p. 2186.
[87] *Ibid.*
[88] *Ibid.,* p. 2187.

as protection, whatever its phase may be, is the controlling economic position of this country, I propose to stand for the protection of the products of my section, whatever my attitude may be upon the question of the tariff as a broad, general proposition."[89]

On March 3, 1903, the Cooper bill (H. R. 15702) was again brought up before the Senate for further discussion. In the course of the debate, Senator Lodge pointed out that while the tobacco industry is one of the most important industries of Massachusetts, none the less he was recommending the passage of the bill, for[90]

> in the vast volume of imports of the United States the small amount of the increase in sugar and tobacco that would come by the passage of this bill would go unnoticed. But, small as it is to us, it may mean life or death to hundreds of those people. We have given them $3,000,000 in the sundry civil appropriation bill to restock their farms and help them buy cattle and start again; but the greatest charity, the largest humanity, that we can show them is to open the channels for reviving business.

However, in spite of the appeals of responsible authorities who had charge of the affairs of the Archipelago, the Senate, for all practical purposes, talked the bill to death. The embattled Senators who were apprehensive of the future of the sugar and tobacco industry in the Philippines won the day. Senator Hoar of Massachusetts gave the epilogue in the following language:

> I think it is my duty to call the attention of the Senate and of the country to the first great object lesson which instructs us as to the absolute unfitness of the American people undertaking to govern distant dependencies.
>
> Here are nine or ten million people, upon whom is impending a terrible famine accompanied by pestilence. This does not rest on the authority of discontent. . . . If nine or ten million Americans had such a calamity impending over them, we would lay aside every thought of other business or affairs; we would have an extra session of Congress; we would sit day and night; the whole resources of the charity and the wealth and the humanity of the American people would be taxed to their utmost.
>
> Now, what have we done? We have appropriated $3,000,000—30 cents, or thereabouts, apiece—to relieve that people. Governor Taft tells us that that will be utterly inefficient, and that unless we make this or some other provision for restoring their industries a terrible fate is not to be averted.[91]

Late in 1903, in the meantime, a group of American business men in the Islands pressed for the modification of the Philippine tariff. In response to this, Governor Taft issued an executive order on Novem-

[89] *Ibid.*
[90] *Ibid.*, p. 2978.
[91] *Ibid.*, p. 3066.

ber 25, 1903, appointing a group of prominent business men of Manila in cooperation with the customs officials[92] to make a report to the Philippine Commission regarding "needed changes in the existing tariff law, to enable the Commission to recommend to Congress amendments to the law in such particulars as experience has shown the said law to be defective, inconsistent with itself, or oppressive in the matter of prohibiting useful importations."[93] The Governor asked the committee to act immediately that he might be able to bring with him to the United States its recommendations and present these to the authorities.

The report of the committee, together with the recommendations of the Philippine Commission, was embodied in a proposed measure to amend the existing tariff laws of the Philippines. Late in 1904 this proposed legislation was transmitted to the Secretary of War, who, as in the previous tariff legislation for the Philippines, had this proposed measure published and invited the suggestions and recommendations of all those in the United States interested in Philippine trade.[94] The significant difference was that at this time there were but few suggestions and recommendations.[95]

In the meantime, on January 23, 1905, Representative Payne of New York introduced a bill (H. R. 18195) the purpose of which was to revise and amend the tariff laws of the Philippines and for other purposes.[96] On February 13, however, Mr. Payne reported another bill, H. R. 18965, as a substitute for his original bill. The purpose of this substitute bill was "to revise and amend the tariff laws of the Philippine Islands, and for other purposes."[97] The latter bill was the proposed legislation recommended by the Philippine Commission as amended by the War Department.

Chairman Payne of the House Committee on Ways and Means, in

[92] The members of this committee were: H. B. McCoy, acting Collector of Customs for the Philippines; W. E. Pullian special deputy collector of customs; J. S. Stanley, acting Insular deputy Collector of Customs; M. F. Loewenstein; Francisco Reyes, President, Filipino Chamber of Commerce; and Frank L. Strong. Mr. Henry Woolfe was appointed to act secretary.

[93] See *Executive Order No. 100*, dated Manila, Nov. 25, 1903 in *Report*, Philippine Commission, 1904, Part I, p. 688.

[94] *Report*, Chief of the Bureau of Insular Affairs to the Secretary of War, Oct. 31, 1904, pp. 1004 *et seq*. attached to the *Annual Report* of the Secretary of War, 1904, Vol. XIII.

[95] *Ibid.*

[96] *Cong. Record*, 58th Cong., 3rd Sess., Part II, p. 1274.

[97] *Ibid.*, Part III, p. 2508. For the debate on this bill, see pp. 2993-3006; 3022; 3131; Part IV, pp. 3528-3529; 3714-3718; 3900.

favorably reporting H. R. 18965 to the House, pointed out that this substitute bill was "the result of much investigation and labor on the part of the insular government and of the Bureau of Insular Affairs of the War Department."[98] No mention was made, however, of the unsatisfactory character of the existing tariff as it affected the Islands. On the other hand, the House Committee reassured the American tobacco and sugar interests that the bill under consideration did not at all affect the question of goods imported into the United States from the Philippines. That is to say, the rates of duty imposed on Philippine sugar and tobacco when imported into the United States as provided for in the Act of March 8, 1902 remained the same. The proposed legislation, therefore, concerned only goods imported into the Philippine Islands.[99]

Furthermore, as an assurance to American exporters that their product would continue to be favored in Philippine markets against foreign competitors, the House Committee pointed out that 224 paragraphs out of 407 in the original bill had not been changed and some of the changes had been made only for the purpose of substituting equivalent *ad valorem* for the specific duties contained in the existing act.[100] In other words, the preference extended to American goods as provided for in the Act of March 8, 1902 was maintained also in the present bill. It was stated further that the proposed measure was exclusively a revenue measure, the average rate of duty being 20 percent or thereabouts.[101]

As a matter of fact, the House Committee on Ways and Means was quite honest in admitting that "the general purpose of this bill, as of the former act, is to give the United States what benefits there are arising from classification of goods."[102]

In answering the question asked by Representative Crumpacker of Indiana as to whether the present bill created any preference in favor of products from the United States, chairman Payne stated that "when the original act was passed two years ago it was so framed as to give advantage to American merchants by the various classifications of goods; the width of goods adapted to American looms and that sort of thing ran through the bill. In this revision the same idea has been carried out, so whatever advantage that could be given to American

[98] *H. R. Report No. 4600*, p. 1.
[99] *Cong. Record*, 58th Cong., 3rd Sess., Part III, p. 2993.
[100] *H. R. Report No. 4600*, p. 1.
[101] *Ibid.* See also *Cong. Record*, 58th Cong., 3rd Sess., Part III, p. 2995.
[102] *H. R. Report No. 4600*, p. 1.

merchants by reason of classification has been effected more fully in this bill, but there is no difference in the rate of duty."[103] It was explained that a reduction in the rate of duty on goods coming from the United States would be extended also to similar goods coming from Spain by virtue of the provisions of the Treaty of Paris.

On being asked to compare the existing rate on cotton and cotton fabrics and manufactured fabrics, with the rates provided for in the proposed measure, Mr. Payne quieted the fears of the cotton interests by assuring them that very little change, if any, had been made in the existing schedules. And this change, according to him, was made solely to give the "United States mills a better chance in the market than foreign mills, through the classification of the goods," which, he confided, was even "improved upon in some respects."[104]

On the whole, the main line of policy laid down in the Tariff Act of September 17, 1901, and the revenue act of March 8, 1902, was maintained in the proposed measure (H. R. 18965).

Among the important provisions of this proposed legislation, which were in the nature of amendments to the existing tariff law of the Philippines, were: the duties on manufactured tobacco imported into the Islands were reduced fifty percent, since it was found that the former rates were prohibitive and, therefore, not productive of revenue; duties on the finer qualities of shoes were slightly increased, while the duty on calfskin and other common shoes remained the same; on agricultural machinery, electrical machinery, and other machinery used largely in the Philippines which can be manufactured in the United States, the duty was reduced to five percent *ad valorem* so as to encourge the introduction and use of machinery into the Islands and still have a slight revenue from it; the duty on gasoline was reduced by fifty percent because of the large use of gasoline engines in the Islands. In order to accommodate "the grand dames in the Philippines" to whom mirrors were a necessity, the duty on mirrors was reduced one third as the existing rate of duty was almost prohibitive. The rates on finer grades of porcelain and crockery were reduced for the same reason.[105]

The existing duties on rice[106] were maintained in the proposed measure, with the additional provision, however, that, the Philippine

[103] *Cong. Record* 58th Cong., 3rd Sess., Part III, p. 2993.

[104] *Ibid.*, p. 2995.

[105] *H. R. Report No. 4600*, pp. 1-2. For the rates of duty levied on the above-named commodities see *Senate Document No. 134*, Exhibit C, pp. 34-36; 55-57; 65.

[106] *Sen. Doc. No. 134*, p. 59.

Commission, within certain limits, might raise the duties on rice in the future. The reason for this grant of power was "to meet the exigencies of the case in the future raising of rice. It may be necessary to increase the duty for the purpose of revenue, and it might be necessary to increase the duty for the purpose of encouragement of the home production."[107]

On being asked by Mr. Burgess of Texas whether the provision in the law regarding rice affected adversely the exportation of American rice to the Philippines, Mr. Payne pointed out that notwithstanding the fact that in 1904 the Filipinos imported rice to the value of $15,000,000, none was imported from the United States. This, continued Mr. Payne, was due to the nearness of the Islands to the rice producing and rice exporting countries of the world. In view of this fact no possible changes in the tariff schedules, according to Mr. Payne, would actually stimulate the exportation of rice from United States to the Islands.[108]

A slight duty on mineral water was imposed. This, it was thought, would be sufficient to protect the mineral water industry of the Philippines from Japanese competition.

At the request of the Philippine Commission and the War Department, an exact copy of the rebate clause of the existing tariff law of the United States was included in the proposed measure together with a similar provision regarding invoices of goods coming from foreign countries requiring the consular certificate. The necessity of such a provision was occasioned by the institution of *ad valorem* instead of specific duties, as heretofore, in a good many commodities. And where the goods came from United States, it was provided that "the invoice has to be made and taken before a notary public and certified by him."[109]

Lastly, with the exception of the export duty on rice which was removed, the present bill maintained the same schedule of export duties on the principal exports of the Archipelago.

This proposed measure was finally passed in the House of Representatives on February 21, 1905,[110] and it was immediately reported to the Senate.[111]

The House bill as amended by the Senate was finally approved and

[107] *H. R. Report No. 4600*, p. 3.
[108] *Cong. Record*, 58th Cong., 3rd Sess., Part III, p. 2994.
[109] *Ibid.*, p. 2995.
[110] *Ibid.*, p. 3006.
[111] *Ibid.*, p. 3022.

passed. And upon signature by President Theodore Roosevelt on March 3, 1905 it became a law.[112]

THE ACT OF FEBRUARY 26, 1906

The merits or demerits of any legislation or part thereof can be demonstrated only by actual experience. We have noted how the classifications of cotton textiles and their rates of duty in the Tariff Act of September 17, 1901, were primarily designed to encourage the importation of American cotton goods.[113] In view of the assurance given by Mr. Payne,[114] chairman of the Committee on Ways and Means of the House of Representatives, and the testimony of Secretary of War Taft,[115] very few changes were made in the Act of March 3, 1905, on the original cotton schedules. Whatever changes were made were intended to favor the Philippine markets for American cotton goods. That the fond expectations of those who arranged the classifications on cotton goods were not fully realized, however, can be gleaned from the following figures: The total cotton imports of the Philippines during the three fiscal years, 1903, 1904, and 1905 were valued at $6,284,-370, $4,962,354, $6,336,962 respectively. During the same years, however, the values of cotton goods imported from the United States were only $389,303, $319,666 and $764,088 respectively.[116]

In order to correct this state of affairs, therefore, Mr. Payne, on December 21, 1905, introduced a bill (H. R. 9978)[117] for the purpose of revising the tariff laws of the Philippines, approved March 3, 1905. On January 25, 1906, however, Mr. Payne reported another bill (H. R. 13104)[118] to the House of Representatives for the same purpose. This bill which was immediately referred to the House Committee on Ways and Means was reported favorably to the House of Representatives.[119] When this proposed measure was finally presented by Mr. Payne on February 9, it was passed by the House on the same day with hardly any debate.[120]

[112] *Ibid.*, Part IV, p. 3715.

[113] *Supra*, pp. 31-32.

[114] See *Cong. Record*, 58th Cong., 3rd Sess., Part III, pp. 2993-2995.

[115] See *Hearings* before the Senate Committee on the Philippines, statement of Hon. William H. Taft, Secretary of War, published in *Cong. Record*, 58th Cong., 3rd Sess., Part IV, pp. 3714-3718.

[116] *Report*, Philippine Commission, 1908, Part II, pp. 587-588, 590.

[117] *Cong. Record*, 59th Cong., 1st Sess., Part I, p. 672.

[118] *Ibid.*, Part II, pp. 1588, 1597.

[119] *H. R. Report No. 582*, 59th Cong., 1st Sess.

[120] *Cong. Record*, 59th Cong., 1st Sess., Part III, pp. 2391-2393.

The proposed measure (H. R. 13104), with the exception of the recommendations by the Philippine Commission for the reduction of the duties in some parts of the shoe schedules and the elimination of the export duty imposed upon fresh coconuts, was primarily designed to amend the existing cotton schedules in order to rectify the "manifest errors" of the Philippine tariff laws.

The motivating factors behind the movement to amend the existing schedules provided for in Paragraphs 117 to 120 inclusive and in Paragraph 123 covering carded textiles of the Act of March 3, 1905 were set forth in the letter sent to Colonel Edwards, Chief of the Bureau of Insular Affairs, by Theodore T. Gorman, secretary of the Merchants' Association of New York, under date of December 18, 1905. Since the reasons advanced by the Merchants' Association for amending the above-noted schedules on textiles coincided perfectly with the opinions of the members of the House Committee on Ways and Means, the letter itself was used as fully expressing the reasons for the proposed legislation and was included textually in the report.[121] As will be shown presently,[122] the same arguments expressed in the letter were used also by the Senate Committee on the Philipines as the reason for its approval of the proposed measure.[123]

In urging the immediate passage of the bill, Mr. Payne pointed out that during the passage of the Act of March 3, 1905 "some gentlemen claiming to represent the cotton manufacturers of the United States secured an amendment, and this amendment became incorporated into the bill on the assurance that the amendment would give advantage to the manufacturers of the United States over the manufacturers of foreign countries, and on that representation the amendment went into the bill and was made part of the law."[124] However, it was discovered later, continued Mr. Payne, that instead of helping the American cotton manufacturers it virtually excluded them from the Philippine trade as the figures[125] tend to show.

One of the principal reasons for the virtual exclusion of American cotton textiles in the Philippine markets was this:[126] Instead of orig-

[121] *H. R. Report No. 582*, 59th Cong., 1st Sess.

[122] *Infra*, p. 69.

[123] *Cong. Record* 59th Cong., 1st Sess., Part III, p. 2718; also *Senate Report No. 1178*, 59th Cong., 1st Sess.

[124] *Cong. Record*, 59th Cong., 1st Sess., Part III, p. 2391.

[125] See *Supra*, p. 64, also *Report*, Philippine Commission, 1908, Part II, pp. 587-588, 590.

[126] *Cong. Record*, 59th Cong., 1st Sess., Part III, pp. 2391-2392; see also *H. R. Report No. 582*, pp. 1-2.

inally weaving the textiles in the widths finally desired as was the practice among American mills, the European manufacturers used a special loom of double the width of the desired textiles. For instance, for a desired print of twenty-five inches in width a loom of fifty-two inches is taken (two inches being allowed for shrinkage in width during the finishing operations). At the center of this wide 52-inch textile two sets of heavy warp threads, slightly separated, are placed and the fabric is woven fifty-two inches wide. Still in this width, the fabric is run through the bleaching, printing, and finishing apparatus. After the completion of manufacturing and finishing, the fabric is "split" or torn lengthwise at the weak center line between the two sets of heavy threads, thus giving two lengths of textiles of the original length woven, but only twenty-five inches wide. These textiles, however, could always be distinguished from American textiles manufactured in single width with true selvage on each edge by the appearance of the false or split selvage along one of the sides.

While it was admitted that the European method of manufacture was much more economical than that prevailing in the United States, it was emphasized that its adoption by the American manufacturers would be economically and practically impossible, since adoption of the European method would mean the "complete loss of the present capital invested in textile machinery and an investment of new capital in wide machinery for this special purpose."[127] Furthermore, adoption of the European method would mean the employment of skilled operators and as a consequence much higher wages. It was pointed out that American wages were already "much higher than among European textile manufacturers."[128] In view of these considerations, and in order to establish a "fair basis" for the introduction in the markets of the Philippines of "American textiles woven with true selvages in all widths," it was urged that a new paragraph and note should be added to read as follows:

> Textiles having a false selvage, on either one or both sides, shall be considered as goods improved in condition, and shall be liable, as the textile, to the duties leviable thereon, plus an additional surtax of one hundred per centum. This provision applies to all cotton fabrics.
>
> *Note:*—By a false selvage shall be understood an edge obtained by cutting, ripping, tearing, or otherwise splitting the textile in the direction of the warp.[129]

[127] *H. R. Report No. 582*, p. 2.
[128] *Ibid.*
[129] *Ibid.*, p. 1.

Hence, by this new provision, a double tax was levied on "false selvage goods" in order that, according to Mr. Payne, "American manufacturers will have at least an equal chance" in the markets of the Philippines "with the manufacturers of other countries."[130]

The second recommendation of the Merchants' Association of New York was a revised schedule of counts to apply uniformly to paragraphs 117, covering plain goods of heavy weave; 118, covering light goods of plain weave; 119, covering heavy goods of twill and fancy weave; and 120, covering light goods of twill and fancy weave. It was maintained that the schedules provided for in the above paragraphs were based upon and in the main followed the original schedule of counts of the Spanish tariff primarily intended for the benefit of the Spanish and European manufacturers. On the other hand, American textiles were manufactured on a wholly different basis.[131] And since the Philippines is now an American possession, it was only fair, so it was maintained, that the counts scheduled in the Philippine tariff law should "conform to the methods used by American manufacturers."[132] Mr. Payne emphasized the fact that "to insure that fairness to the American products it is absolutely necessary that the system of counts should be made to conform to the American schedules."[133]

Hence, the rates of duty and the schedule of counts in the above-named paragraphs were revised in order that American textiles of this class should have "the best possible position" in the Philippine markets, "in competition with the products of other countries."[134]

With reference to paragraphs 117 and 119 a proviso in the form of a "note" was attached providing that "Textiles woven with a colored yarn on the selvage or with a colored selvage stripe not exceeding 2 millimeters in widths shall not be considered as manufactured with dyed yarns."[135]

The above proviso was made necessary, according to the Merchants' Association, because of a custom prevalent among the American manufacturers of sailcloths, twills, ducks and the like, that a blue line, usually two millimeters in width, is interwoven to serve as a guide in sewing two widths together. It was expected, therefore, that the above proviso would overcome the possibility in the existing tariff that

[130] *Cong. Record*, 59th Cong., 1st Sess., Part III, p. 2391.
[131] *H. R. Report No. 582*, p. 4.
[132] *Ibid.*
[133] *Cong. Record*, 59th Cong., 1st Sess., Part III, p. 2392.
[134] *Ibid.*
[135] *H. R. Report No. 582*, p. 4.

American fabrics so manufactured might be required to pay the duty imposed upon "fabrics colored throughout."[136]

As its last recommendation, the Merchants' Association offered the following amendments to paragraph 123 covering the carded textiles, such as blankets and other similar articles. The two changes recommended were: the "admission of blankets by schedule in accordance with the percentage of color" and secondly, the admission of "hemmed blankets."[137]

According to the letter of the Association, a large proportion of American blankets is manufactured without color except the small stripe or set of stripes known technically as the "border." Colored yarns in these borders form but a very small percentage of the total yarn composing the blanket. On the other hand, under the existing tariff any particle of colored yarn added to a blanket would place the latter in the category of blankets composed entirely of colored yarn, thus making it subject to an additional duty of six cents per kilo. Since blankets with a large percentage of colored yarns were more expensive than the plain ones, and ought to be subject to a high rate of duty, it would be consistent, so it was maintained, to permit the entry of American blankets with colored borders at lower rate of duty.

Concluding its letter, the Merchants' Association maintained that the above-mentioned amendments were "necessary and essential," and that in submitting them the Association had always been guided by the "necessity of maintaining the revenues of the Philippine Islands." Representing as it did "the greater part of the cotton manufacturers of the United States," with millions of capital invested in the industry and "giving employment to hundreds of thousands of American citizens," the Merchants' Association of New York, therefore, urged the immediate adoption of its recommendation.[138]

As previously noted,[139] there were other minor changes proposed in the bill which were recommended by the Philippine Commission. These were the reduction of duties in some parts of the shoe schedules and elimination of the export duty levied on fresh coconuts.[140]

So convinced were the individual members of Congress of the importance of the amending legislation and the necessity for its immedi-

[136] *Ibid.*

[137] *Ibid.*, p. 5.

[138] *Ibid.*, p. 5.

[139] *Supra*, p. 67.

[140] See the Letter of the Secretary of War Taft under date of January 16, 1906, addressed to Hon. Sereno E. Payne, published in *H. R. Report No. 582*, pp. 7-8.

ate passage that it was unanimously reported by the House Committee on Ways and Means, passed by the House on the day it was presented and immediately sent to the Senate which referred it to the Senate Committee on the Philippines. On February 20, 1906, the Senate Committee not only reported the bill H. R. 13104 favorably to the Senate but also adopted the arguments presented in the letter of Theodore T. Gorman, secretary of the Merchants' Association of New York, as its own in recommending the passage of the bill.[141] When Mr. Lodge presented the bill to the Senate two days later, it was approved without any debate and passed in record time.[142] On February 26, 1906, upon signature by the President it became a law.[143]

Because of the lack of sufficiently early information as to the enactment of the above law, many importers of English and German goods who had placed contracts for large quantities of fabrics were not able seasonably to countermand their order, thereby finding themselves obliged to pay very heavy duties upon the arrival of their goods in the Philippine Islands and so suffered heavy losses, as they claimed, by reason thereof. It was also charged that in view of the changes made in the cotton schedules foreign manufacturers would be virtually excluded from the Philippine markets, and thus, with the elimination of foreign competition, the American cotton manufacturers, so it was maintained, would raise the cost of cotton goods to the natives of the Philippine Islands.[144] The following figures showing Philippine importation of cotton goods from all countries for the fiscal years ending June 30, 1904 to June 30, 1908, did not justify the fear.[145]

Imported from:	1904	1905	1906	1907	1908
All other countries	$4,642,688	5,572,874	6,363,533	7,263,751	7,325,915
The United States	319,666	764,088	278,796	1,056,328	685,919
Total	$4,962,354	6,336,962	6,642,329	8,320,079	8,011,834

NOTE:—Values expressed in United States currency. Amounts in cents were omitted.

It can be seen from the above figures that under normal conditions the total Philippine importation of cotton goods from America should

[141] See *Senate Report No. 1178*; also *Cong. Record*, 59th Cong., 1st Sess., Part III, p. 2718.

[142] *Cong. Record*, 59th Cong., 1st Sess., Part III, p. 2835.

[143] *Ibid.*, p. 3069.

[144] See *Report*, Philippine Commission, 1906, Part III, pp. 14-15.

[145] *Ibid.*, 1908, Part II, pp. 287, 588.

have increased steadily. The encouraging figures of 1907 following the passage of the tariff act of February 26, 1906 were not maintained, and Philippine imports of American cotton goods which were increased by $777,532 in 1907 over that of the previous year, declined to $685,919 in 1908. On the other hand, Philippine imports of cotton goods from all other countries continued to increase—nothwithstanding the Act of February 26, 1906—although the increase for 1908 over the imports during 1907 was only $62,164. Three reasons seemed to explain this singular fact.

In the first place, Philippine importers of British and German fabrics, because of previous contracts, were not able to cancel their orders. Philippine importation of foreign textiles, being practically the same during the fiscal years 1907 and 1908, tended to substantiate the claim of great losses suffered by importers of British and German fabrics.

In the second place, the Japanese victory over Russia in 1905 electrified the Chinese people and aroused in them a new sense of nationality. "Engineered by the Cantonese in Canton and in San Francisco, California, and fomented by the students of the new era, especially by those who had studied in Japan" a boycott of American trade—subsequently extended to other countries—was instituted by the Chinese people "as a means of strengthening the hands of their government to permit the unrestricted immigration of Chinese into the United States."[146] This boycott of American trade found its way into the Philippines where it gained momentum due to the losses suffered by the Chinese traders as a result of the immediate operation of the Act of February 26, 1906.[147] The effectiveness of such a boycott could not be under-estimated since the Chinese were, and still are, the principal retailers in the Philippines and to some extent they were also the direct importers of some commodities including wheat flour and cotton goods.

While it was true that as a result of the representations by the Powers, including the United States, strong measures were taken by the Imperial Chinese Government to stamp out the boycott movement in China,[148] the effects of the Chinese boycott in the Philippines against American manufactures continued to be felt there until 1907 as far as wheat flour was concerned. And as far as cotton importation

[146] H. B. Morse and H. F. MacNair, *Far Eastern International Relations*, pp. 548-549.
[147] *Report*, Philippine Commission, 1906, Part III, p. 18 ff.
[148] Morse and MacNair, *op. cit.*, p. 459.

from the United States was concerned, it seemed that the unfavorable effects of the boycott must have been in part responsible for the unfavorable showing in 1908, in view of the precipitous decline in Philippine importation of American cotton goods during this fiscal year.

And thirdly, the reduced values in all the large items of cloths, knit goods, yarn and thread during the fiscal year 1908 must have been offset, to some extent, according to the Philippine Commission, by the increases in cotton goods of minor importance by reason of the increase of Philippine importation from foreign countries represented by the sum of $62,164.[149]

The increase in Philippine importation of foreign textiles as shown in the figures for the fiscal years 1907 and 1908 seemed to refute the claim[150] that the Act of February 26, 1906 would tend toward an American monopoly of the Philippine market on textiles.[151] This is obviously due to the following reasons, namely, the lower cost of European methods[152] and the better adaptability of European products to Philippine conditions. And finally, any act which tends to divert the old-established channels of trade must of necessity take into account the time element.

General Summary[153] 1901 to 1908

We have noted that from the enactment by the Philippine Commission of the Tariff Act of September 17, 1901—later incorporated as part of the Tariff Act enacted by the Congress on March 8, 1902—to the passage by the Congress of the Act of February 26, 1906, Philippine tariff rates were arranged not only to bring in more revenue for the Philippine government but also to encourage Philippine importation of American goods. On the American end of the line it had been deemed necessary to maintain the Dingley rates with the twenty-five percent reduction on Philippine goods subject to customs duty when imported into the United States. As a consequence of this trade policy, Philippine import from the United States had been greatly increased

[149] *Report*, Philippine Commission, 1908, Part III, p. 18. See also *Infra*, p. 73.

[150] *Supra*, pp. 69-70.

[151] *Report*, Philippine Commission, 1908, Part III, p. 18.

[152] *Supra*, pp. 66-67.

[153] Summary is drawn from the *Report* of the Collector of Customs for 1908 attached to the *Report* of the Secretary of Finance and Justice under date of October 26, 1908 to the Philippine Commission. See *Report*, Philippine Commission, 1908, Part II, pp. 587-588.

under the tariff legislation[154] in effect, both in actual value and in proportion to the goods imported from foreign countries.[155]

For instance, the values showing Philippine imports of cotton goods from the United States from 1901 to 1905 inclusive is quite instructive. While Philippine importation in 1901 was only $94,655, this amount had been increased steadily, and in 1903 it reached the value of $389,303. This value for 1903, however, was decreased by $69,637 during the following year. But in 1905, Philippine imports of American cotton goods reached the value of $764,088. On the other hand, Philippine importation of cotton goods from all other countries during the fiscal years 1901 to and including 1905 were valued at $9,346,-382; $6,798,091; $5,895,067; $4,642,688; and $5,572,874 respectively.

In view of this fact, therefore, American cotton interests urged the amendment of the Tariff Act of March 8, 1902. Hence, in the Tariff Act of March 3, 1905, amendments were made in some of the cotton schedules for the purpose of encouraging further importation into the Philippines of American cotton goods. The results of these amendments, however, were not satisfactory as shown by the figure representing Philippine imports of American cotton goods for the fiscal year 1906. Thus, on February 26, 1906 the Congress enacted other tariff legislation for the Philippines to amend the Tariff Act of March 3, 1905. On the whole, the amending legislation of February 26, 1906 was quite satisfactory notwithstanding the fact that the value of $1,056,328, representing the Philippine cotton imports from the United States for the fiscal year 1907, was not maintained in 1908. It is safe to assume that had it not been for the Chinese boycott in the Philippines against American manufactures, the importation into the Islands of American cotton goods would have been much more than the imports for 1907. This was borne out in the subsequent data showing Philippine importation of this commodity from the mother country.

Since Philippine tariff schedules had been arranged generally to favor the Philippine markets for American goods over similar goods from foreign countries, it follows that, on the whole, and with few exceptions, the percentage of Philippine importation of American goods must show a tendency to exceed the importation into the Islands of

[154] While in later years other reasons than tariff preferences—such as better and superior quality of American products—may have actuated Philippine importation from the United States, there is no doubt that during the early years of the American régime in the Islands, American tariff legislation played a decisive part in diverting the channels of Philippine trade and commerce.

[155] See *Appendix II*, Table No. 4.

similar products from foreign countries. This is obvious in the above comparative table showing the value of Philippine imports from the United States and from all other countries. It is interesting to note the fact, however, that from the fiscal year ending June 30, 1902 to and including the fiscal year 1908, the United States did not rank first as an exporting country to the Philippines. The relative rank of the United States with other exporting countries was in 1902, third; 1903, fourth; 1904, second; 1905, second; 1906, second; 1907, second; 1908, third.

It should be noted that government free entries are not included in these tabulations. That is to say, commodities or materials to be used by the United States Government in the Philippines and also those which were to be used by the Insular government were admitted into the Islands free of duty. While no exact figures as to the actual value of that merchandise are obtainable, it would be safe to assume, however, that had its value been added to the total value of the merchandise coming from the United States, it would be more than the value of the merchandise coming from any other countries.

On the whole, Philippine exports to the United States did not increase in proportion to the increase in the imports of the Islands therefrom.[156]

The principal imports of the United States from the Philippines for the fiscal years 1901 to 1908 inclusive were hemp and sugar, the latter being a poor second.[157] The tremendous fluctuations of the sugar imports of the United States from the Islands during the fiscal years 1906 and 1907 deserve explanation. Sugar exports of the Islands from 1905 to 1907 inclusive were 168,798; 131,000; and 124,901 tons respectively. Although the quantities exported during 1906 and 1907 were greater than the exports for 1905 the values received for the 1906 and 1907 exports were less in view of the reduced prices on sugar during the two years. Hence, out of the total sugar exports of 131,000 tons for 1906 and 124,901 tons for 1907 only 7,187 and 6,506 tons were exported to the United States during 1906 and 1907 respectively at values of $260,104 and $234,074. Thus, during these two years Philippine sugar found an almost exclusively Oriental market.[158]

Copra and tobacco, on the other hand, were not as important. Yet, in spite of this fact, it is interesting to know that from 1902 to 1908 the United States—as far as the total value of imports is concerned—

[156] See *Appendix II*, Tables No. 4 and 5.
[157] *Ibid.*, Table No. 5.
[158] See *Report*, Philippine Commission, 1907, Part I, pp. 15, 62.

ranked as the largest importer of goods from the Philippine Islands because of the great importation of hemp by American cordage manufacturers.[159]

The provision of the Act of March 8, 1902 regarding the withdrawal of the export duty of $7.50 a ton on hemp when sent directly to the United States for use and consumption therein, played an influential part in augmenting American importation of the product. At times American cordage manufacturers were able to offer a higher price for Manila hemp because of this rebate.[160] None the less, foreign importations continued.

American importations of Philippine copra, while showing a tendency to increase and which, like hemp, had its export duty of 10 cents a 100 kilograms removed when sent direct to the United States, remained negligible, however, when compared with foreign importations.

Philippine sugar and tobacco, on the other hand, were not favorably received in American markets—in so far as the customs duties levied on them were concerned. Although a twenty-five percent reduction of the Dingley rates was provided for sugar and tobacco, in addition to a further reduction equivalent to their respective export duties when imported into the United States, it seems obvious that these reductions were inadequate—as the table of Philippine exports[161] indicates.

In spite of the petitions and memorials of the Philippine sugar planters and tobacco operatives regarding the necessity of reducing the rates of duty levied on Philippine sugar and tobacco to twenty-five percent of the Dingley rates, Congress deemed it proper to maintain the existing seventy-five percent rates on the above products of the Archipelago. The reasons for this polciy are not hard to discover.

Be it recalled that the political party that sponsored the acquisition of the Philippine Islands was the Republican party, the party of protection. In 1900 it made a "distinct promise" to the farmers that they need not fear that the Republican party would permit the cheap labor and the cheap sugar and tobacco of any tropical territory to be brought to the United States in a manner which would destroy the domestic sugar and tobacco industries "which the farmers of the United States have, under the fostering care of the Republican party,

[159] *Appendix II*, Table No. 6.

[160] See *Census of the Philippine Islands*, 1918, Vol. IV, Part II, p. 714; see also *Appendix II*, Table No. 5.

[161] See *Appendix II*, Tables No. 1, 2 and 5.

been building up during the last few years."[162] In 1904, the Republican platform declared the principle of protection which "guards and develops" American industries to be "a cardinal policy of the Republican party,"[163] and the extent of such protection was to be measured by the difference in the cost of production at home and abroad.[164] And in 1908, the same political party, while it favored a "free interchange" of products between the Philippines and the United States, maintained that products of the Archipelago should be placed under "such limitations as to sugar and tobacco as will afford adequate protection to domestic interests."[165]

Throughout the period under review, the Republican party was in control of the executive and the legislative branches of the Government. The above declarations, therefore, were an index of governmental policy. How far the Republican party followed its 1908 platform as far as American tariff policy in the Philippines is concerned will be revealed in the chapter that follows.

[162] *Republican Party Campaign Textbook*, 1900, p. 152.
[163] *Ibid.*, 1904, p. 486.
[164] *Ibid.*
[165] *Ibid.*, 1908, p. 462.

3: *Attempts to Revise the Philippine Tariff Laws during 1905-1908*

AUGUST 5, 1909 TO OCTOBER 3, 1913

THERE HAD BEEN efforts to establish free trade between the United States and the Philippines or to obtain a reduction of the rates of duty on products of the Islands, especially sugar and tobacco, to twenty-five percent of the Dingley rates. Bills had been introduced periodically in the Congress for this purpose. While two tariff acts were enacted into law, on March 3, 1905 and on February 26, 1906, both of these measures, as previously indicated, were merely concerned with goods imported into the Philippines. Hence the rates of duty levied by the Act of March 8, 1902 on Philippine goods imported into the United States continued to be enforced.

On April 30, 1908 a bill was introduced in the House of Representatives to amend and revise the Tariff Act of March 3, 1905. Like the two acts of Congress above-noted, this proposed measure (H. R. 21449) dealt only with goods imported into the Archipelago. Specifically, the purpose of this bill was to amend and revise the rates of duty in the act of March 3, 1905, on cocktails, liqueurs, buttons, agricultural implements and machinery, machinery and apparatus for mining and the reduction and smelting of ores, and all other machinery including materials for road and shipbuilding.[1]

It was not until 1909, however, when the provision of Article IV of the Treaty of Paris lapsed[2] and after the proponents of tariff reduction for the Philippines were able to wrest concessions from American

[1] *Cong. Record*, 60th Cong., 1st Sess., Part VIII, pp. 7092-7097.

[2] In a note under date of Oct. 30, 1908, the Spanish Government proposed the continuation of the provision of Article IV of the Treaty of Paris regarding Spanish wines imported into the Philippines. In return for this, the Spanish Government promised to extend to articles coming from the Philippines her minimum rates of duty. While Secretary of State Elihu Root recognized "the desirability of some such reciprocal understanding, beneficial alike to Spain and the Philippine Islands," he pointed out, however, that the Government of the United States did not have the authority to make such arrangement. Furthermore, such an arrangement at that time, he indicated, would be "inexpedient" since it would tend "to limit the freedom of the national Congress in considering and establishing future relations between the United States and the Philippine dependencies." *Papers Relating to the Foreign Relations of the United States*, 1909, copy 2, pp. 546-549.

sugar and tobacco interests in the form of quotas, that a bill was finally enacted into law providing that a limited quantity of sugar and tobacco from the Archipelago might be admitted into the United States free of duty. In order to better understand the forces that stood against the movement to extend a substantial tariff reduction to Philippine goods imported into the United States, a brief review of the efforts to revise the Philippine tariff laws from 1905 to 1908 might now be in order.

On January 14, 1905 Representative Charles Curtis of Kansas introduced a bill (H. R. 17752) to amend the Tariff Act of March 8, 1902.[3] Among the most important provisions of this bill were the reduction of the duties on Philippine sugar and tobacco imported into the United States to twenty-five percent of the Dingley rates, and the admission free of duty into the United States[4] of all other articles wholly the growth and product of the Philippines. This bill, while it was favorably reported by the Committee on Ways and Means, never had a chance to be voted upon on the floor of the House of Representatives. Its importance, however, lies in the fact that its presentation marked the beginning of a series of public hearings.

During the year 1905 hearings were held on the much-mooted question of tariff reduction on Philippine products especially sugar and tobacco; the extension of American coastwise navigation laws to the Archipelago; and the general economic conditions existing therein.

On January 23-28 and February 3, 1905 the Committee held hearings[5] on the Curtis bill. During the month of August there were public hearings in the Philippines before the Secretary of War, William Howard Taft, and the Congressional party which accompanied him there on a tour of inspection. The questions regarding tariff reduction on Philippine sugar and tobacco, the proposed extension of the coastwise navigation laws of the United States to the Islands and the general economic conditions of the Archipelago were the subjects covered during these public hearings.[6]

[3] *Cong. Record*, 58th Cong., 3rd Sess., Part I, p. 890.

[4] *H. R. Report No. 4867*, pp. 1-4.

[5] See *Hearings* before the Committee on Ways and Means, House of Representatives, January 23-28 and February 3, 1905.

[6] See *Public Hearings in the Philippine Islands* upon the proposed reduction of the tariff upon Philippine sugar and tobacco, the extension of the United States coastwise and navigation laws to the Philippines and the general economic conditions of the Islands, held during the month of August, 1905, before the Secretary of War and the Congressional Party accompanying him to the Islands, attached as Appendix to *Senate Document No. 277*, pp. 213-378.

On December 13-16 and 18 another hearing was held on the Payne bill.[7] Mr. Payne introduced this bill in the House of Representatives on December 4, 1905. It is interesting to note that the provisions of the Curtis bill of January 14, 1905 were substantially adopted in this bill.[8]

After the approval by the House of Representatives of the Payne bill it was sent immediately to the Senate which referred it to the Senate Committee on the Philippines. This body, however, found it advisable to hold another public hearing on this proposed measure which lasted from January 20, 1906 to February 28.[9] The result of all these public hearings was to bring out clearly the fundamental objections against the proposal of reducing the duties on Philippine sugar and tobacco and the establishment, ultimately, of free trade between the United States and the Philippine Islands.

During the public hearing which was held on the Curtis bill, Representative Joseph W. Fordney of Michigan started the broadside against tariff reduction by reminding the members of the House Committee on Ways and Means that Michigan produced a good deal of beet sugar and that the whole beet sugar interest of the country was against reducing the duties to twenty-five percent of the Dingley rates as provided for in the proposed measure. In answering the question of Mr. Needham of California as to whether he would maintain permanent tariff duties on goods and merchandise coming from a territory belonging to the United States, Mr. Fordney assured the members of the House Committee of his coöperation in doing something for the Filipinos provided that doing so would not be injurious to an industry in the United States. He maintained, however, that the proposed reduction of duty on Philippine sugar would be injurious to both the cane and the sugar beet industries of the United States since "in the Philippine Islands they can produce sugar today under the present old-fashioned machinery without installing farm implements . . . and can put it at our markets at one cent or more per pound less than it can be produced in this country."[10]

Mr. Watts S. Humphrey, representing a Michigan refining com-

[7] See *Hearings* before the Committee on Ways and Means of the House of Representatives, 59th Cong., 1st Sess., Dec. 13-16 and 18, 1905.

[8] See *House Report No. 4867*, pp. 1-4, 58th Cong., 3rd Sess.; also see *House Report No. 20*, pp. 1-7, 59th Cong., 1st Sess.

[9] See *Hearings* before the Committee on the Philippines of the United States Senate, 59th Cong., 1st Sess., Jan. 20, 1906 to Feb. 28.

[10] *Hearings* Jan. 23-28, Feb. 3, 1905, p. 23.

pany, was another defender of the home sugar interests. He informed the House Committee that discharged soldiers of the American Army were buying up sugar lands and were going into the production of sugar in the Philippines.[11] He stated also that there were millions of dollars ready to be invested in sugar production in the Archipelago awaiting only the passage of the Curtis bill. Asked by Mr. John S. Williams of Mississippi whether such a contingency was not a welcome part of the general plan for the benevolent assimilation of the Filipinos and whether it would not enable the American people to assimilate and christianize those wards, Mr. Humphrey agreed that such a policy was correct from a philanthropic standpoint. He complained, however, against the readiness of some people "to christianize and enlighten all the heathen on the face of the earth at the expense of our home sugar industry."[12]

The American Beet Sugar Association expressed its opposition to the Curtis bill through its secretary, Mr. Truman G. Palmer, who maintained that the passage of the pending legislation would bring the American sugar industry in closer competition with cheap Oriental labor.[13] He pointed out that the American factories were being operated in a protected tariff market under the most expensive conditions in the world. The American beet sugar industry paid its labor from $1.50 to $2.50 a day, while in the Philippines labor commanded about $0.30 a day. Under such conditions, therefore, it would be impossible for the American sugar industry to survive Philippine competition. It was recalled that the sugar interests of the country were promised that, should they not oppose the ratification of the Cuban treaty,[14] they could go on and develop their industry without fear of competition. Mr. Palmer urged the Filipinos to devote more time for the production of coffee, hemp or rubber rather than sugar, for, in the long run, it would be more beneficial for them "to produce as much as possible of those things we can not produce rather than to induce them, through special legislation to produce those things which compete with us." To his mind, this not only was a "common-sense view" but also "a fair proposition."[15]

[11] *Ibid.*, p. 31.

[12] *Ibid.*, p. 23.

[13] *Ibid.*, p. 31.

[14] The Administration, although it failed to obtain through legislation a reduction of duty on Cuban sugar entering the United States, later succeeded in obtaining the same in a reciprocal treaty with Cuba signed in 1903.

[15] *Hearings*, Jan. 23-28, Feb. 3, 1905, pp. 37-38.

A representative of another Michigan sugar company indicated that what the domestic sugar interests were up against was the future prospect of the Philippine sugar production.

It is not for the present, but for the future that we plead, and when the Philippine Commission specifies plainly and clearly that there are 50,000,000 acres of land in the Philippine Islands that are well adapted to sugar and tobacco, and when in addition to that they go forward still further and advocate that 25,000,000 acres of these lands be not sold, but given to capitalists, who will go into those islands and develop the sugar plantations on those islands, and when the same Commission's report specifies that each one of those acres can produce five tons of sugar, I affirm . . . that it is not for the present but for the future that we are looking forward.[16]

In voicing the interest of a third Michigan sugar company against the passage of the Curtis bill, its representative made mention of his belief in the "present system of protection." He confided his fondness of quoting the statements of "the apostles and high priests of the protective policy of the Republican party"; that he was made to believe that "the policy of protection was a fixed and firm policy"; and that it would continue to form a "part of the Republican policy of government."[17] To his mind, however, the bill under consideration seemed to indicate a departure from the time-honored policy of protection. Of course, if in the wisdom of the Congress, legislation should be enacted that would drive the home industries to hopeless ruin, he requested that "some one of the famous leaders of the Republican Party (perhaps he now sits at this table) be delegated to clamber to the top of our falling smoke stack—the same smoke stack that furnished the text of our most effective campaign oratory—and there plant the victorious banner bearing the inscription, 'Protection and Prosperity.' "[18]

Mr. David Eccles of Ogden, Utah, gloomily admitted that should the proposed legislation pass it would be "only a matter of time, and a short time at that," when the domestic sugar factories "will shut up."[19]

Colonel James D. Hill of New Orleans called on the Democratic members of the House Committee on Ways and Means "to help maintain the present tariff on goods brought from the Philippines."[20]

While it was true that the public hearing on sugar occupied much

[16] *Ibid.*, p. 66.
[17] *Ibid.*, pp. 72-73; statement of Mr. Carman N. Smith.
[18] *Ibid.*, p. 77.
[19] *Ibid.*, p. 79.
[20] *Ibid.*, p. 112.

of the attentoin of the Committee on Ways and Means American tobacco and its manufactured products were by no means neglected. Among those that composed the tobacco delegation were the President of the New England Tobacco Growers' Association; the President of the National Cigar Leaf Tobacco Association; the President of the Lancaster County Tobacco Growers' Association of Pennsylvania; the President of the Cigar Makers' International Union of America with headquarters in Chicago, Illinois, and Representative Michael E. Driscoll of the State of New York.

In objecting to the passage of the Curtis Bill, Mr. H. S. Frye, president of the New England Tobacco Growers' Association, could not entertain a belief that the Republican party, "our old friend and benefactor is liable to go back on us now, and largely, too, as a matter of sentimentality, there being no question of national honor or repudiation involved."[21]

Mr. A. Bijur of the National Cigar Leaf Tobacco Association called attention to the great disparity in the cost of tobacco and cigar production in the Philippines and in the United States. He pointed out that American tobacco field hands were being paid $1.50 per day and that cigar makers averaged considerably more, while in the Philippines field hands receive from $0.15 to $0.25 per day, and cigar makers averaged just below $0.40 per day.[22] To his mind, a tariff rate which, after making due allowances for transportation and other necessary expenses, did "not fully equalize the difference in labor cost" would mean "either lower wages for our working people or the transfer of the industry to the point of cheaper production."[23] He was equally apprehensive that the proposed reduction of duty on Philippine tobacco to twenty-five percent of the Dingley rates might serve to increase exportation of Sumatra tobacco to the United States through the Philippines. This was possible, so Mr. Bijur maintained, because the Philippine tariff levied only 22½ cents per pound on Sumatra tobacco imported into the Islands. With the addition of 46½ cents plus an *ad valorem* tax of only 6¼ percent, which would result from the adoption of the Curtis bill, it would be profitable to send Sumatra tobacco to the United States by way of the Philippines.[24]

On being reminded by Mr. Payne that the reduction contemplated in the bill under review applied only to articles wholly the growth and

[21] *Ibid.*, p. 82; statement of Mr. Carman N. Smith.
[22] *Ibid.*, p. 87.
[23] *Ibid.*
[24] *Ibid.*, p. 89.

products of the Philippines, Mr. Bijur was willing to bet that no one could distinguish a Sumatra wrapper in a cigar. Continuing Mr. Bijur pointed out that since the declared policy of the American Government was "to put every business interest of the community on an adequately protected basis, we feel justified in assuming that the measure of protection accorded the tobacco interests is ours by right, and as long as the policy of universal protection obtains our rate of protection should not be lowered in favor of anyone else whatever against our welfare."[25] Asked by Mr. Williams of Mississippi whether he regarded the import duty on tobacco as a matter which should be determined by his interests and not by the representatives of the people, Mr. Bijur pointed out that the complaints of the American tobacco interests were based on the fact that no attempt was made to find out whether the reduction contemplated in the proposed measure would not injure the American tobacco industry. Concluding, Mr. Bijur said that inasmuch as "we have to buy protected shoes and everything else . . . we ought to have the right to sell protected cigars and tobacco, or we are at a disadvantage."[26]

The Lancaster Tobacco Growers' Association of Pennsylvania registered its "solemn protest" through its President, Mr. B. E. Herr, against the proposed reduction of duty provided for in the Curtis bill. He maintained that should the proposed reduction be adopted it would cause a great injury not only to Pennsylvania but also to Ohio since both were "the great filler-tobacco raising States" of the country.[27]

On the other hand, Mr. Payne pointed out that Philippine tobacco would not injure the domestic industry, for, according to the report of the *Daily Bulletin* at Manila, December, 1904, the price of Philippine leaf tobacco went all the way from $9.50 to $42 per quintal (a quintal is equivalent to 101 pounds). This would mean an average price of from $0.09 to $0.42 per pound. Then too, there was the $0.46 duty to be levied on Philippine tobacco when imported into the United States as provided for in the Curtis bill. But according to the *Reporter,* also of December, 1904, continued Mr. Payne, the market price for leaf tobacco in the United States was between $0.08 and $0.09 a pound. It would be apparent therefore, concluded Mr. Payne, that American leaf tobacco would withstand the so-called Philippine competition.[28]

[25] *Ibid.*, p. 94.
[26] *Ibid.*, p. 95.
[27] *Ibid.*, pp. 99-100.
[28] *Ibid.*, p. 101.

Nevertheless, Mr. Herr maintained, the future of American tobacco must be safeguarded from the menace of Philippine competition.[29]

The Cigar Makers' International Union of America, speaking through its president, Mr. G. W. Perkins, could not understand "by what right the Congress can justify legislation that will surely result in lowering the standard of living of such a large army of loyal American citizens."[30] It was emphasized that no legislation on the part of Congress could lift the Filipino people up to the American standard. He believed that the enactment into law of the pending bill would "have a tendency to and will drag us down nearer their level."[31]

Representative Michael E. Driscoll of New York intimated the readiness of the Tobacco Growers' Association of the State of New York to compromise on a reduction of the duty on Philippine tobacco to fifty percent of the Dingley rates. He was of the opinion that it would be wise for the House Committee on Ways and Means to seek first this compromise rather than report the Curtis Bill as constituted, otherwise it would meet "a stubborn opposition in the House and perhaps in the Senate, and I do not know what the result may be, but the people interested in tobacco all over the country will feel sore about it."[32] This question of tariff reduction on Philippine goods opened up another phase, he continued. Should the rates of duty levied on Philippine products imported into the United States be lowered as provided for in the pending legislation it would tend "to hitch the Philippines closer to us than now. There are a lot of people, and Republicans, who would not like to do that and who are ready to get rid of the Philippines in any honorable way."[33]

The Philippine side of the question was ably presented by Colonel Clarence R. Edwards, Chief of the Bureau of Insular Affairs; Colonel George R. Colton, then collector of customs for the port of Iloilo in the island of Panay, who buttressed his remarks with a memorial from the Iloilo Chamber of Commerce and Agriculture; and the Secretary of War, William Howard Taft.[34]

In the course of his statement, Colonel Edwards showed that the exportation of sugar from the Philippines into the United States during the calendar years 1895-1904 had not been materially increased[35] al-

[29] *Ibid.*
[30] *Ibid.*, p. 103.
[31] *Ibid.*, p. 104.
[32] *Ibid.*, p. 108.
[33] *Ibid.*, p. 109.
[34] *Ibid.*, pp. 138-211 for the statement of these three officials.
[35] *Ibid.*, pp. 139-140: statement of Colonel Edwards; Also *Appendix II*, Table No. 7.

though sugar consumption in the United States during the same period was so far beyond domestic production that more than 1½ million tons continued to be imported from foreign countries.[36]

In regard to Philippine tobaccos and their exportation to the United States, Colonel Edwards showed also that because of the high Dingley rates on tobacco, Philippine exports of tobacco and its manufactures to the mother country were negligible.[37]

Colonel Colton opened his testimony by pointing out how the Filipinos had suffered during the previous six years. This, according to him, could have been relieved by timely action on the part of the Congress. He added that the Filipinos had been "resting securely in the belief that when the fact should be known to the American people justice would speedily be done, as it must."[38] Continuing, he added that the Filipinos, "having been deprived, through the change in sovereignty, of the markets and considerations formerly extended by the Spanish Government," should have every reason to believe that the American people would extend "to them the markets of the United States as unrestrictedly as the Spanish markets were extended in former times by the [then] mother country."[39] Furthermore, he urged the passage of the pending legislation as a means of compelling the Chinese buyers of Philippine products to pay a competitive price for those products.

Asked by Mr. Charles H. Grosvenor of Ohio what good the reduction of the present import duty would be to the Philippine sugar industry if Philippine sugar would not be sent to the United States anyway, Colonel Colton explained that what the Philippines needed most was for the United States market to fix the price of Philippine sugar. Thus, "if it is worth ten dollars in New York the Chinese merchants will pay the ten dollars, less the freight to New York."[40] While he admitted that Philippine sugar was also exported to the United States he was of the opinion, however, that the natural market of Philippine sugar was China where the Chinese were less fastidious and consumed it in its raw (muscovado) form.[41]

Concluding his remarks, he emphasized the fact that the approval of the Curtis bill would benefit the Filipinos "to the extent of the pres-

[36] *Appendix II*, Table No. 8.
[37] *Ibid.*, Table No. 9.
[38] *Hearings*, January 23-28, February 3, 1905, p. 168.
[39] *Ibid.*, p. 169.
[40] *Ibid.*
[41] *Ibid.*, p. 170.

ent tariff less the freight to New York; enable the employment of our available labor in the remunerative production of sugar; bring back prosperity to our impoverished islands, and with it contentment and appreciation on the part of these loyal people, while not adding materially to the exports from the islands to New York and in no way competing with the beet-sugar growers of America."[42]

In urging the approval of the pending legislation, Secretary Taft reminded the House Committee that the Philippine Islands belonged to the United States and that "we have held it on the altruistic principle that being forced into a position where we had to take control, we are not permitted to release control so long as a release will be to the detriment of the body of the people of the islands. We thus have imposed on us the trust of developing those islands so far as we may politically, educationally and in a business way. In a business way especially, because if a parent or guardian does not keep his child's or ward's stomach full, all the political or moral maxims and all the liberty that can be given will be entirely useless and unsatisfactory."[43]

In trying to quiet the fears of the American sugar interests Secretary Taft reminded those interests that since the beginning of the American regime up to and including 1903, Philippine sugar exported to the United States did not reach such a proportion as to occasion a justified apprehension on the part of the domestic interests with regard to the future of the Philippine sugar industry. From 1898 to 1903 inclusive the annual sugar importation to the United States from foreign countries was more than one and one half million tons. He indicated furthermore that during the first ten months of 1904 only 25,489 tons of sugar were imported from the Philippines, while the United States imported around 1,600,000 tons of sugar from foreign countries.

Secretary Taft recalled that when the question of free trade with Puerto Rico was before the same House Committee "these same gentlemen, representing the same especial interests, were just as certain that by granting to Puerto Rico the privilege of our markets you were going to destroy these two industries and affect most injuriously the labor interests of this country."[44] Of course, these prophecies have not proven true; and while the sale of Puerto Rican sugar and tobacco in the United States had been of great benefit to the people of Puerto Rico, these products have not created the slightest ripple in the price

[42] *Ibid.*, p. 172.
[43] *Ibid.*, p. 182.
[44] *Ibid.*, p. 183.

of the same products in the American market. Now these same interests, continued Secretary Taft, claimed that should Philippine sugar and tobacco come to the United States at the reduced rates provided for in the proposed measure, these products would bring calamity to like products of the United States. In the light of Puerto Rican experience their claim against Philippine sugar and tobacco therefore was merely "a repetition of the same timorous but unfounded cry."[45]

Of the claim that there were 50,000,000 acres of undeveloped lands in the Philippines suitable for sugar production; that these lands with machinery would be capable of producing five tons of sugar per acre; and that the owners could and would produce 250,000,000 tons of sugar, Secretary Taft observed that this line of argument reminded him of one of Mark Twain's famous characters, Colonel Sellers, who "calculated the number of people in China that needed eye-water at a dollar a bottle, and he would sell it to them, and he would make $400,000,000 a year."[46]

Mention may be made of the fact that the values of Philippine sugar exported to all countries for 1903 and 1904 were $3,955,568 and $2,668,507 respectively. On the other hand, the values of Philippine sugar exported to the United States for the corresponding period were only $1,335,826 and $354,144.[47]

Turning to the case of tobacco, Mr. Taft again appealed to figures. By way of comparison he spoke of the 105,000,000 cigars exported from the Philippines in 1904, while in the same year the United States produced a total of 7,000,000,000 cigars.[48] During the years 1903 and 1904 Philippine cigars exported to the United States were merely 332,000 and 96,000, valued at $3,866 and $1,796 respectively.[49] Mr. Taft indicated further, that 140,000,000 pounds of domestic leaf tobacco were consumed in making cigars and that over 30,000,000 pounds more were imported while the Philippines was exporting only a total of 19,000,000 pounds of both filler leaf and smoking tobacco.[50] It is quite evident, however, that only a very limited amount of this exportation found its way into the markets of the United States since the values of

[45] *Ibid.*

[46] *Ibid.*, p. 185.

[47] *Report*, Chief of the Bureau of Insular Affairs to the Secetary of War, dated Washington, Oct. 15, 1905, attached to the *Report*, Philippine Commission, 1905, Part I, p. 22.

[48] *Hearings*, January 23-28, February 3, 1905, pp. 208-209.

[49] *Senate Report No. 9*, p. 102, 61st Cong., 1st Sess.

[50] *Hearings*, Jan. 23-28. Feb. 3, 1905, p. 209.

all unmanufactured Philippine tobacco exported to the United States were listed at $46,162 for 1903 and $1,857 for 1904.[51]

In the month of August, 1905, Mr. Taft and a Congressional party went to the Philippines to see "the actual conditions" in the Islands. Public hearings were held in the most important cities and towns of the Archipelago not only on the tariff question and the effects upon the Islands if the American navigation laws should be extended thereto, but also on the general economic conditions of the country.

Native sugar planters together with American officials in the Insular government and other Americans engaged in commerce and trade in the Islands emphasized the prostrate condition of Philippine agriculture. They presented statistics to show that taking all the items in the cost of production, including interest, freight rates and insurance charges, Philippine sugar and tobacco, even with the complete removal of the Dingley rates, would not be able to go to the American market and compete with American products. Reduction of duty or its entire removal was also urged as a measure of compelling Chinese and Japanese buyers to offer better prices for Philippine sugar.

Señores Leon Heras and Francisco Liongson, both from Pampanga, were agreed on the advisability of establishing an agricultural mortgage bank in the Islands to supply the much-needed capital for the country's development.[52] On the question of the extension of the American coastwise shipping laws to the Philippines, Mr. Liongson was of the opinion that the future shipping monopoly which would result therefrom would render null the favorable effects of the removal of the Dingley tariff on Philippine products imported into the United States.[53]

Mr. Esteban de la Rama, a sugar planter in the Provinces of Iloilo and Occidental Negros, blamed "the seven years of calamity, with a war and plagues, failures of crops" and the ravages of locusts for the

[51] *Appendix II,* Table No. 5.

Mr. H. S. Frye, president of the New England Tobacco Growers' Association, in a speech delivered before the members of the Association on January 10, 1906, admitted that should the present acreage devoted to tobacco culture in the Philippines be not extended, "the prospective output of leaf and cigars in the islands would not be large enough to permit of serious competition here with our domestic tobacco interests." *Senate Document No. 95,* 59th Cong., 1st Sess.

[52] *Public Hearings in the Philippine Islands,* etc., 1905, p. 217; see also statement of Mr. Francisco Liongson, *Ibid.,* pp. 227-232.

[53] *Ibid.,* p. 232; also see statement of John T. Macleod regarding this matter, *Ibid.,* pp. 333-343.

general deplorable state of the country.[54] While there was a general increase in the cost of living, he continued, prices paid for Philippine sugar were relatively low. Therefore, he concluded, the only recourse left for the Filipinos was to urge the governmnt of the mother country to remove her duties levied upon Philippine products.[55]

Mr. W. C. Welborn, chief of the Bureau of Agriculture of the Philippines, was asked by Senator Murphy J. Foster of Louisiana whether in his opinion the removal of duty on Philippine sugar and tobacco entering the United States would not work out at the expense of other industries of the Islands, namely, the raising of hemp, coconuts and rice. Mr. Welborn assured the Senator that sugar and tobacco could not encroach upon the raising of hemp or coconuts. Coconuts and hemp, he continued, are grown as in an apple orchard. They are permanent.[56] Nor would sugar and tobacco encroach upon rice production, since rice is grown upon land which could not grow good sugar.[57]

In answering the question asked by Senator Francis G. Newlands whether the removal of duty levied upon Philippine tobacco would not increase its importation into the United States, Mr. W. S. Lyon, also of the Philippine Bureau of Agriculture, indicated that an increase in the exportation of Philippine tobacco to the United States would depend entirely upon its coming "into favor with American smokers"—a contingency hard to foretell. He informed the Congressional delegation that "the taste for [a] Philippine cigar is an acquired taste" and that "many people do not like it at first."[58] For instance, "the first time I tasted a Philippine cigar I thought it was simply vile," but "now I prefer it to anything else." American smokers, therefore, would have to "cultivate a taste for Philippine cigars" before they could like them.[59]

At this juncture, the ever-resourceful Collector of Customs for the Philippines, Mr. Shuster, presented an ingenious plan to get around the obstructions in Congress. Briefly stated this proposal was as fol-

[54] *Ibid.*, pp. 235-236.

[55] *Ibid.*, p. 237. See also statement of Mr. Maurice Lowenstein of the Castle Brothers, Wolf and Sons, importers and exporters at Manila, *Ibid.*, pp. 243, 252-253.

[56] This is not an accurate statement, for the abaca plant—where hemp is derived—can be transplanted.

[57] *Public Hearings in the Philippine Islands*, etc., p. 275. See also statement of Mr. P. Kraft of the firm of Baer, Senior and Company, pp. 281-290; also statement of Mr. Justo Guido of the Germinal Cigar and Cigarette Factory, pp. 291-294.

[58] *Ibid.*, p. 300.

[59] *Ibid.*

lows: the Philippine Commission should enact a law granting to exporters of Philippine products to the United States a refund of the duties paid to the customs authorities of the United States. This could be done without any further legislation by Congress, as under the present law all amounts collected as customs duties by the United States on Philippine products were refundable to the Insular government. Under this plan such refunds made to the Insular treasury would at once, by act of the Commission and on submittal of the proper documents, be returned to the exporter. This would practically amount to free trade relations with the United States.

The Governor General of the Philippines, although he was desirous of seeing American markets opened freely to Philippine products, was nevertheless reluctant to adopt the plan since it might excite an unfavorable reaction in Congress and result in the enactment of legislation hostile to the general interests of the Archipelago. It was further asserted by the Governor that with the institution of the Shuster plan, the Insular government might in the future find itself in the awkward position of opposing Congress. The immediate effect of this statement was to dampen the ardor of the supporters of the Shuster scheme.[60]

After the Congressional party came back from the Philippines, another public hearing was held by the Committee on Ways and Means of the House of Representatives. This hearing, which lasted from December 13 to 18, 1905, was occasioned when Representative Payne, inspired perhaps by what he saw and learned in the Philippines about conditions there, introduced a bill[61] on December 4 to amend the Philippine tariff of March 8, 1902. The tariff acts of March 3, 1905 and February 26, 1906, be it recalled, did not affect the rates of duty levied on Philippine sugar and tobacco imported into the United States as provided for in the Act of March 8, 1902.

At this hearing[62] there developed a veritable war of figures, now fought with increased vigor. Prophecies of the future were dragged in as concrete arguments against the proposal of tariff reduction. Domestic sugar and tobacco interests painted a dismal picture of the future of these industries should the proposed measure be allowed to

[60] For the Shuster proposal see *Manila American*, Feb. 14-16 and 18, 1905. See also *Manila Times*, Feb. 14, 1905, quoted as Exhibit B of the testimony of Daniel D. Colcock of Louisiana, representing the American Cane Growers' Association in the *Hearings* Before the Committee on Ways and Means of the House of Representatives, Dec. 13-18, 1905, pp. 2-7.

[61] *H. R. 3*, 59th Cong., 1st Sess., Part I, p. 45.

[62] *Hearings*, etc., December 13-18, 1905.

pass. On the other hand, government officials took the Philippine side of the debate. In support of their statements they offered evidence which they thought ought to be sufficient to convince reasonable people. Experts were summoned, but as usual they disagreed.

American sugar interests argued further that the passage of the Payne bill (H. R. 3) would mean the exclusion of Philippine sugar from Europe. This would mean, so it was contended, that the sale of Philippine sugar would be concentrated in the markets of the United States in view of the provision of the Brussels Sugar Bounty Convention signed on March 5, 1902 which became effective on September 1, 1903.[63] In view of this consideration, the Ways and Means Committee of the House of Representatives called on Mr. Wallace P. Willett of New York, publisher of the Statistical Sugar Trade Journal, *Willett and Gray,* to explain the working of the Brussels Convention relating to sugar bounties.[64] Mr. Willett informed the House Committee that the recent decision of the permanent commission[65] charged with watching the execution of the provisions of the Convention ruled that "regarding the Philippines there exists a surtax, but the Commission has decided that this surtax can not be construed to mean a bounty for raw or refined sugar."[66]

In the light of the above ruling, continued Mr. Willett, Philippine sugar could still be exported to the United Kingdom or Europe although the Philippines received from the United States a gift of duties or a practical exemption from taxation granted to 84-test sugar equivalent to 33.9 cents per one hundred pounds. This being less than the required limit of forty-nine cents per one hundred pounds on raw sugar the surtax was not placed in the category of a "bounty" by the permanent commission. Should this 33.9 cents per one hundred pounds be increased to about the rate of forty-nine cents per one hun-

[62] *Hearings*, etc., Dec. 13-18, 1905, pp. 41-46; statement of Mr. Fred Hathaway of Saginaw, Michigan.

The signatory countries to the Brusells Convention were, Germany, Austria, Bohemia, Belgium, Spain, France, United Kingdom (which included Great Britain, Ireland, British Dominions and India), Italy, Netherlands, Sweden, Norway and Roumania.

[64] *Ibid.*, pp. 189-200, statement of Mr. Wallace P. Willett.

[65] This body ascertains also whether any bounty exists in signatory or non-signatory states and to estimate the amount for the purpose of assessing a special duty thereon. Also, to pronounce an opinion on contested points. Reports are made to the Belgian Government, which shall convoke a conference to take such decisions or measures as the circumstances demand. Their decisions to take effect within two months time at least.

[66] *Ibid.*, p. 190.

dred pounds allowed by the Convention, the permanent commission would undoubtedly consider such excess as being an "indirect bounty" granted by the United States to the Philippines. In this case, duties would be assessed against Philippine sugar or prohibit its importation.[67]

Mr. Willett observed, however, that should the United States Government decided to increase the Philippine preferential by reducing the existing duty on Philippine sugar to twenty-five percent of the Dingley rate, the Islands could still send sugar to Hongkong because this British colony was not within the Convention. China and Japan not being signatories to the Brussels Convention and not being exporters of sugar, could continue to import Philippine sugar without being affected by the provisions of the Convention. He pointed out at the same time that should the Philippines send sugar to Europe the proposed reduction of seventy-five percent would be considered as "an indirect bounty of 97.1 cents per one hundred pounds, which is 48.1 cents per one hundred pounds in excess of the 49 cent-surtax." Under these circumstances there would be "a positive certainty that the permanent commission would assess against this a countervailing duty on Philippine sugars, thus shutting them out from European markets."[68]

Nevertheless, should the proposed measure[69] be adopted, Philippine sugar could still be exported to Hongkong since that British colony was not within the Convention. Likewise, Philippine sugar could still be exported to China and Japan they being non-signatories of the Brussels Convention and furthermore these two countries were not exporters of sugar. It was apparent, however, that the proposed reduction of seventy-five percent of the Dingley rates on Philippine sugar would, in point of practice, tend to force all sugar from the Islands to enter the United States.

Nevertheless, the proposed measure was successfully piloted through the House by Representative Payne and was ultimately passed with a substantial majority.[70] It was then sent to the Senate which referred it to the Senate Committee on the Philippines and that body, as previously indicated, had a public hearing of its own on this measure, lasting from January 20 to February 28, 1906. The subjects which were covered during the public hearings in 1905, already noted, were dis-

[67] *Ibid.*, pp. 190-191.
[68] *Ibid.*, pp. 192-193.
[69] *H. R. 3*, 59th Cong., 1st Sess.
[70] See *Cong. Record*, 59th Cong., 1st Sess., Part II, pp. 1163-1164; 259 yeas, 71 nays, 7 answered present, 48 not voting.

cussed further. The same arguments were presented and practically nothing new was added.[71]

This Payne Bill[72] aimed not only at reducing the duties on Philippine sugar and tobacco to twenty-five percent of the Dingley rates, but also provided for the establishment of free trade between the United States and the Philippines after April 11, 1909, when the equality provisions of the Treaty of Paris should terminate.[73]

Although this bill had the backing of the Administration, it died an unnatural death in the hands of the Senate Committee on the Philippines in whose files the bill was buried without benefit of further consideration.[74] "Wiser counsels" had prevailed indeed, and "the quickened conscience of the protection sentiment" had shamed the petty, miserable arguments of expediency that were pressing for the ultimate passage of this measure.[75] The prevailing sentiment was lyrically expressed by Representative Mondell of Wyoming, one of the strongest opponents of tariff reduction, when he quoted a song[76] that was sung during a banquet of the "Military Order of the Carabao."

The next attempt to revise the existing tariff laws of the Philippines was on April 30, 1908 when Representative Payne introduced a bill (H. R. 21449) to amend and revise the Tariff Act of March 3, 1905.[77] This proposed measure dealt only with goods imported into the Islands. In so far as Philippine goods imported into the United States were concerned, the Tariff Act of March 8, 1902, continued to be enforced.

This amending legislation adopted substantially the recommendations of the Philippine Commission of December 31, 1907.[78] Among the most important of these recommendations were the increase of the

[71] See *Hearings*, published as *Senate Document No. 277*.

[72] *H. R. 3*, 59th Cong., 1st Sess.

[73] *H. R. Report No. 20*, pp. 1-7, 59th Cong., 1st Sess.

[74] All that the Senate Committee on the Philippines did was to hold public hearings on this bill from Jan. 20 to Feb. 28, 1906. See *Senate Document, No. 277*, 59th Cong., 1st Sess.

[75] For the debate on this bill see *Cong. Record*, 59th Cong., 1st Sess., Part I, pp. 694-710; 724-746; 753-777; 833-836; 852-880; 913-935; 950-979; 986-1008; Part II, pp. 1009-1012; 1017-1053; 1085-1109; 1139-1164.

[76] I am only a common beet-sugar man, and as for the Philippines, They tell me I have a brown brother there who wants to beat me out of my means.
I like the word fraternity, but at this I draw the Line;
He may be a brother of Secretary Taft, but he ain't no friend of mine. *Cong. Record*, 59th Cong., 1st Sess., Part I, p. 772.

[77] *Cong. Record*, 60th Cong., 1st Sess., Part VI, p. 5509. For a copy of this bill, see *Ibid.*, Part VIII, p. 7092.

[78] *Report*, Philippine Commission, 1907, Part I, pp. 64-73.

tariff duty on spirituous liquors; the lowering of the duties on some agricultural and other machinery, including machinery and apparatus for mining and smelting of ores; the adoption of some adequate measures designed to protect an infant button industry of the Islands and the repeal of Section 22 of the Tariff Act of March 3, 1905, which provided that importations exceeding $100 in value should be accompanied by a consular invoice. This amendment was urged by the Philippine Commission in order to improve customs collections in the Islands.[79]

During the public hearing that was held regarding the bill, both General Clarence Edwards, chief of the Bureau of Insular Affairs, and his assistant, Major Frank McIntyre, urged the approval of the proposed measure since it would not only be beneficial to the people of the Philippine Islands but also it would be advantageous to American agricultural machinery.[80]

On May 6, 1908, the Committee on Ways and Means reported the proposed measure[81] to the House of Representatives with some amendments, the most important of which was to add the notary public among the list of persons[82] before whom invoices required for American goods exported to the Philippines shall be sworn.

When the bill was finally discussed on the floor of the House of Representatives on May 27, it evoked biting criticisms from some Democratic members. Mr. Henry D. Clayton of Alabama pointed out that the bill under consideration was an "affirmation of the Massachusetts Republican idea of what the tariff ought to be." It should give him "free raw material that he wants to use in manufacturing the goods that he sells to the country, but a high protective tariff on the manufactured goods that he compels the American consumers to buy."[83]

Mr. John S. Williams of Mississippi spoke sarcastically of the readiness of the Committee on Ways and Means to "bless the poor Filipinos by putting agricultural implements and machinery to carry on various industries upon the free list" while the same Committee "do not put the mower, the reaper, the plow, the hoe, the ax, the cotton gin, the bagging, and ties of the American farmer on the free list to save

[79] *Ibid.*, p. 67.

[80] *Hearings*, before the Committee on Ways and Means of the House of Representatives, May 5, 1908 (60th Cong., 1st Sess.).

[81] *H. R. 21449* (60th Cong., 1st Sess.).

[82] These persons were the U. S. Commissioner, Collector of Customs, and Deputy Collector of Customs.

[83] *Cong. Record*, 60th Cong., 1st Sess., Part VIII, p. 7093.

their lives."[84] On the other hand, Mr. William Sulzer of New York characterized the pending legislation as "an emergency hodgepodge tariff bill—a sort of cross between the good and bad—a miserable compromise."[85]

Certainly, the Filipinos ought to be congratulated, remarked Mr. Oscar W. Underwood, since they could obtain favorable tariff reductions while Americans could not. He maintained that "the doors of the Ways and Means Committee locked hard against the American people, but it seems that if we were Filipinos we could get the doors opened. . . ."[86] He agreed with his colleague, Mr. Clayton, that in some respects, "so far as the tax by the Federal Government is concerned, the American farmer had better be a Filipino than American."[87]

To the above criticisms, and as an answer to the direct question asked by Mr. Ollie M. James of Kentucky whether he would also agree to an amendment for the benefit of the American farmers by putting agricultural implements on the free list, Mr. Payne reminded the House that the Philippines manufactured only cigars and buttons. In the United States, on the other hand, "with our varied industries, with hundreds of thousands of men employed in those industries, with the happiness and prosperity and luxury that we have brought to the homes of these people, it is necessary that we should have more progressive ideas." It was a pity, continued Mr. Payne, that there were many gentlemen who "do not seem to understand the difference between the two countries." He was thankful, however, "that we have the Philippine Islands, if for no other purpose than to furnish education to gentlemen like the gentleman from Kentucky (Mr. Ollie M. James). I thank God that those islands are attached to us, that they may learn some new ideas from us, and that the Filipinos are learning the valuable lesson of employing their labor at home to make those articles which they need, and every time they ask us to take a step in this direction I am in favor of it." He concluded by saying that such a step was not only a progressive idea but also it was "the Republican doctrine."[88]

The proposed measure (H. R. 21449) was ultimately passed in the House of Representatives on May 27, 1908 and was immediately sent

[84] *Ibid.*
[85] *Ibid.*
[86] *Ibid.*, p. 7096.
[87] *Ibid.*
[88] *Ibid.* For the debate on this bill see pp. 7093-7097.

to the Senate which referred it to the Committee on the Philippines. However, the Senate Committee on the Philippines deemed it proper to shelve the House bill, consequently it was never reported to the Senate.[89]

Section V of the Payne-Aldrich Law of August 5, 1909

The next phase of America's tariff policy in the Philippines was expressed in Section V of the Payne-Aldrich Law of August 5, 1909. When Congress convened after the election of 1908, the operation of the equality provisions of the Treaty of Paris was about to terminate, and this opened anew the question of the Philippine tariff. It was felt that if American products were to be allowed free entry into the Philippines some liberal concessions should be extended to the products of the Archipelago entering the United States.

The Philippine Commission, in its report for the fiscal year 1908, showed that the production of sugar and tobacco in the Islands and their exportation to the United States had not materially increased, and that there was no indication that sugar and tobacco production in the Archipelago might increase considerably in the near future.[90] Again, the mistaken belief "fostered by much of the ultra-protectionist talk, that a duty brings a burden on foreign producer, not on the domestic consumer" placed the case of the Philippine sugar and tobacco producers in a favorable light. It was urged, therefore, that the Philippine producers of these products should not be treated as foreigners "by maintaining what was supposed to be a burden on them."[91] These considerations enabled President Taft to obtain concessions from the domestic sugar and tobacco interests that a limited quantity of like products of the Philippines might be admitted free of duty into the United States.[92]

Thus, when on March 17, 1909, Representative Payne of New York introduced a bill (H. R. 1438) "to provide revenue, equalize duties, and encourage the industries of the United States and for other purposes," a provision was inserted in this proposed measure—subsequently amended by the Senate,[93] to whose amendments the House later acquiesced—to govern the commercial relations between the United

[89] *Ibid.*, p. 7104.

[90] See *Report*, Philippine Commission, 1908, Part II, pp. 590-592.

[91] Frank W. Taussig, *The Tariff History of the United States*, 1931, p. 397 *et seq.*

[92] See *Tariff Hearings* before the Committee on Ways and Means of the House of Representatives, 1908-1909, 60th Cong., 2nd Sess., Vols. III and IV, schedules E and F respectively.

[93] *Cong. Record*, 61st Cong., 1st Sess., Part III, pp. 3177-3218; 3251; 3326-3336.

States and the Philippine Islands. This provision, granting quotas to Philippine sugar and tobacco for free entry into the United States, was dictated by the American sugar and tobacco interests.[94] It became Section V of the Payne-Aldrich law of August 5, 1909.[95]

This section provided that sugar, whether refined or unrefined, and tobacco, manufactured or unmanufactured, imported into the Philippines from foreign countries should be subject to the same rates of import duty imposed upon them by the tariff laws of the United States. The continuance of free importation of Manila hemp into the United States was also provided. Other articles, the growth, product or manufacture of the Philippines (except rice) shipped directly into the United States were to be admitted therein free of duty with the following significant limitations:[96]

1. Only 300,000 gross tons of sugar were to be admitted yearly into the United States free of duty.

2. In any year only 150,000,000 cigars from the Islands were to be admitted duty free into the United States. The amount of wrapper tobacco and filler tobacco when mixed with more than fifteen percent of wrapper tobacco could not exceed 300,000 pounds, and filler tobacco, 1,000,000 pounds.

3. Philippine manufactured articles, in order to be admitted free of duty into the United States, could not contain foreign materials to the value of more than twenty percent of the total value of the manufactured product.

In consideration for the above privileges extended to all articles, the growth, product or manufacture of the Philippines entering the United States, it was provided also in the above-noted Section that "all articles, the growth, product, or manufacture of the United States, upon which no drawback of customs duties has been allowed therein, shall be admitted to the Philippine Islands from the United States free of duty," provided that their free entry—as in the case of articles from the Philippines—should "be conditioned upon the direct shipment thereof from the country of origin to the country of destination."[97]

In the course of the debate in Congress occasioned by the introduction of the above-noted Section, one could not help but be impressed

[94] See *Infra*, pp. 97-98.
[95] See *Appendix I.*
[96] *Ibid.*
[97] *Ibid.*

by the fact that political expediency was the rule—and this is also true up to the present time—rather than the exception in America's Philippine tariff policy. This was graphically illustrated in the following developments.

Recall that on January 16, 1906, Mr. Taft, then Secretary of War, permitted Representative Payne to quote him on the floor of the House as not in favor of the limitation upon Philippine sugar and tobacco contemplated in Mr. Fordney's amendment.[98] Three years later, when Mr. Taft became the occupant of the White House, a change in his attitude in respect to the same question set in.[99] On March 26, 1909, Mr. Fordney, the consistent defender of the beet sugar interests, tells of an agreement with President Taft. He said in part:

We are trying to do something for the Philippine Islands. . . . I will stand by the bill and the compromise on sugar, the free importation of 300,000 tons per year from the Philippine Islands into the United States.

I am willing to stand by that, and the sugar men of the country whom I have consulted are also satisfied. . . .

Our present good President, Mr. Taft, agreed in my presence that during his administration he will not permit, as far as he can avoid it by his action, any further reduction in the sugar schedule if we will accept this agreement and let 300-000 tons come in free from the Philippines.[100]

Commenting on Mr. Fordney's amendment to his bill (H. R. 3) of

[98] Representative Fordney's amendment to *H. R. 3* which was presented on Jan. 16, 1906 read in part as follows:

That on all sugars in excess of 200,000 tons, wholly the growth and product of the Philippine Islands coming into the United States from the Philippine Islands, each calendar year from and after the passage of this act, there shall be levied, collected, and paid the full rates of duty as now provided by law on all sugars coming into the United States from foreign countries, other than Cuba and territory belonging to the United States; and that the rates on tobacco shall apply as follows:

	Cigars (*Numbers*)	*Wrapper Leaf* (*Pounds*)	*Filler Leaf* (*Pounds*)
Free of Duty	50,000,000	300,000	3,000,000
At 25 percent Dingley rates..........	100,000,000	400,000	4,000,000
At 50 percent Dingley rates..........	150,000,000	No Limit	No Limit
At 75 percent Dingley rates.........	200,000,000	No Limit	No Limit

—Quotation taken from *Cong. Record*, 59th Cong., 1st Sess., Part II, p. 1146.

[99] Perhaps the reason for this reversal of attitude on the part of President Taft may be due to the defeat of early legislation in the Congress which contemplated a more liberal trade relation with the Philippines. He may have entertained the belief, therefore, that it should be better to accept the concessions offered by the American domestic interests rather than risk the prospect of not having those concessions at all.

[100] *Cong. Record*, 61st Cong., 1st Sess., Part I, p. 333.

December 4, 1905, Mr. Payne on January 16, 1906 spoke of America's "plain duty" to the people of the Philippine Islands, and concluded by saying:

I do not know what I should think of myself if I should catch myself thinking it was our plain duty to give this concession of tariff up to 300,000 tons and then put up 75 percent of the Dingley rates on whatever came beyond that. . . . You might just as well not pass any bill at all as pass a bill with this amendment.[101]

On March 23, 1909, however, Mr. Payne, in speaking about Section V of the general tariff bill (H. R. 1438) which provided for a limited free trade between the Philippines and the United States, indicated that that provision was "a sort of compromise between the friends of the sugar and other outlying industries."[102] And that as far as he was concerned he would not put on these limitations, but "a majority of the committee favored it."[103]

The official attitude of the Filipino people regarding the trade relation between the Philippines and the United States as provided for in Section V of the general tariff bill (H. R. 1438) was expressed on the floor of the House of Representatives on April 3, 1909, by Honorable Benito Legarda, one of the Philippine Resident Commissioners in Washington. In the course of his remarks, Commissioner Legarda pointed out that had this legislation been presented before the Philippine Assembly was constituted[104] there would have been very little, if any, opposition regarding the trade relation contemplated in the proposed measure. Today, however, continued the Commissioner, the Filipinos "have a duly constituted popular body of men elected by the people as their representatives to care for their interests and to voice their aspirations." Acting in their behalf, therefore, the Philippine Assembly instructed the Resident Commissioners in Washington to present to the Congress the wishes of the Filipino people concerning the Philippine trade policy contemplated in this legislation.[105]

It was emphasized by Commissioner Legarda that the forthcoming trade relations between the two countries would tend to divert Philippine sugar and tobacco products from their natural markets in China and Japan to a market several thousand miles away. While admitting the wisdom exercised by the House Committee on Ways and Means in

[101] *Ibid.*, 59th Cong., 1st Sess., Part II, p. 1147.
[102] *Cong. Record,* 61st Cong., 1st Sess., Part I, p. 190.
[103] *Ibid.*
[104] *Ibid.*, p. 930.
[105] *Ibid.*

imposing a quota on the free entry into the United States of sugar and tobacco as a means of protecting similar industries which had been built up under a protective tariff in the United States, Mr. Legarda observed that it would be natural that "an equal interest" should be taken also in protecting the industries in the Islands "which were created under conditions parallel to those which obtain here. . . ."[106]

Furthermore, the unlimited free entry of American products into the Philippines, continued Mr. Legarda, would mean a deficit for the Insular treasury estimated at $2,500,000. He was especially apprehensive of the seriousness of this problem since both the Philippine Assembly and the Philippine Commission had not as yet taken the necessary steps to replace this loss in revenue. And in view of the depressed economic conditions in the Archipelago and the relative rate of taxation then existing therein, it would be "impossible to create new additional revenue, at least until such time as a new era of prosperity may make itself felt."[107] On the other hand, concluded Commissioner Legarda,

> If, instead of the free admission without limitation as to quantity of American products into the Philippine Islands, this bill provided only the free entry there of agricultural machinery and other commodities of prime necessity, such as cotton cloth, and which are needed for the agricultural and industrial development of those islands, or if this bill provided only for such reciprocal exchange of commodities custom-duty free as would balance the limited quantity of American products to be sent from here—if such were the provisions of this bill, it would be our pleasant duty as representatives of the Philippine people to make manifest to this House their gratitude. . . .[108]

Resident Commissioner Pablo Ocampo, in an interview printed in the *Washington Post*[109] elaborated further the official stand of the Filipinos against the provision of Section V of the tariff bill (H. R. 1438). He maintained that the passage of the proposed measure would not only embarrass the Philippine government financially but also the "constant and profound desire" of the Filipino people for an independent existence "would be imperiled by such commercial ties." The thought of independence, concluded Mr. Ocampo, "is stronger with us than the desire for more economic gain, and while we would like the greatest possible commercial prosperity, we are willing to defer it

[106] *Ibid.*
[107] *Ibid.*, p. 931.
[108] *Ibid.*
[109] For a copy of this interview which was printed in the *Washington Post*, May 17, 1909, see *Cong. Record*, 61st Cong., 1st Sess., Part II, pp. 2240-2241.

rather than forever lose our hope of independence by an artificially rapid development through American corporations."[110]

Notwithstanding the representations made by the Philippine Resident Commissioners against the provision in Section V of the general tariff bill and the vigorous attacks against it by Senator Elihu Root of New York, who insisted that that provision would secure for the United States "an undue advantage over the weak people of the Philippine Islands,"[111] and by Senator Tom P. Gore of Oklahoma, who saw the American sugar trust as the real beneficiary of the above provision rather than the Filipinos,[112] this Section (which Senator Newlands of Nevada called a "monumental blunder") ultimately formed a part of the general tariff bill (H. R. 1438). The approval of the American sugar and tobacco interests both outside and in the Congress having been previously obtained with regard to Philippine quotas on sugar and tobacco,[113] the passage of Section V both in the House of Representatives and in the Senate was less thorny than that of the Payne bill of December 4, 1905. Upon the signature of President Taft on August 5, 1909 the general tariff bill became law and was known as the Payne-Aldrich law after its sponsors in the House and in the Senate.[114]

The Philippine Tariff Act of August 5, 1909

Shortly after the approval on April 9, 1909 of the general tariff bill (H. R. 1438) by the House of Representatives another bill (H. R. 9135) was introduced by Representative Payne on May 3. The purpose of this proposed measure was to revise the existing tariff in the Philippines.[115]

Two important reasons motivated the introduction of the new bill. In the first place, in spite of the establishment of virtual free trade

[110] *Ibid.*

[111] *Ibid.*

[112] *Ibid.*, pp. 3335-3336. Particularly pointed was the statement of Frank C. Lowry, Secretary of the Committee of Wholesale Grocers, formed to assist in obtaining cheaper sugar for consumers through reduction of duties on raw and refined sugar, embodied in a pamphlet entitled *Our High Tariff on Sugar and its Effects*, pp. 10-11.

[113] See *Supra*, p. 97.

[114] For the debate on Section V of this measure see *Cong. Record*, 61st Cong., 1st Sess., Parts I, II, III, IV.

[115] *Ibid.*, Part II, p. 1689; for the debate on this bill see *Ibid.*, Part II, pp. 1975-2012; 2119-2125; 2126.

between the Philippines and the United States as provided for in Section V of the general tariff bill then under consideration in the Senate, Congress felt the necessity of maintaining a separate tariff law for the Islands as heretofore. However, it was felt desirable that the customs tariff and regulations of the two countries should conform as nearly as possible to each other. Secondly, while virtual free trade between the Philippines and the United States would, ultimately, be beneficial to Philippine sugar and tobacco, one of the immediate effects of this trade, on the other hand, would be a loss of revenue for the Philippine treasury which Mr. Payne had estimated would be around $1,000,000.[116]

Mr. Payne based his estimate on the memoranda which General Clarence Edwards, chief of the Bureau of Insular Affairs, sent him on May 6, including the cable communication from Governor General Smith the day before showing an anticipated loss of $1,746,747.[117]

Representative Payne, chairman of the House Committee on Ways and Means, in favorably reporting the proposed measure (H. R. 9135) with various amendments,[118] pointed out that the bill under consideration substantially followed the draft of the bill prepared by Colonel George R. Colton, the Insular Collector of Customs, and by John S. Hord, Collector of Internal Revenue for the Philippines, with the "concurrence of ten or fifteen tariff experts who were active in the preparation of the bill."[119] Then after extensive public hearings which were held to give all those interested in the subject an opportunity to speak, the schedules agreed upon were submitted to the Bureau of Insular Affairs which in turn "gave them wide publicity throughout the United States for suggestions and recommendations."[120]

In explaining the nature of the amendments[121] made by his Committee, Mr. Payne declared that most of the amendments were merely in the phraseology of the bill, some as to punctuation, and only a few

[116] *Ibid.*, Part II, p. 1998.

[117] See *H. R. Report No. 7*, pp. 3-5. 61st Cong., 1st Sess.

[118] *H. R. Report No. 7*, 61st Cong., 1st Sess.

The House amendments included the institution of two additional sections, namely, 25 and 26. Section 25 provided for the imposition of an internal-revenue tax on foreign goods, in addition to other taxes, when imported into the Islands. Section 26 conferred upon the courts of the Philippines original jurisdiction over all cases arising in the Islands. Senate Amendment number 182, later acceded to by the House, became Section 12 of the Philippine Tariff Act. See *H. R. Report No. 22.* (Conference Report to accompany *H. R. 9135*), pp. 2-3.

[119] *Cong. Record*, 61st Cong., 1st Sess., Part II, p. 1998.

[120] *H. R. Report No. 7*, pp. 1-2.

[121] See *H. R. Report No. 22*, pp. 1-3.

material changes were made from the original draft.[122] The only changes the Committee made were to reduce the duty on light rails and sugar machinery.

Chairman Payne mentioned how some American manufacturers insisted upon this discriminatory duty on light weight rails and sugar machinery and that the Philippine Tariff Board and the Bureau of Insular Affairs, not wanting to see the bill fail, "had accommodatingly given way to the demands of these interests."[123] Of course, Mr. Payne disclaimed absolute knowledge regarding the correctness of the information which he and his Committee members had been able to obtain.

Other provisions of the bill worth mentioning were those providing protection to the manufacture of matches and of bolts and units of structural steel which were claimed to be "infant industries" of the Philippines. Then, too, on the following important exports, copra, hemp, sugar and tobacco, export duties were re-enacted. Although the Committee conceded that the imposition of export duties is "foreign to the policy of our Government and prohibited by our Constitution," the fact that export duties had "always been a feature of the revenue laws in the Philippine Islands," and the ruling of the Supreme Court in the famous Insular Cases, seemed to justify the Committee's action.[124]

General Edwards in a letter to the Secretary of War, dated Washington April 1, 1909,[125] transmitting the proposed tariff revision law drawn by a board of tariff experts in the Philippines and later revised by the Bureau of Insular Affairs, intimated his belief that the proposed tariff would be passed. His optimism was based on the fact that since contending parties had been reconciled as far as schedules were concerned, there should be no further opposition.[126] He pointed out that the schedules regarding tobacco, Sumatra leaf, and sugar imported into the Philippines were made identical with the schedules in the pending general tariff bill then being considered in the Senate. The imposition of identical schedules on these products, continued General Edwards, should remove the apprehension of the domestic interests

[122] See *The Proposed Tariff Revision Law 1909 for the Philippine Islands,* published as *House Document No. 14,* 61st Cong., 1st Sess.

[123] *Cong. Record,* 61st Cong., 1st Sess., Part II, p. 1998.

[124] See *H. R. Report No. 7,* pp. 1-2, 61st Cong., 1st Sess.

[125] *Report* of the Chief of Bureau of Insular Affairs to the Secretary of War, dated Oct. 31, 1909, attached to the *Report,* Philippine Commission, 1909.

[126] *Ibid.* For the rates on imported sugar and tobacco into the Philippines see p. 44-47 of *The Proposed Tariff Revision Law for the Philippine Islands,* Paragraphs 240-244 and 304 respectively.

that these goods might be imported into the Philippines at a lower tariff rate and thence into the United States free as the growth and product of the Archipelago.[127]

In the course of the debate that followed, Representative Harrison of New York maintained that the present bill (H. R. 9135) was not designed for the benefit of the Filipinos but was "simply and solely a selfish exploitation of the islands in behalf of certain American industrial monopolies." He supported his statement by citing the case of structural steel and matches. He said that the structural steel plant in Manila "used really to import steel from the United States and assemble it there to the extent of putting in bolts and screws." The rate of duty on this product was 56/100 of one cent while the Payne bill (H. R. 1438) and the Dingley law imposed 3/10 of one cent. Since by the same bill under consideration, American products went to the Philippines free of duty this "protective rate" of 56/100 of one cent did not at all protect the so-called infant industry in Manila, for structural steel could be imported from the United States completely finished and free of duty. "So it is obvious that this thing is a ridiculous farce."[128]

Taking the case of another infant industry, the match industry in the Islands, Mr. Harrison discovered that the match company in Manila used American match machinery. When the match interests in the Archipelago asked for protection they were given the rate in the Payne bill (H. R. 1438). "In other words," concluded Mr. Harrison, "so long as they are helping to exploit an American industry they are entitled to a protection which is prohibitive to all the rest of the world."[129]

Representative Underwood of Alabama, while admitting that the bill as a whole "is a great boon to the people of the Philippine Islands as compared with the laws we have written on the statute books for our own people at home,"[130] decried the re-enactment of the export tax as "not justified by any economic principle of government."[131] He pointed out that it was not only unconstitutional but also an unsound economic practice, for an imposition of an export tax means a taxa-

[127] See *Report* of the Chief of the Bureau of Insular Affairs to the Secretary of War dated October 31, 1909, attached to the *Annual Report*, War Department, Vol. VIII, pp. 3-7.

[128] *Cong. Record*, 61st Cong., 1st Sess., Part II, p. 2003.

[129] *Ibid.*

[130] *Ibid.*, p. 2005.

[131] *Ibid.*, p. 2008.

tion imposed upon those people who engage in an export trade, hence "limit their ability to successfully meet their foreign competitor and reduce the territory in which they can successfully dispose of their surplus products abroad."[132]

In view of the fact that many other countries produce copra and with the same class of labor reach foreign markets as easily and as cheaply as can copra from the Philippines, an export tax on this product would mean a taxation to be paid by the Philippine copra producers. This being the case, it would be necessary for them either to produce their copra much cheaper than their competitors in order to be able to compete with them or they must lower their cost of living to that extent below their competitors to have an even chance to succeed.[133]

Mr. Underwood maintained that an export tax on Philippine products imported into the United States is not fair to American producers of similar articles. With prophetic insight, he observed that:

> If there were equal terms and equal conditions in the sale of the export sugar from the Philippine Islands between this country and the Orient, I have no doubt that a large amount of the Philippine sugar would not come to the United States but would go to the markets of the Orient; but when you put an export tax on Philippine sugar of 5 cents a hundred kilos, you drive that Philippine sugar to the American market and out of the Orient, because when it comes to the American market it comes free.[134]

While Mr. Underwood did not deny that the export duty on sugar was but five cents for every 220 pounds, he reminded Representative Slayden of Texas that the greatest of fortunes in this world have been made by saving a cent on a very large product, and a few cents difference in the cost of a product will determine its destination. He pointed out that

> the tax on copra and tobacco amounts to a good deal more. On tobacco it amounts to $1.50 a hundred kilos in some classes of tobacco. On copra it amounts to ten cents on a hundred kilos; but the tendency of this export tax would be to drive other exports to the American markets and interfere with their having fair competition in the markets abroad.[135]

Representative Hill of Connecticut, while conceding the arguments presented by Mr. Harrison of New York, reminded the House, how-

[132] *Ibid.*
[133] *Ibid.*
[134] *Ibid.*
[135] *Ibid.*, p. 2009.

ever, that the bill was primarily a revenue measure the average rate of duty of which would not exceed twenty per cent *ad valorem*. Speaking of structural steel he pointed out that it was "not an ordinary article of commerce" in the Philppines, that "only $200,000 worth all told was imported last year, and that was chiefly for bridges or public buildings built by the government."[136] Mr. Hill mentioned an establishment in Manila which was engaged in the steel and iron industry employing a thousand or more Filipino laborers in the manufacture or bringing together of steel and iron of various forms. He observed that under these circumstances, it would be exceedingly desirable that this labor should be so employed. It might be mentioned here, that this rate was made in compliance with the request of the Collector of Customs of the Islands to give this differential of $8.50 a ton, so that these people might be continued in their present employment.[137]

Regarding the match question, Mr. Hill assured his colleagues that the match factory in Manila was not at all "an industry," but it was merely "an isolated case.[138] They want to keep it there and I guess the duty is sufficiently high enough to keep the plant there." Although the rate of twenty cents a kilo imposed upon this article was the same as that of the Act of March 8, 1902, this schedule was nowhere as high as was imposed under the Spanish régime, when the manufacture of matches was a government monopoly.[139]

Mr. Hill informed us that the proposed legislation had been made with reference to two things, a revenue bill for the Philippines, and the hope of bringing trade to the United States, where it belongs "without exploiting the islands." While admitting the difficulty of divorcing these two things he was equally determined not to "exploit" the Filipinos "one particle." In the next breath he was equally desirous that the Philippine trade must be with the United States, for

> we have a right to it, and it is our duty to the American people to make this tariff bill without wronging them, being absolutely fair to them, so that trade will come to us, and I think it will do it under this bill.[140]

When this proposed measure was finally referred to the Senate Committee on the Philippines on May 25 that body reported it favorably to the Senate with certain amendments,[141] among the most important

[136] *Ibid.*
[137] *Ibid.*
[138] *Ibid.*, p. 2010.
[139] *Ibid.*
[140] *Ibid.*
[141] For a complete list of these amendments, see *Senate Report No. 9*, pp. 1-96.

of which, and subsequently acceded to by the House of Representatives, were the following:[142]

Firstly, the Senate Committee recommended the reimposition of the 25 percent duty on one hundred kilos of petroleum and products thereof. This would mean, so it was maintained, an *ad valorem* duty of about ten percent for illuminating oil. The Committee based its recommendation on the fact that petroleum and its products "cover a wide range of articles most of which the Philippines imported from foreign countries."[143] It was the belief of the Senate Committee that the Ways and Means Committee of the House of Representatives had not fully considered the effects of its action in placing these products on the free list.

For instance, during the fiscal year 1908 the Philippines imported from India and Borneo illuminating oil valued at $167,567 upon which $55,174 was collected as duty. From Japan, parafin and wax were imported, the value of which amounted to $42,000 out of which $5,000 was collected as duty. And, finally, Philippine importation of candles, principally from Spain, Belgium and India, was valued at $74,461 and $18,077 collected as duty. Now then, in view of the difference in freight rates between the United States and the Philippines on the one hand, and on the other hand between the Philippines and other countries from which these articles were imported, the retention of the duty on petroleum and its products would mean also the retention of all the existing revenues derived from them. This, concluded the Senate Committee, would be extremely desirable[144] because of the general loss in revenue which would follow the establishment of the trade relationship as contemplated in the proposed measures.[145]

Secondly, a new Section was incorporated in the bill and, as finally agreed upon by the House and the Senate conferees, read as follows:

> Section 12—That all articles, except rice, the growth, product, or manufacture of the United States and its possessions to which the customs tariff in force in the United States is applied and upon which no drawback of customs duties has been allowed therein, going into the Philippine Islands shall hereafter be admitted therein free of customs duty when the same are shipped directly from the country of origin to the country of destination: Provided, that direct shipment shall include shipments in bond through foreign territory contiguous to the United States said articles shall be as originally packed without having

[142] *Ibid.*, pp. 2-3, 7-8, 9-10; also see p. 18 for the proposed paragraph 22.
[143] *Ibid.*, p. 3.
[144] *Ibid.*, pp. 2-3.
[145] Section 5 of *H. R. 1438* and *H. R. 9135*. Also *Supra*, pp. 95-97; 100-101.

been opened or any manner changed in condition: Provided, however, that if such articles shall become unpacked while *en route* by accident, wreck or other casualty, or so damaged as to necessitate their repacking, the same shall be admitted free of duty upon satisfactory proof that the unpacking occurred through accident, or necessity, and that the merchandise involved is the identical merchandise originally shipped from the United States, or its possessions, as hereinbefore provided, and that its condition has not been changed except for such damage as may have been sustained.[146]

Thirdly, the following provisions regarding tobacco were inserted in the bill, and read as follows:

(a) Leaf tobacco of any kind, unstemmed, kilo, $4.08.
(b) Leaf tobacco of any kind, stemmed, kilo, $5.52.
(c) Cigars, cigarettes, and cherootes of all kinds, kilo, $9.93 and 25 percent *ad valorem*, and paper cigars, and cigarettes, including their wrappers, shall be dutiable under this clause.
(d) Other tobacco manufactured or unmanufactured, not otherwise provided for, kilo, $1.25.[147]

The above changes were recommended to simplify the provisions regarding those articles. It was also pointed out that the agreement with the domestic tobacco interests called for these changes. It was intimated that as far as the Islands were concerned the above changes were of little importance since the Philippines did not import filler tobacco and "whatever wrapper tobacco is imported would be subject to re-exportation to any foreign country."[148]

And finally, with reference to the export duty on tobacco, the following provisions were inserted:

Tobacco gross weight
(a) Manufactured or unmanufactured, except as otherwise provided, 100 kilos, $1.30.
(b) Stems, clippings, and other wastes of tobacco, 100 kilos, $0.50.[149]

These changes were recommended in order to simplify the collection of export duties on tobacco. According to the Senate Committee "the rate proposed is an average of all export duties collected and will raise the same amount of revenue."[150]

On August 4 this proposed legislation was ultimately pushed

[146] See *Senate Report No. 9*, pp. 1 and 9, also *H. R. Report No. 22* (Conference Report to Accompany H. R. 9135), p. 2.
[147] *Senate Report No. 9*, pp. 7-8.
[148] *Ibid.*, p. 8.
[149] *Ibid.*, pp. 9-10.
[150] *Ibid.*

through both Houses of Congress, and, like the Payne-Aldrich bill, received President Taft's approval on August 5, 1909.[151]

The Free Trade Provisions of the Acts of 1909 and Their Effects upon the Channels of Trade and Commerce in the Philippines

Summarizing the contents of Section V of the Payne-Aldrich Act of August 5, 1909, which provided for the trade relations thenceforth to exist between the United States and the Islands, and Section 12 of the Philippine Tariff Act of the same date, we find the following:

According to the above Sections and the regulations issued thereunder,[152] goods, (except rice), the growth, product, or manufacture of the United States were to be admitted into the Philippine Islands free of duty provided shipment conformed to the following conditions:

1. That no drawback of customs duty be allowed.
2. That they were shipped direct, direct shipment to include shipment in bond through foreign territory contiguous to the United States. Goods shipped must make the entire ocean trip in one bottom. If such articles were unpacked while *en route* by accident, wreck or other casualty, or so damaged as to require repacking, the same were to be admitted free of duty upon satisfactory proof regarding the cause of unpacking and that the merchandise was the identical merchandise originally shipped. The vessel on which this merchandise was shipped could call at foreign ports *en route* and the shipment still be regarded as direct; but if the goods were transshipped *en route,* shipment could not be regarded as direct and were dutiable upon entry into the Philippines.
3. That a certificate of origin of each shipment, properly executed in accordance with Treasury Department regulations, should be presented to the collector of customs at the port of entry.

Similarly, with the exception of rice, goods, the product or manufacture of the Philippine Islands, could be shipped to the United States free of duty under identical conditions, with the following significant exceptions:

1. That the number of cigars admitted free of duty in any one year should be limited to 150,000,000; filler tobacco when mixed with more

[151] *Cong. Record,* 61st Cong., 1st Sess., Part V, p. 5096.

[152] See *Report,* Chief of the Bureau of Insular Affairs to the Secretary of War, dated October 31, 1909, attached to the *Report,* Philippine Commission, 1909, pp. 3-7.

than fifteen percent of wrapper tobacco should not exceed 300,000 pounds; filler tobacco was limited to 1,000,000 pounds; and sugar to 300,000 gross tons.

2. That manufactured articles from the Philippines should be admitted free of duty into the United States provided that they did not contain foreign materials to the value of more than twenty percent of the total value of the manufactured article.

Shipments either way which did not, in all respects, fulfill the foregoing conditions were subject to the duty imposed on shipments of like articles from foreign countries.

On the whole, the passage of these acts, like previous tariff acts for the Philippines, was motivated by the general policy of extending American trade in the Archipelago.

While an adequate appraisal of the effects of the trade provisions of the laws of August 1909 would be hard to make in view of the limited period during which they were in operation, some concrete evidence tending to show their influences on the general flow of Philippine trade and commerce may be gleaned through an examination of the volume of trade and commerce of the Islands during the years 1909 to 1913 inclusive.

It is essential, however, that a brief résumé of Philippine trade and commerce from 1899 to and including 1908 in the light of the Tariff Acts of September 1901, March 1902, March 1905 and February 1906 should first be made, for it would tend to be an invaluable aid to an understanding of subsequent figures covering the years 1909 to 1913 inclusive. It should be recalled, therefore, that the passage of the Philippine Tariff Acts above-noted was immediately followed by an increase in Philippine importation of American goods. Of the total imports of the Islands in 1899, amounting to $19,192,986, only $1,352,086 represented the total importation of the Archipelago from the United States. In 1902, however, out of total imports of the Islands, amounting to $33,342,166, Philippine imports from the mother country were listed at $4,153,174, or, an increase of from seven percent in 1899 to twelve percent in 1902. In 1908, the total imports of the Philippines reached the amount of $79,186,125 while her total imports from the United States amounted merely to $5,101,836, or, 17 percent of the total imports of the Islands.[153]

On the other hand, out of the total exports of the Philippines, listed

[153] *Annual Report,* Insular Collector of Customs, 1921, p. 50.

at $14,845,582 in 1899, the exports of the Islands to the United States were valued at $3,935,255. In 1902, the total exports of the Archipelago reached the amount of $28,671,904 and the value of Philippine exports to the mother country was at this time listed at $11,475,948. In other words, Philippine exports to the United States, which were twenty-six percent of her total exports in 1899, reached forty percent in 1902. However, of the total exports of the Islands in 1908 ($32,601,072), the total exports to the mother country were listed at $10,450,755, or thirty-two percent of the total exports of the Philippines.[154] Under the Act of August, 1909, there was a decided increase in both imports of American goods into the Islands and exports to the United States from the Philippines.[155]

Three important facts are worth noting. In the first place, Philippine imports from the United States continued to increase, and in 1913 the imports of the Islands from the mother country reached $26,676,261 as against Philippine imports in 1908 from the same source of $5,101,836. Thus, for a space of six years Philippine importations from the United States increased from seventeen percent in 1908 to fifty percent of the total imports of the Islands in 1913. This remarkable increase not only indicated the then growing importance of the Philippines as a customer for American goods, but also tended to show the effectiveness of the tariff policy of the United States in the Philippines as expressed in the Tariff Act of August 5, 1909, in diverting the flow of trade and commerce of the Islands from their original course. For instance, of the total trade of the Philippines in 1899 only sixteen percent was with the United States and in 1902 this percentage reached twenty-five percent.[156] In 1909, however, America's share of Philippine trade reached thirty-two percent, and in 1913, forty-two percent of the total trade of the Islands was with the United States.

Secondly, Philippine exports to the United States showed, on the whole, a steady increase. The total exports of the Philippines to the United States, which in 1899 were only twenty-six percent of the total exports of the Islands, rose to forty percent in 1902. Although this favorable showing was not maintained in 1908 when the mother country consumed only thirty-two percent of the total exports of the Philippines, a recovery seemed to have been made in 1911 when the total imports of the United States from the Islands amounted to $19,922,627, or forty-

[154] *Annual Report,* Insular Collector of Customs, 1921, p. 50.
[155] *Ibid.*
[156] *Ibid.*

four percent of the total exports of the Archipelago.[157] Because of the great fall in the price of sugar in the United States in 1913,[158] however, Philippine sugar exports to that country were listed at only 30,231 long tons against 131,763 long tons the previous year. Coupled with the decrease in Philippine exportation of sugar to the United States was the decline in the importation by the latter of Philippine copra (except coconut oil for which American importation had increased from $205,-052 in 1908 to $1,095,438 in 1913), hemp and tobacco. Only thirty-four percent of the total exports of the Islands went to the United States in 1913 in comparison with forty-one percent of the previous year. But fifty percent of the total exports of the Islands in 1914 went to the mother country and in 1920 this rose to 70 percent.

During the five-year period represented in the table previously noted, Philippine imports from the United States exceeded its exports thereto to the extent of $5,444,241. With the exception of the year 1909, when the Islands enjoyed a "favorable balance" in its trade with all countries amounting to $3,839,819, from 1910 to 1913 inclusive the Philippines had "unfavorable trade balances" to the amount of $9,090,898, $3,187,280 and $5,539,803 respectively.

The reasons for these unfavorable trade balances of the Philippines may be seen in the growing investments for agricultural and commercial development of the Islands as a result of the new trade relation between the United States and the Philippines established by the laws of August 5, 1909,[159] as tangible indications of which there were increases in Philippine importation of iron and steel and their manufactures. For instance, in 1908 the total importation of the Islands for these commodities amounted merely to $2,164,907, but in 1910 this amount rose to $5,559,458 and in 1913 to $8,613,904.[160]

As a further indication of these developments the following data are worth noting. In 1903 there were only 1,075 sugar mills in the Philippines, with a total capitalization of $8,466,747 and with an annual production averaging $3,301,503. In 1918, however, there were 2,663

[157] See *Appendix II*, Table No. 10.

[158] Prices for sugar not above No. 16, Dutch Standard, per pound: 1910—2.59 cents; 1911—2.45 cents; 1912—2.81 cents; 1913—2.18 cents. Taken from Department of Commerce, *Statistical Abstract of the United States*, 1913. The average prices per kilo of Philippine sugar in Manila in 1910, 1911, 1912 and 1913 were .11894; .10596; .09945; and .08940 cents respectively. See Table XI, *Annual Report*, Insular Collector of Customs, 1923, p. 71.

[159] *Report*, Philippine Commission, 1910, pp. 5-8.

[160] *Statistical Bulletin No. 1*, Philippine Islands, 1918, p. 9.

sugar mills in the Islands with a total capitalization of $26,403,757, and an annual production averaging $41,072,981.[161]

And, finally, the Philippine Census for 1918 reported that in 1903 there were only 2,184 manufacturing establishments in the Islands with a total investment in money and real and personal property amounting to $18,113,042 paying a total average in monthly wages of $378,920 and with an annual production totaling $17,548,604. On the other hand, the number of manufacturing establishments in the Philippines in 1918 was listed at 5,239 with a total investment in money and real and personal property of $82,372,934, paying a total average in monthly wages of $1,097,591 and with a total yearly production of $115,242,-833.[162]

There were two fundamental factors, however, which tend to indicate that during the period under review American and foreign investments for agricultural developments in the Philippines were, on the whole, negligible. In the first place, well-meaning Americans were apprehensive of the United States Government's colonial policy in the Philippines. They were opposed to the colonial policy, for they believed that its institution in the Islands would be followed by a system of large grants of land, as in the Dutch East Indies, and this would be likely to be prejudicial to the well-being of the Filipinos. The American domestic sugar producers and tobacco interests, not wanting to see large areas of land in the Philippines opened up to sugar cane and tobacco culture, joined hands with the opponents of colonial policy.[163] The result of this unholy alliance was the provision in Section 15 of the Phillippine Organic Act of July 1, 1902, that only sixteen hectares of public land (a hectare is equal to 2.47 acres) should be acquired by an individual person and that 1,024 hectares was fixed as the maximum amount of public land a corporation could acquire.[164] This provision, according

[161] *Ibid., No. 5*, 1922, p. 45.

[162] *Census of the Philippine Islands*, 1918, Vol. IV, Part I, pp. 199-209.

[163] H. P. Willis, *op. cit.*, p. 368 *et seq.*

[164] There were instances when American corporations bought more public lands than allowed by law. In 1909, for instance, an American corporation bought 55,000 acres of friar lands in the island of Mindoro for the sum of $361,000. The Hawaiian sugar planters followed suit and bought 20,000 acres from the Calamba convent in the province of Laguna to establish a sugar central on the spot. In the opinion of the Attorney General of the United States, the limitations of the public land act did not apply to these sales.

In 1910, however, the legality of these sales was questioned in Congress apparently at the instigation of the domestic sugar interests, and because of the fact that American capitalists identified with cane sugar interests were among the purchasers. A searching investigation was made by a Committee on Insular Affairs of the House of

to former Governor General William Cameron Forbes, was intended "to cripple the Philippine sugar industry by preventing corporations from holding enough land to supply a modern sugar central."[165] And in the second place, the Filipinos through their leaders, did not look with favor on the unlimited entry of American and foreign capital into the Islands, for they feared that these investments might hamper their chances in obtaining independence from the United States in the future.

And thirdly, another fact worth noting is the continued increase of Philippine importations from all other countries in spite of the free entry of American goods into the Philippines.[166] This development seems to be indicative of either the need for adaptability of American manufactured goods (especially cotton textiles) to Philippine conditions, or of the inevitable part that the time element has had to play in re-directing old-established habits of trade and commerce—as well as their natural channels—as changed conditions warranted.[167] Nonetheless, one fact is certain which is germane to the present study: as a result of the new trade relation between the Philippines and the United States established by the Act of August 5, 1909, agricultural production in the Islands, in the main, would be greatly enhanced and consequently, the purchasing power of the Filipinos would be increased. The Philippines being an agricultural country the increase in price of its basic products would have a very salutary effect on the general commerce and trade of the Archipelago.[168]

Speaking of the newly established trade relation between the Philippines and the United States the Philippine Commission, while expecting that henceforth the Filipinos would be able to augment their purchases from the mother country, expected also that duty-paying imports from other countries would not be cut off very greatly thereby enabling the Insular treasury to continue to collect "a respectable revenue from customs."[169]

Whether the Philippine Commission succeeded or not in its prediction will be shown in the following chapter.

Representatives, but the action of the Philippine Government was upheld, the Committee dividing practically on party lines. For testimony and evidence brought out during the investigation see *H. R. 2289*, 61st Cong., 3rd Sess.: also see *Cong. Record*, 61st Cong., 2nd Sess., Part IV, pp. 3801-3806.

[165] W. C. Forbes, *op. cit.*, Vol. I, p. 324.

[166] See *Appendix II*, Table No. 4.

[167] See *Report*, Philippine Commission, 1909, pp. 5-7.

[168] *Ibid.*, 1910, pp. 158-160; *Ibid.*, 1911, pp. 148-150; also *Appendix II*, Tables No. 4 and 10.

[169] *Ibid.*, 1909, p. 5.

4: *Development of Policy*

OCTOBER 1913 TO MARCH 1934

IN VIEW of the platforms of the Democratic party[1] and the statements of its responsible leaders regarding general American-Philippine relations[2] the victory of this party during the national election of 1912 gave the Filipino People reasons for optimism regarding their future relations with the mother country and the prospects for their national independence.

Meanwhile, as already noted, the trade relation which was inaugurated in 1909 between the United States and the Philippines was diverting the channels of Philippine trade and commerce from their original course to the United States. On the other hand, this trade relation with the mother country gave the necessary impetus to the production of the basic export products of the Archipelago.

For instance, the total area devoted to sugar cane in 1910 was listed only at 83,168 hectares while in 1911 this area reached 120,313 hectares, in 1912 it rose to 164,261 hectares, and in 1913 to 176,118 hectares.[3] Although the area devoted to hemp had steadily declined from 475,136 hectares in 1910 to 368,211 in 1913 only to recover somewhat in 1914 when it rose to 437,470 hectares, the total value of this product, however, continued to increase. In 1910 the total value of hemp amounted to $13,476,172 and in 1913 this sum rose to $16,159,838[4]

The total area devoted to coconut planting was listed at 164,193 hectares in 1910. In the following year it reached 208,476 hectares and in

[1] *Campaign Textbook of the Democratic Party*, 1900, p. 4; *Ibid.*, 1904, p. 7; *Ibid.*, 1908, pp. 7, 50, 135-137; *Ibid.*, 1912, p. 30. Hereafter cited as *Democratic Textbook*.

[2] See Hon. William J. Bryan's speech accepting the democratic nomination for the Presidency of the United States, in *Democratic Textbook*, 1900, pp. 15-32. See also statement of Senator Joseph L. Rawlins of Utah in *Cong. Record*, 57th Cong., 1st Sess., Part II, pp. 1060-1061. See also statement of Representative Oscar W. Underwood, *Ibid.*, 61st Cong., 1st Sess., Part II, p. 2008. See also Hon. Woodrow Wilson's speech accepting the nomination of the Democratic Party for President of the United States in the *Democratic Textbook*, 1912, pp. 351-352.

[3] *Statistical Bulletin No. 3*, Philippine Islands, 1920, Table No. 22, p. 23.

[4] *Ibid.*

1912 rose to 230,682 hectares. In 1913, however, there were only 223,212 hectares devoted to coconuts.[5]

Regarding tobacco, there were only 53,626 hectares devoted to its cultivation in the Islands in 1910. In 1911, however, it rose to 69,015 hectares. While a decline was experienced in 1912 when there were only 57,041 hectares planted with tobacco in the Philippines, in 1913, on the other hand, there were 68,991 hectares devoted to this commodity.[6]

Notwithstanding the general increase in the cultivation of sugar cane and tobacco in the Philippines, the quotas set forth in Section V of the Payne-Aldrich Act of August 5, 1909 were not reached[7]

In view of this fact and because of the belief entertained by influential leaders of the Democratic party that an export tax on some of the most important exports of the Philippines was not only unconstitutional but also restrictive to the growth of Philippine industries concerned,[8] and that it would be manifestly unfair to enact a law allowing the unlimited free entry of American products into the Islands while denying the same privilege to the products of the Archipelago imported into the United States, a provision was inserted in the general tariff bill (H. R. 3321) the chief features of which—those which are germane to the present study—were the following:[9]

1. Rice, sugar and tobacco from the Philippines were to be granted unlimited free entry into the United States, provided, however, that all manufactured tobaccos of the Islands such as cigars, cigarettes, and other manufactures of tobacco, should be admitted free of customs duty into the United States only when these products did not contain foreign material to the value of more than twenty percent.

2. Export taxes, as provided for in Section 13 of the Philippine Tariff Act of August 5, 1909, and levied upon the chief exports of the Islands, were repealed.

3. On the recommendation of the Chief of the Bureau of Insular Affairs of the War Department the foreign-material content of all Philippine manufactured articles (except manufactures of tobacco)

[5] *Ibid.*
[6] *Ibid.*
[7] *Ibid.*
[8] *Supra*, pp. 103-104; see also *Cong. Record*, 61st Cong., 1st Sess., Part II, p. 2008 for the complete statement of Representative Underwood; see also *Senate Report No. 80*, 63rd Cong., 1st Sess.
[9] *H. R. Report No. 5*, 63rd Cong., 1st Sess.

was raised from twenty to fifty percent. This was recommended so as to encourage embroidery and lace-making industries in the Islands.[10]

4. In consideration for the above privileges it was provided that all articles the growth, product or manufacture of the United States (if no drawback of customs duties was allowed on them—as in the case of all articles the growth, product or manufacture of the Philippines entering the mother country free of duty)—were to be admitted into the Philippines free of duty.

5. And finally, the free entry of all articles, the growth, product or manufacture of the United States into the Philippines, and vice versa, were conditioned on their direct shipment under a through bill of lading from a country of origin to a country of destination. Direct shipment, as similarly provided for in the Payne-Aldrich Act, included shipment in bond through foreign territories contiguous to the United States.

During the debate in the House of Representatives with respect to the proposed measure (H. R. 3321), Mr. Luther W. Mott of New York on April 28, 1913, fired the opening shot against the provision allowing the unlimited free entry of Philippine tobacco and its manufactures into the United States. Such a proposal, according to him, would be "unfair and unjust" to a vast army of American citizens employed in the production of tobacco and its manufactures, for they would be compelled "to submit to the unlimited competition of the Malayas in the Philippine Islands."[11]

Following the above line of argument, Mr. Frederick H. Gillett of Massachusetts on May 7 offered to amend the Philippine section of the proposed legislation by retaining the existing annual quota of 150,000,000 cigars from the Islands to be allowed free entry into the United States.[12]

Speaking in favor of the above amendment, Mr. Frederick A. Britten of Illinois indicated that the unlimited free entry of Philippine manufactured tobacco into the United States would impose a severe hardship on the manufacturers and cigar makers of the country. He backed this statement with the petition of the Cigar Maker's Union of Chicago signed by its 1,500 members.[13] Asked by Mr. Richard Bartholdt of Missouri whether the adoption of the proposed provision would not become an incentive for the American Tobacco Trust to extend operations

[10] *H. R. Report No. 5*, pp. 1-2.
[11] *Cong. Record*, 63rd Cong., 1st Sess., Part I, p. 712.
[12] *Ibid.*, Part II, p. 1328.
[13] For a copy of this petition, see *Ibid.*, pp. 1328-1329.

to the Philippines in view of the comparatively low wages existing there, Mr. Britten replied that there was no provision in the pending legislation which would restrain the Trust in going to those Islands. He recalled that as a result of the establishment of free trade between the United States and Puerto Rico the American Tobacco Trust extended its operations to that island. Since then, he continued, the Trust controlled eighty percent of the cigar manufacturing and leaf tobacco industry of Puerto Rico. Mr. Britten was of the opinion that the same result would follow should Congress allow the unlimited free entry of Philippine tobacco and its manufactures into the United States.[14]

In supporting Mr. Britten's position, Mr. Frank B. Willis of Ohio pointed out that organized labor was opposed to the contemplated provision regarding Philippine tobacco. He submitted the petition of the Cigar Maker's International Union of America under date of May 3, 1913, indicating the desirability of limiting the free entry of Philippine cigars to 73,000,000 annually. The great disparity in labor costs between the Islands and the United States and the belief that one-half of the cigar factories in Manila were owned by "Chinese coolies"[15] were the reasons given for the above proposal.

In voicing the position of the majority Party against Mr. Gillett's amendment and the arguments therefor, Mr. Underwood of Alabama, chairman of the Committee on Ways and Means of the House of Representatives, gave a scathing indictment of the selfish interests behind the amendment. He pointed out that in the pending tariff legislation (H. R. 3321) "nearly every man that has been concerned in business in the United States has had his duties reduced from the present law." On the other hand, he continued, the Committee decided to maintain the existing differential—the difference between 35 cents a pound on filler tobacco and $1.85 on wrapper tobacco—in favor of the American tobacco manufacturers not only because this differential "was on a fair revenue basis" but also because this advantage made it possible for the domestic tobacco interests to build up their business in the United States. To his mind, therefore, it was unreasonable that the American tobacco manufacturers should insist on depriving the Filipinos of a "reciprocal market in the United States" when "under our law [they] are compelled to give us free trade."[16]

[14] *Cong. Record*, 63rd Cong., 1st Sess., Part II, p. 1328.
[15] For a copy of this petition see *Ibid.*, pp. 1328-1329.
[16] *Ibid.*, p. 1329.

It should be borne in mind, concluded Mr. Underwood, that the existing law which allowed the Philippines to export 150,000,000 cigars annually to the United States free of duty had been on the statute books for four years. And that in spite of the fact that the tobacco industry of the Islands was not new but one which had already been developed when the United States acquired sovereignty over the Philippines, the total number of cigars imported into the United States therefrom was only 63,852,000 for the fiscal year ending June 30, 1912.[17]

Asked by Mr. William F. Murray of Massachusetts whether it would not be wise to retain the existing limitation since the Philippine quota had not even been reached and therefore there was no necessity for adopting the proposed provision regarding Philippine cigars, Mr. Underwood pointed out that while Congress had the legal right to maintain the existing limitations such act nevertheless would be "to the shame of every American citizen." "We could not face these dependent people who give us free trade in their markets," he continued, "if we close our doors to the only imports that they might possibly send here." "No man who understands the honor and integrity of his own country," he asserted, "is going to attempt to make a one-sided contract of that kind with a dependent people."[18]

Mr. Gillett's amendment to retain the existing provision regarding Philippine cigars imported into the United States was finally brought to a vote but the House of Representatives decided to vote it down.[19]

Close on the heels of this decision Mr. Fordney of Michigan offered to amend the whole Philippine section (Section IV, Paragraph C) of the proposed measure by maintaining the existing provisions stipulated in Section V of the Payne-Aldrich Act of August 5, 1909.[20]

Speaking in favor of Mr. Fordney's amendment, Mr. Mondell of Wyoming noted the "unexplainable inconsistencies" of the Democratic party. He observed that it was the avowed purpose of that party to grant the Philippine Islands its independence and at an early date provide for its complete separation from the United States. Yet in the next breath, he pointed out, this very same party—as exemplified in the provision of Section IV Paragraph C—proposed "to establish conditions under which it will be less desirable to those people to leave us, conditions under which an increased number of those people shall desire to

[17] *Ibid.*
[18] *Ibid.*
[19] *Ibid.*
[20] See *Appendix I.*

remain bound to us, and conditions under which, if separation shall come, the industries of the islands shall be thrown into infinitely greater confusion than they would otherwise be." On the other hand, it would be little short of tragedy to "highly paid American labor," should Philippine products, produced under "wages far below ours," be allowed unlimited free entry into the United States.[21]

Of the proposal regarding the increase from twenty to fifty percent in the foreign material-content of Philippine manufactured products, except tobacco, Mr. Mondell saw in it a chance for the Philippines "to secure from India, the Malay States, China, and Japan, and from all over the East, products in unlimited quantities, and ship them here free of duty provided they declare that fifty percent of the value of such products is of Philippine origin."[22]

However, Mr. Fordney's amendment was finally voted down and the Philippine section of the proposed measure (H. R. 3321) as originally constituted[23] remained intact. And on May 8, 1913, this proposed legislation was pushed through the House of Representatives and immediately sent to the Senate which referred it to the Senate Finance Committee.[24] The following day (May 9) debate in the Senate regarding this proposed measure was actually begun.

The opening broadside was given by Senator Newlands of Nevada, who, in the course of his remarks against the proposed free entry of sugar from whatever origin three years after the passage of the pending legislation, found occasion to criticize the mistaken generosity of the Congress regarding its Philippine tariff policy. He pointed out that instead of preparing and starting the Filipinos on a career of individualized life Congress, as exemplified in the bill under review, was undertaking to bring those people under the American protective system in the belief that in doing so a favor was being extended to them. In view of the expressed willingness of the Democratic party to ultimately give the Philippine Islands its independence Senator Newlands asked whether it was not mistaken generosity to accustom the Filipinos "to a hothouse system of protective tariff . . . when the very process of cutting them off involves the destruction of the hothouse methods." With their independence granted, he continued, "the Philippine Islands will then drift into their individual life, compelled to compete not under favored laws

[21] *Cong. Record*, 63rd Cong., 1st Sess., Part II, p. 1334.
[22] *Ibid.*
[23] *Ibid.*, p. 1427; also *supra*, pp. 115-116.
[24] *Senate Report No. 80*, 63rd Cong., 1st Sess.

with this country but with the entire world—a competition which they were not able to bear before their annexation to this country."[25]

Senator Joseph E. Ransdell of Louisiana, while not making any direct reference against the proposed unlimited free entry of Philippine sugar into the United States provided for in the bill under consideration, pointed out that the provision regarding the free entry of sugar into the United States was a violation of the Democratic platform adopted in Baltimore and which assured the preservation of legitimate industry against foreign competition.[26] The adoption of this provision, Mr. Ransdell continued, would enable the American Sugar Trust and other American refiners to gain "complete control of the market, and after a brief period of three or four years, under free sugar, would raise prices as high or higher than now." Furthermore, not only would the national government lose $52,000,000 a year in revenue, but also the American people would get "no cheaper sugar, except for a few years necessary to ruin the domestic producers, after which the trust and other refiners would pocket immense profit."[27]

Senator Lodge of Massachusetts was caustic in his remarks against the free entry of sugar into the United States. The adoption of such a provision, he maintained, would mean the giving up for nothing an annual revenue derived from sugar and of which no one complained. On the other hand, while the free entry of raw sugar into the United States would be beneficial only to the three great refineries of the country, this provision, continued the Senator, would cause an irreparable damage to our domestic sugar industries and would tend to destroy our "great and growing trade" with our territories and dependencies "which want only to trade with us, and must trade practically only with us." The inability of their sugar to withstand foreign competition in our market would also mean a "reduction in their ability to buy from us." To his mind therefore the present measure was "not only cruel to the industries involved, but . . . economically it is the most indefensible action that can possibly be taken in any revenue bill."[28]

On the question of tobacco, however, and on the recommendation of the Boston Central Labor Union,[29] the learned Senator offered to amend the Philippine section of the pending bill by retaining the existing an-

[25] *Cong. Record,* 63rd Cong., 1st Sess., Part II, p. 1602.
[26] See *Democratic Textbook,* 1912, pp. 2 and 40.
[27] *Cong. Record,* 63rd Cong., 1st Sess., Part II, p. 1845.
[28] *Ibid.,* Part IV, p. 3487.
[29] For a copy of this petition by the Boston Central Labor Union under date of July 16, 1913, see *Ibid.,* p. 3954.

nual quota of 150,000,000 cigars from the Islands to be admitted free of customs duty into the United States. Senator Lodge pointed out that the above amendment was made necessary because the cigar makers of the country believed that the unlimited competition of cheap cigars from the Philippines would "be extremely severe and detrimental to them, and they desire to have the limitation of the present law preserved."[30]

Both Senator John D. Works of California, in behalf of the cigar makers of that state and Senator Lawrence B. Sherman of Illinois, speaking for the International Cigar Maker's Union and all the local unions of those states strongly urged the adoption of Senator Lodge's amendment. Like the previous amendment in the House which was offered by Representative Gillett also of Massachusetts, Senator Lodge's amendment was rejected.[31]

Shortly thereafter Senator Lodge, speaking for the cordage interests of Massachusetts, offered another amendment which urged the removal of the phrase "under a through bill of lading" in the following clause of the Philippine section of the pending legislation, to wit:

> and provided further, that the free admission, herein provided, of such articles, the growth, product, or manufacture of the United States into the Philippine Islands, or the growth, product, or manufacture, as hereinbefore defined, of the Philippine Islands into the United States, shall be conditional upon the direct shipment thereof, *under a through bill of lading,*[32] from the country of origin to the country of destination. . . .[33]

In explaining the reason for his amendment, Senator Lodge recalled how that same phrase was urged upon the Senate Finance Committee, of which he was then the chairman, when that body was considering the provisions of Section V of the Payne-Aldrich bill of 1909. He asserted his belief then—and still entertained the same belief—that should that "risky" phrase be inserted in the Philippine section of the pending legislation, it would "enable hemp to go through London" and he feared that that "would undo all that has been done in that direction."[34] In other words, Senator Lodge was fearful that the operation of the above provision might tend to deprive the American cordage interests of the $7.50 per ton rebate.[35]

[30] *Ibid.*
[31] *Ibid.*
[32] *Italics* are mine.
[33] *Ibid.*
[34] *Ibid.*
[35] See *Supra*, pp. 50-53.

On the suggestion of Senator Williams of Mississippi the above amendment offered by Senator Lodge was sent back to the Senate Finance Committee for further study. Ultimately, however, this amendment was not acceded to.[36]

Senator Boies Penrose of Pennsylvania, after showing the great disparity in the rate of wages between those prevailing in the United States and those in the Philippines, warned his colleagues of a movement by American and British financial interests to invest large sums of money in the exploitation on a gigantic scale of Philippine tobacco industries. These interests, he warned his colleagues, were awaiting only the passage of the measure providing for an unlimited free entry of Philippine tobacco into the United States. Hence, the benefits of the "unrestricted free trade will not go to the building up of the general prosperity of the Philippine Islands" but would "go into the pockets of these capitalists."[37]

Speaking of labor, Senator Penrose reasoned that since Chinese and Japanese laborers were, for the most part, employed in the cigar factories of the Islands, it would therefore be inconsistent "to exclude this oriental labor from our shores and yet admit freely the products of that labor."[38] Consequently, he offered to amend the Philippine section of the proposed measure by reenacting the then existing provision with regard to the importation into the United States of raw and manufactured tobaccos from the Islands. However, by a vote of 36 to 46 (16 not voting), this amendment was rejected.[39]

The Philippine provisions of H. R. 3321 drafted by the Committee on Ways and Means of the House[40] was adopted with one important exception. This was the Senate amendment reimposing the then existing twenty percent proviso regarding the foreign material content of Philippine manufactured products exported to the United States.[41] Subsequently, however, the House acceded to this amendment[42] and the Philippine provisions of the proposed measure as amended became part of the general tariff law when President Wilson approved it on October 3, 1913.[43]

[36] See *H. R. Report No. 86* (Conference Report to accompany H. R. 3321); also *Appendix I.*

[37] *Cong. Record,* 63rd Cong., 1st Sess., Part V. pp. 4289-4290.

[38] *Ibid.,* p. 4290.

[39] *Ibid.,* p. 4617.

[40] *H. R. Report No. 5,* pp. L-LI, 63rd Cong., 1st Sess. Also *Supra* pp. 115-116.

[41] See *Senate Report No. 80,* pp. XXVIII-XXIX, 63rd Cong., 1st Sess.

[42] See *H. R. Report No. 86* (Conference Report to accompany *H. R. 3321*), 63rd Cong., 1st Sess.

[43] *Public No. 16,* United States Statutes at Large, Vol. XXXVIII, p. 113.

With three exceptions the Philippine section (Section IV, Paragraph C) of the Act of October 3, 1913, commonly known as the Underwood-Simmons law, was identical in language and provisions with Section V of the Payne-Aldrich Act of August 5, 1909. These exceptions were: the unlimited free entry of Philippine products into the United States; the repeal of export taxes imposed by the Philippine government upon some of the principal exports of the Islands; and the insertion of a phrase "under a through bill of lading" to follow the clause which provides that the free entry of Philippine products into the United States should be conditioned upon their direct shipment thereto.[44]

It might be noted also that while Section IV, Paragraph C of the Underwood-Simmons Act removed the quotas imposed by the Payne-Aldrich law of 1909 on the free entry of Philippine products into the United States annually, it could be stated that actually the Philippine section of the Underwood-Simmons Act merely continued the same preferential treatment that was enjoyed by the products of the Archipelago in the American market. This was due to the fact that the quotas imposed on Philippine products by the Act of 1909 had never been reached.[45] This preferential treatment, especially with respect to Philippine sugar—which is practically a subsidy—would be equivalent to the duty levied on similar products imported into the United States from a foreign country.

It should be borne in mind that the Underwood-Simmons Act provided also that hemp and copra should be admitted duty free into the United States, and that beginning May 1, 1916 all raw sugar should be allowed free entry into the United States. This would mean that sugar from the Philippines would be admitted into the United States on the same basis as all other foreign sugar. Therefore these provisions relative to copra, hemp and sugar would leave only to Philippine tobacco and a few minor products the advantages of the trade privileges granted in the Underwood-Simmons Act. It was in the light of this consideration that the Manila Merchants' Association addressed a petition under date of April 2, 1914 to the President and the Congress of the United States.[46]

It was pointed out that the free entry into the United States of Manila hemp and copra and the provision allowing all foreign sugar free

[44] United States Tariff Commission, *Comparison of Tariff Acts of* 1909, 1913 *and* 1922, *prepared for the use of the Committee on Ways and Means of the House of Representatives*, 1923, pp. 163-165.

[45] *Statistical Bulletin No. 3*, Philippine Islands, 1920, p. 23.

[46] For a copy of this petition see *Cong. Record*, 63rd Cong., 2nd Sess., Part XII, pp. 11437-38.

of customs duty into the American market after May 1, 1916, would be tantamount to a withdrawal of the "compensation" the Philippines had for admitting "all articles the growth, product or manufacture of the United States . . . free into the Philippine Islands without restriction or limitation of any kind." In view of the restrictive character of Philippine exports the above provision regarding the ultimate free entry into the United States of all raw sugar would be obviously unfair to the Islands, and moreover it would not be compatible "with the traditional justice of the American Nation and the generous character of the American people."[47]

The petitioners, therefore, urged the modification of the Underwood-Simmons Act by maintaining the duty on sugar under the old law. They recommended also the imposition of such duty on other articles not then subject to duty which were produced, or could be successfully produced in the Philippines. The adoption of such a measure, it was pointed out, would not only serve as an incentive to the development of industries in the Islands, the growth of commerce, and the economic rejuvenation of the Filipino people but also it would tend to "equalize the benefits" derived from "reciprocal trade" relations between the Philippines and the United States. Furthermore, the mother country "would profit in full measure with these islands from the increased commerce and the enhanced prosperity that would certainly follow."[48]

On the other hand, by importing from foreign countries such "tropical products" as cocoa, coffee, fibers, rubber, raw silk, sugar, and so forth, the United States suffered an unfavorable trade balance of nearly $400,000,000 a year. Should there be a moderate duty on the above products, continued the petitioners, the Philippines, which is capable of producing them would be able to supply the needs of the mother country. This would enable the American people to obtain from their own territory the above-noted articles and obviously there would be available to the United States "a compensating trade subject directly to its control." In other words, increased production in the Philippines would mean also enlarged purchasing power of the Filipino people. This in turn would necessarily be reflected in a "corresponding increased trade for the United States [serving] to reduce in equal measure the balance against the United States in its trade with other tropical or semi-tropical countries."[49]

[47] *Ibid.*, p. 11437.
[48] *Ibid.*
[49] *Ibid.*

It was not until February 14, 1916, however, that a bill[50] was introduced in the House of Representatives, the purpose of which was to amend paragraphs 177 and 178 of the Underwood-Simmons Act of 1913[51] relating to the free entry into the United States of sugar, molasses and other articles, and consequently, to maintain the existing rate on raw sugar of about 1.25 cents a pound according to the polariscope test.[52]

The majority members of the House Committee on Ways and Means in urging the immediate passage of the amendatory legislation pointed out that were it not for the abnormal conditions occasioned by the World War the Act of 1913 would have raised sufficient revenues to take care of the expenses of the Federal Government and still permit sugar to go upon the free list in 1916.[53] This was borne out by the fact, according to Mr. Claude Kitchin, Chairman of the Committee on Ways and Means, that from January 1 to August 1, 1914, the only time when the Underwood-Simmons law had a fair trial, and just before the World War broke out, that revenue act produced over $17,426,008.90 more than had been collected under the Payne-Aldrich Act for the corresponding months in 1913. But conditions did not remain normal; consequently there was a necessity for retaining the present duties.[54]

The Democratic majority in Congress defended its stand on the measure on the ground that an emergency existed as a result of the World War while the "conversion" of the Democrats to the Republican doctrine of protectionism was summarized by Mr. Nicholas Longworth of Ohio in the following language: "I am glad that the Democracy has experienced a change of heart; I rejoice that a great light has burst upon them. . . . I welcome you, my friends of the Democracy, to at least limited membership in the Republican Party. I rejoice that at last you are with us in our efforts to maintain American industry."[55]

On the whole, the traditional line of cleavage between the two major

[50] *H. R. 11471*, 64th Cong., 1st Sess.

[51] The free-sugar provisions of paragraphs 177 and 178 of Schedule E of the Underwood-Simmons Act, provided that on and after May 1, 1916, sugar, tank bottoms, syrups of cane juice, melada, concentrated melada, concrete and concentrated molasses, molasses, sugar drainings and sugar sweepings, maple sugar and maple syrup, glucose or grape sugar, and sugar cane in its natural state, or unmanufactured, shall be admitted free of duty into the United States.

[52] *Cong. Record,* 64th Cong., 1st Sess., Part IV, pp. 4147-4148.

[53] *Cong. Record,* 64th Cong., 1st Sess., Part IV, pp. 4147-4148. See also *H. R. Report No. 266,* 64th Cong., 1st Sess., pp. 1-2. For the estimated revenue resulting from the Underwood-Simmons Act see *Senate Document Nos. 180* and *217,* 63rd Cong., 1st Sess., pp. 1-22 respectively.

[54] *H. R. Report No. 266,* p. 2.

[55] *Cong. Record,* 64th Cong., 1st Sess., Part IV, pp. 4159-4160.

parties was practically brushed aside when the proposed measure (H. R. 11471) was under discussion.[56] On April 27, 1916 this legislation received the approval of President Wilson.[57]

The next indication of American tariff policy in the Philippines was expressed in a bill which was introduced in the House of Representatives on December 6, 1915. This bill was entitled "an Act to Declare the Purpose of the People of the United States as to the Future Political Status of the People of the Philippine Islands, and to Provide a more Autonomous Government of those Islands."[58] This bill was passed in both Houses of the Congress and President Wilson approved it on August 29, 1916.[59]

This law provided that while "the Philippine government shall have the authority to enact a tariff law, the trade relations between the islands and the United States shall continue to be governed exclusively by the laws of the Congress of the United States." Furthermore, "tariff acts or acts amendatory to the tariff of the Philippine Islands shall not become law until they shall receive the approval of the President of the United States, nor shall any act of the Philippine Legislature affecting immigration or the currency or coinage laws of the Philippines become a law until it has been approved by the President of the United States. . . ."[60]

Representative William A. Jones of Virginia, chairman of the House Committee on Insular Affairs, in answering the question asked by Mr. Henry A. Cooper of Wisconsin regarding the above provision, explained that henceforth all propositions regarding changes in the existing laws to be made by the Philippine Legislature must first receive the approval of the President of the United States "before they are passed by the legislature."[61]

In Section 10 of this Act there was also inserted a provision specifically forbidding the Insular legislature to restore export duties in the Philippines.

Thus, subject to the approval of the President of the United States,

[56] For the debate on this bill, see *Ibid.*, Part IV, pp. 4146-4172; Part V, pp. 4214-4252; Part VI, pp. 5775-5788; 5797-5807; 5875-5898; Part VII, pp. 6441-6443; 6477-6478; 6631-6652.

[57] *Ibid.*, Part VII, p. 6991; Also *Public No. 61.*

[58] *H. R. 1,* but ultimately superseded by *Senate Bill 381.* See *Cong. Record,* 64th Cong., 1st Sess., Part I, pp. 14, 80; also see *H. R. Report No. 499* (to accompany *S. 381*) 64th Cong., 1st Sess.; also *Senate Document No. 527 and No. 530* (Conference Reports on *S. 381*).

[59] *Public, No. 240.*

[60] *Ibid.*, Section 10.

[61] *Cong. Record,* 64th Cong., 1st Sess., Part XIII, p. 12835.

the Act of August 29, 1916, gave the Philippine Legislature a partial tariff autonomy with regard to the enactment of customs duties on all foreign goods entering the Islands. It was provided, however, that the trade relations between the United States and the Philippines should continue to be governed exclusively by the Congress of the United States. Since all articles the growth, product or manufacture of the United States were admitted (and still are admitted)[62] free of duty into the Islands, it follows that whatever rates of customs duty should be levied by the Insular government on foreign goods would, on the whole, redound to the advantage of similar products from the United States imported into the Philippines. Similarly, this would hold true also with regard to the products of the Philippine Islands imported into the mother country, subject, however, to the exception imposed by the proviso regarding the twenty percent foreign material-content of Philippine manufactured products imported into the United States.

The trade relation between the Philippines and the United States outlined above remained in force until the Jones-Costigan Sugar Act was approved by President Franklin D. Roosevelt on May 9, 1934.[63] By virtue of this legislation the Secretary of Agriculture was authorized to fix quotas for sugar imported from Cuba, Hawaii, and the Philippine Islands, Puerto Rico, and the Virgin Islands.

However, in spite of President Roosevelt's recommendation that the sugar quota from the Philippines should be set at 1,037,000 short tons[64] the sugar quota for the Islands was finally fixed at 1,015,185 short tons to commence retroactively on January 1, 1934.[65] The following year this quota was further reduced to 981,042 short tons.[66]

Meanwhile, as a substitute measure for the Hare-Hawes-Cutting Act which the Philippine Legislature allowed to lapse,[67] a new Philippine Independence Act commonly known as the Tydings-McDuffie Law was approved by President Roosevelt on March 24, 1934.[68] This was subse-

[62] As of July 3, 1946.

[63] *Public No. 213*, see *Cong. Record*, 73rd Cong., 2nd Sess., Part VIII, p. 8412.

[64] See President Roosevelt's message of February 8, 1934, in *Cong. Record*, 73rd Cong., 2nd Sess., Part II, p. 2176.

[65] *Public No. 213*, 73rd Cong., 2nd Sess.; see also New York Trust Company, *The Index*, October 1935, Vol. XV, No. 10, pp. 197-204.

[66] *The New York Times*, August 18, 1935, Section 3, p. 8 f.

[67] This Act authorized the Philippine Legislature to meet not later than January 17, 1934 to consider the calling of a convention to frame a constitutional form of government for the Islands. But the Insular Legislature allowed the law to lapse. See *Cong. Record*, 73rd Cong., 2nd Sess., Part I, p. 258 for President Roosevelt's communication with the Congress regarding this matter.

[68] *Public No. 127*, 73rd Cong., 2nd Sess.

quently accepted by the Philippine Legislature on May 1.[69] This new Independence Act—to which reference will be made shortly—not only promised independence for the Philippines at the end of a transition period of ten years but also provided that during the intervening period prior to the granting of ultimate independence, the trade relations between the United States and the Philippines should be as heretofore provided by law, subject to the following exceptions:[70] that in any calendar year only a limited quantity of sugar, manufactures of Manila hemp (such as cord, cordage, and so forth) and coconut oil should be allowed free entry into the United States from the Philippine Islands.

Furthermore it was provided that during the sixth year after the inauguration[71] of the government of the Commonwealth of the Philippines, a graduated export tax should be levied on all products of the Islands that might be imported into the United States. Thus from November 15, 1941, the Philippine government should levy an export tax of five percent of the regular rates of duty which may be levied in the United States on like articles from foreign countries. Then during the seventh year this rate should be raised to ten percent; in the eighth year to fifteen percent; in the ninth year to twenty percent; and after the expiration of the ninth year this export tax should be twenty-five percent.[72]

Finally, after the Philippines had become a free and independent nation, products from the Islands imported into the United States should be subject to the same rates of duty levied upon like articles imported from other foreign countries.[73]

On the other hand, the Philippine Independence law maintained the existing provisions regarding products from the United States imported into the Philippines. That is to say, American products shall continue to be admitted free into the Islands. And the fact that since 1909 practically the same rates of duty were levied on imports from foreign countries into the Philippines as those levied in the United States, would tend to give to similar American products imported into the Islands the monopoly of the market therein.[74]

On May 11, 1934, however—that is, ten days after the acceptance by the Philippine Legislature of the Tydings-McDuffie Independence Act—Congress imposed an excise (or processing) tax of three cents a pound

[69] See *Infra*, p. 139.
[70] *Public No. 127*, Section 6; see also *Appendix I*.
[71] The new government in the Philippines was inaugurated November 15, 1935.
[72] *Public No. 127*, Section 6.
[73] *Ibid.*, Section 13.
[74] See *Supra*, Chapter III.

on coconut oil from the Philippines or oil pressed in the United States from Philippine copra.[75] This tax was pushed through Congress in spite of President Roosevelt's insistence that such a measure would be a violation of the spirit and intent of the Tydings-McDuffie Act.[76]

On April 11, 1934, when the Senate was considering section 602½ of the Revenue bill (H. R. 7835) providing for the imposition of an excise tax of five cents a pound on Philippine copra and coconut oil, that body by a vote of 59 to 17 accepted Senator George W. Norris' "perfecting amendment" to the revenue bill. This amendment provided that the proceeds of the tax should be turned over to the Philippine treasury. If, on the other hand, the Philippine government "by any law provides for any subsidy to be paid to the producers of copra, coconut oil, or allied products, then this proviso shall at once become null and void."[77]

There had been a good many differences between the House of Representatives and the Senate regarding the provision of the House bill (H. R. 7835). One of these differences was the Senate's amendment reducing the original rate of five cents a pound excise tax on the Philippine coconut oil and copra to three cents a pound. As a result, a joint conference was called to iron out these differences. The conference agreed to accept not only Senator Norris' amendment but also the reduced rate of three cents a pound on copra and coconut oil from the Philippines. It was in this form that President Roosevelt signed the bill on May 11, 1934.

That the amendments referred to above had done something toward meeting the objections to Section 602½ of the Revenue law (H. R. 7835) as originally passed in the House could not be denied. Nonetheless, the fundamental fact remained that that Act imposed a tax upon Philippine copra and coconut oil which, in the language of Senator Pat Harrison, is certainly "a violation of the independence act."[78]

President Roosevelt, in a special message to Congress under date of May 28, 1934, urged the reconsideration of the excise tax on Philippine copra and coconut oil. He gave three reasons for this recommendation. Firstly, the tax implied the "withdrawal of an offer made by the Congress of the United States to the people of the Philippine Islands." Secondly, the enforcement of the "provision at this time would produce serious conditions among many thousands of families in the Philippine Islands." And finally, since there had been "no effort to work out some

[75] *Cong. Record*, 73rd Cong., 2nd Sess., Part VI, p. 1061 *et seq*.

[76] See copy of President Roosevelt's letter to Senator Pat Harrison of Mississippi, chairman of the Senate Finance Committee in *Ibid.*, p. 6317.

[77] *Cong. Record*, 73rd Cong., 2nd Sess., Part VI, p. 6380.

[78] *Ibid.*, p. 6317.

form of compromise which would be less unjust to the Philippine people and at the same time attain, even if more slowly, the object of helping the butter and animal-fat industry in the United States" the necessity for reconsidering the excise tax on Philippine copra and coconut oil becomes apparent.[79]

Although it was indicated that the excise tax on Philippine copra and coconut oil was for the purpose of extending the processing tax of the Agricultural Adjustment Act to these products of the Islands in order to protect the butter and animal-fat industries of the United States,[80] it can be claimed that for all practical purposes Section 602½ of the Revenue law of May 11, 1934 is an amendment to Section 6, Paragraph (b) of the Tydings-McDuffie Independence law, which provides that:

> There shall be levied, collected, and paid on all coconut oil coming into the United States from the Philippine Islands in any calendar year in excess of two hundred thousand long tons, the same rates of duty which are required by the laws of the United States to be levied, collected, and paid upon like articles imported from foreign countries.[81]

That the Congress of the United States has the legal right to enact laws regarding Philippine-American trade relations in any manner it sees fit cannot be denied. But whether Congress has not broken faith with the Filipino people by enacting an excise tax on Philippine copra and coconut oil after having "covenanted " with them in the Tydings-McDuffie Independence law, is, of course, another question.[82]

In this connection, however, one is reminded of the ringing words of the late Senator Henry Cabot Lodge of Massachusetts who said that "while we regard the welfare" of the Filipino people "as a sacred trust, we regard the welfare of the American people first."[83] Almost thirty-four years later this sentiment found its echo in the words of Senator Walter F. George of Georgia, who, in spite of differences in political faiths, expressed the same feeling but in different words. While haranguing in favor of levying an excise tax on Philippine copra and coconut oil, Senator George found occasion to point out that the reason why he voted for Philippine independence was merely "to do something

[79] See *Cong. Record*, 73rd Cong., 2nd Sess., Part IX, p. 9682.

[80] *Ibid.*, Part VI, p. 6317.

[81] See *Appendix I.*

[82] Senator Millard Tydings' (of Maryland) remark on this matter is very illuminating. See *Cong. Record*, 73rd Cong., 2nd Sess., Part VI, p. 6309.

[83] See *Supra*, p. 36.

for the American farmer."[84] Certainly, in the game of politics one should expect to discover, not infrequently, such strange bedfellows!

Free Trade versus Independence

Philippine Economic Development:

For decades the Filipinos had been repeatedly advised with paternal solicitude to be more material-minded and devote more serious attention to their country's economic development. Those in close contact with Philippine conditions were fully appreciative of this need. The annual reports of the Philippine Commission[85] and those of the Governors-General[86] continuously reiterated a demand for economic development of the country—essential if the Philippines were to take its place as an independent country afterwards. Governor General William Cameron Forbes in his inaugural address went even further and said:

> We must bend our efforts to advance the day when each individual supplies the articles which he is best fitted to produce, which he sells to his fellow men, and uses the money thus gained to purchase of others the things which they can produce better and cheaper than he. This is the essence of trade. . . .
>
> Our success in accomplishing our principal object in the Islands,—namely, that of bettering the conditions of the people—may be best measured by the increase from time to time in the rate of wages and the value of imports and exports.[87]

In fact, from the administration in 1900 of Honorable William Howard Taft as President of the second Philippine Commission to the passage in March 1934 of Public Law No. 127, commonly known as the Tydings-McDuffie Philippine Independence Act, the economic development of the Islands had been systematically encouraged for it was rightly thought that upon it the governmental and political future of the Archipelago rested.[88] Governor-General Henry L. Stimson, in his inaugural address delivered upon his arrival in the Philippines on March 1, 1928, reminded the Filipinos that "individual freedom and the practice of self-government are found to be most prevalent and firmly held

[84] *Cong. Record*, 73rd Cong., 2nd Sess., Part VI, p. 6321.

[85] See *Reports*, Philippine Commission. 1899-1913.

[86] See *Annual Reports* of the Governors-General of the Philippine Islands to the Secretary of War from 1902 to 1934.

[87] Extracts from inaugural address of Governor-General William Cameron Forbes quoted from F. Chamberlain, *The Philippine Problem*, pp. 192-193.

[88] *Report* of the Special Mission on investigation to the Philippine Islands to the Secretary of War, pp. 33-37.

in those communities and nations which have a highly developed system of industry and commerce as a foundation" and that "only in such communities and nations can the average citizen attain the degree of individual comfort, education and culture which modern civilization is coming to demand."[89]

On July 16, Governor Stimson delivered his first message to the Insular legislature. While he was generous in praising the Filipinos for their remarkable progress in political education and other fields of knowledge, the Governor, on the other hand, could not understand why in the Philippine Islands, a country rich in natural resources and possessed of a political relationship with the foremost industrial nation in the world, many of its citizens were under-nourished from lack of a proper food supply and suffered greatly from diseases arising from malnutrition. "What is the cause of this singular anomaly," he asked?

> Why is it that a people who have shown such remarkable interest in and adaptability for the advantages of modern civilization, and have exhibited so much intelligence, self-sacrifice and zeal in their pursuit, and who at the same time are the heirs of such wonderful natural resources, should be held up and turned back at the very entrance to the Promised Land, like a thirsty tantalus at the vision of his springs of living waters?[90]

As if to answer his own questions, Mr. Stimson advised the Philippine Legislature to pass laws to attract American capital to the Islands.[91] This recommendation resulted in the modification of the Philippine Land Laws.[92] While corporations may continue to lease only 1,024 hectares of agricultural public lands in the Philippines, shareholders, bondholders, or officers of the corporations may acquire additional public lands for agricultural purposes not in excess of 144 hectares.[93]

Governor-General Dwight F. Davis, like Mr. Stimson, has emphasized also the importance of economic development. Taking cognizance of the movement in the United States to limit the free entry of Philippine products, notably sugar, he urged the formulation in the Islands of "such a sound and progressive solution of the existing economic problems" of the Archipelago as "may tend to insure that material prosperity

[89] *Inaugural address* of Governor-General Henry L. Stimson delivered on March 1, 1928.

[90] *Message*, Governor-General to the Philippine Legislature delivered on July 16, 1928, attached as *Appendix* F, p. 29 of the *Annual Report*, Governor-General of the Philippine Islands etc., 1928.

[91] *Ibid.*

[92] See *Supra*, p. 112.

[93] See Sections 33 and 34 of *Public Law No. 3517* approved Jan. 30, 1929 in *Official Gazette of the Philippine Islands*, 1929. Vol. XXVII, Part I, pp. 970-971.

which is so essential to political, industrial, and social well-being" of the Filipino people.[94]

A year later, impatient for quick action on the part of the Insular Legislature to enact adequate measures to meet the immediate problems of the Islands, Governor Davis reminded the members of the Philippine Legislature that what the Philippines needed most was "more economics" and "less politics." Continuing, Governor Davis pointed out that

> Government is essentially a practical business. Words no matter how eloquent, will not solve our problems. Sound common sense, not high sounding phrases, are needed. True progress in government is measured not by abstract theories, eloquent verbiage, abstruse doctrines, but by high standards of living for all the people, by advancement in culture, by the physical, mental, and moral well-being of its citizens.
>
> The condition of the average man, not of the powerful, is the standard by which we will be judged.[95]

When Governor-General Theodore Roosevelt arrived in Manila on February 29, 1932, one of the many important problems that confronted him was the critical situation of the Insular treasury occasioned by the fall in the prices of the chief exports of the Islands,[96] which with the exception of cigars and cigarettes, had been especially pronounced in 1932. Although the Philippine exports of cigars from 1929 to 1935 inclusive averaged three percent of the total exports of the Islands, cigarette exports, on the other hand, did not reach an average of one half of one percent of the total exports.[97] Taken as a whole, however, the total tobacco exports of the Philippines during the same period averaged six percent of the total exports of the Islands. Around fifty-one percent of the average total value of all tobacco exports was to the United States.[98]

In spite of the precipitate decline in 1932 in the prices of the four leading exports of the Philippines, sugar, coconut oil, abaca, and copra,—which during the calendar years 1929 to and including 1935 had averaged forty-eight, twelve, ten and nine percent respectively of the total ex-

[94] *Message*, Governor-General to the Philippine Legislature delivered on July 16, 1929, attached as *Appendix A* to the *Annual Report*, Governor-General of the Philippine Islands etc., 1929, pp. 20-21.

[95] *Ibid.*, 1930, pp. 34-35.

[96] *Message*, Governor-General to the Philippine Legislature delivered on July 16, 1932, attached as *Appendix 2* to the *Annual Report*, Governor-General etc., 1932, pp. 56-69.

[97] *Annual Report*, Insular Collector of Customs, 1935, pp. 92-93.

[98] *Ibid.*, p. 94.

ports of the Islands,—the balance of trade of the Archigelago as expressed in the excess of exports over imports continued to be favorable.[99] This was due primarily to the great quantity of sugar exported during the calendar year 1932. For instance, during the calendar years 1929 and 1930 the total quantity of sugar exported to all countries was 695,868,138 and 743,979,730 kilos for which was paid $53,244,149 and $52,240,266 respectively. During the calendar year 1932, however, the Islands exported 1,016,568,150 kilos of sugar and received therefor the sum of $59,801,885.[100]

It should be noted that during the calendar years 1929, 1930 and 1932 sugar exports from the Philippines to the United States were 670,952,762; 737,195,480 and 1,016,265,923 kilos respectively with the following corresponding values: $52,153,929; $52,038,675; and $59,792,293. It follows, therefore, that the percentages of the total value of sugar going to the mother country during the calendar years 1929, 1930 and 1932 were 98 percent, 99.6 percent, and 99.9 percent respectively.[101] In point of fact, ever since 1925 the total value of Philippine sugar going to the United States had never been less than 90 percent of the total value of that product exported.[102]

In view of the dependence of the Philippines upon its five chief exports Governor Roosevelt felt the necessity for practical education in an agricultural community like the Islands. Therefore, he recommended that the Department of Agriculture and Natural Resources with the co-operation of the Bureau of Education should work out suitable courses for agricultural schools and that the Bureau of Commerce should work out similar courses for vocational schools.[103]

Governor-General Frank Murphy considered diversification of crops as the primary problem of Philippine agricultural development. He found the Islands too dependent upon sugar, copra, hemp, and tobacco, and that the purchasing power provided by these products "has been used altogether in too large a proportion for the purchase of foodstuffs

[99] In 1930, excluding the exports in gold and silver both bullion and coin, the Philippines had a "favorable trade balance" of $10,074,174: in 1931 this balance had declined to $4,793,355; but in 1932 this balance reached $15,942,995. Figures taken from *Annual Report,* Insular Collector of Customs, 1935, pp. 66-67.

[100] *Annual Report,* Insular Collector of Customs, 1935, pp. 66-67, 90.

[101] *Ibid.,* p. 90.

[102] *Ibid.*

[103] See *Message* of Governor-General Theodore Roosevelt to the Philippine Legislature delivered on July 16, 1932. See also his article entitled "Our Economic Policy Should be to Develop Local Industries," *Commerce and Industry Journal* (July and August 1932), Vols. VIII and X, Nos. 7 and 8.

that could very well have been produced in the Islands." Since "the Philippines are perfectly adapted for the production of all their food-stuffs," continued Governor Murphy, "the spectacle of large imports of such articles as poultry products, canned fish, meat products, and a host of other articles that can be produced in the islands is incongruous in the extreme."[104]

It might be mentioned here in passing that the annual report of the Director of the Bureau of Plant Industry for the calendar year 1930 estimated the total area in the Philippines under cultivation at 3,756,504 hectares. This, continued the report, was less than one-fourth of the whole area considered to be suitable for agricultural purposes in the Islands. This area was planted to the following leading staple products of the Archipelago in the following percentages:[105]

Rice	48.25 percent	Sugar cane	6.89 percent
Coconuts	14.64 "	Tobacco	2.13 "
Corn	13.76 "	Maguey	1.04 "
Abaca (Manila hemp)	13.21 "	Cacao	.05 "
		Coffee	.03 "

Concluding, the report pointed out that the total land under cultivation was sixty-five percent greater than that which was under cultivation twenty years ago.

That the early encouragement for the economic development of the Philippines has been productive of the desired results is indicated further in the general increase of the volume of trade in the Islands both with the United States and with all other countries. This mounted from an average of $45,519,848 in the period 1899-1901 to $222,796,924 in the period 1928-1935.[106] It seems obvious therefore that the American tariff policy in the Philippines had greatly affected the development of trade and commerce of the Islands.

But trade with the United States in 1934 amounted to seventy-five percent of the total trade of the Islands, and of their exports eighty-three percent went to the United States. These figures show the dependence of Philippine products upon the American market, a dependence even more marked in the case of sugar, coconut and tobacco

[104] *Report,* Governor-General of the Philippine Islands etc., 1933, pp. 12-13.

[105] See *Hearings* before the Committee on Insular Affairs of the House of Representatives, 72nd Cong., 1st Sess., on *H. R. 7233*, a bill to provide for the independence of the Philippine Islands, statement of Speaker Manuel Roxas, pp. 20-21.

[106] *Appendix* II, Table No. 10; See also W. C. Forbes, *op. cit.,* Vol. I, pp. 243-244; Vol. II, pp. 333, 460, 533.

products. Of sugar exported from the Philippines 99.9 percent went to the mother country, 45.32 percent of copra, 94.13 percent of the coconut oil and 64.76 percent of the tobacco.[107]

It should be recalled, in this connection, that the Payne-Aldrich Act which inaugurated a partial free trade for Philippine products imported into the United States became effective late in 1909. This Act was superseded by the Underwood-Simmons law of 1913, which extended unlimited free trade to Philippine products subject only to the existing proviso that Philippine manufactured articles imported into the United States free of duty should not contain foreign material to the value of more than twenty percent.

On the American end of the line, the unlimited free entry of American products imported into the Philippines, inaugurated by the Payne-Aldrich Act of 1909, was continued. Hence, with the exception of the proviso relating to the foreign-material content of Philippine manufactured products when imported into the United States, the trade relation between the Philippines and the United States as outlined above remained until the passage in 1934 of the Jones-Costigan Sugar Act coupled with the enactment in March 1934 of the Tydings-McDuffie Independence law.

An interesting sidelight on American tariff policy in the Islands is the working of Section IV, paragraph C of the Underwood-Simmons law (which still applies to American goods and manufactured articles imported into the Philippines.) It provides that these products should be admitted into the Islands free of duty. Before the War, America imported raw silk from Japan free of duty, out of which were manufactured dresses, lingerie, handkerchiefs, and so forth. In the light of the above provision these manufactured products should have been admitted into the Philippines duty free. Were the above articles imported from the United States into the Philippines embroidered, and then re-exported back to the United States, the twenty percent foreign-material content proviso regarding Philippine manufactured products applied.[108]

Less important exports of the Islands such as embroideries, lumber and hats, comprising a little over five percent of the total exports, were sent to the following countries: the United States was the principal market for the Philippine embroideries[109] while lumber found its way

[107] *Annual Report,* Insular Collector of Customs, 1935, pp. 81-94.

[108] *Hearings* before the Committee on Insular Affairs of the House of Representatives, 72nd Cong., 1st Sess., on *H. R. 7233,* statement of Speaker Manuel Roxas, pp. 70-71.

[109] *Annual Report,* Insular Collector of Customs, 1935, p. 68.

not only to the markets of the mother country but also to Japan, Great Britain and China. According to the figures for 1934 the United States imported thirty-six percent, Japan thirty-three percent, Great Britain ten percent, China eight percent. Of hats the United States imported sixty-one percent, France sixteen percent, Great Britain thirteen percent and Italy six percent.[110]

It may be stated in passing that in view of the above data, it would be hard indeed to entertain an optimistic attitude regarding the economic future of the Islands.

The Tydings-McDuffie Act of March 24, 1934

The passage on January 17, 1933 over President Hoover's veto[111] of H. R. 7233, generally known as the Hare-Hawes-Cutting Act, marked the culmination of the movement to re-impose limitations on the free entry into the United States of Philippine products. While the Philippine Independence Mission then in Washington and the Philippine Resident Commissioners there endorsed this Act,[112] the Philippine Legislature deemed it proper not to act upon it, as provided for in Section seventeen of the law.[113]

It was pointed out that the United States Congress failed to meet the demands made by the Philippine Legislature in November 1932.[114] The most important of those which are germane to the persent study were the failure of the Congress to grant a maximum tonnage of 1,500,000 tons of Philippine sugar to be admitted annually into the United States free of duty and its failure to write a "reciprocal tariff clause" in the Act.[115]

Consequently, the Philippine Legislature appointed a committee "to

[110] *Ibid.*, 1934, p. 50 *et seq.*

[111] See *House Document No. 524*, 72nd Cong., 2nd Sess., containing *H. R. 7233* and President Hoover's message vetoing the proposed measure. The House of Representatives passed the bill over his veto on Jan. 13, the Senate on Jan. 17.

[112] See *Report of the Philippine Independence Commission to the Philippine Legislature*, published by *The Tribune*, Manila, July 30, 1933, quoted in its entirety by Senator Key Pittman of Nevada as a part of his speech on the floor of the Senate on March 22, 1934. See *Cong. Record*, 73rd Cong., 2nd Sess., Part V, pp. 2119-5160.

[113] See *Official Gazette of the Philippine Islands*, Vol. XXXII No. 7, pp. 118-119 for *House Concurrent Resolution No. 61*, adopted by the Philippine Legislature on October 17, 1933. Section 17 of *H. R. 7233* provided that, "The foregoing provisions of this act shall not take effect until accepted by concurrent resolution of the Philippine Legislature or by a convention called for the purpose of passing upon that question as may be provided by the Philippine Legislature."

[114] Philippine Research Bureau, *The Philippine Islands and the United States*, 1935, pp. 29-30.

[115] *Ibid.*

proceed to the United States at the earliest practicable time to seek amendments to the said act of Congress or the enactment of such new legislation as will fully satisfy the aspirations of the Filipino people to become at the earliest practicable date a free and independent nation, under conditions and circumstances that will not imperil the political, social and economic stability of the country."[116] In the meantime, an announcement was made that should President Roosevelt give assurance that the United States Congress would consider amendments to the Hare-Hawes-Cutting Act, Senate President Quezon would be ready to recommend to the Philippine Legislature that it withdraw its opposition and formally adopt the Act before its expiration on January 17, 1934.[117] Apparently, however, this assurance was not given, for on November 4, 1933 the new Independence Mission left Manila for the United States. By the middle of January 1934 Senate President Quezon as the head of the new Mission made "counter proposals" at the request of President Roosevelt.

In a message to Congress on March 2, 1934, President Roosevelt recommended the re-enactment of the Hare-Hawes-Cutting Act provided that its provisions regarding military and naval bases should be amended. The President found no necessity for changing other provisions for he was confident that "where imperfections or inequalities" existed, they could be "corrected after proper hearing and in fairness to both peoples."[118] He added that to grant independence to the Philippines "without allowing sufficient time for the necessary political and economic adjustments would be a definite injustice to the people of the Philippine Islands themselves little short of a denial of independence itself. To change at this time the economic provisions of the previous law would reflect discredit on ourselves."[119]

On the basis of President Roosevelt's proposal Representative John McDuffie of Alabama introduced a bill on March 10, 1934, "to provide for the complete independence of the Philippine Islands, to provide for the adoption of a constitution and a form of government for the Philippine Islands, and for other purposes."[120] On March 13 the House Committee on Insular Affairs to which the bill was referred, reported it back favorably to the House of Representatives without amendment.[121]

[116] See *Concurrent Resolution No. 46* of the Philippine Legislature.

[117] Philippine Research Bureau, *op. cit.*, p. 34.

[118] See *Cong. Record*, 73rd Cong., 2nd Sess., Part IV, p. 3580.

[119] *Ibid.*

[120] *H. R. 8573, Cong. Record*, 73rd Cong., 2nd Sess., Part IV, p. 4225.

[121] *H. R. Report No. 968*, 73rd Cong., 2nd Sess.

And on March 19, acting on the information[122] supplied by Mr. McDuffie that Senator Quezon, President of the Philippine Senate and chairman of the new Independence Mission then in Washington, had given him assurance that the bill as constituted would be ratified by the Philippine Legislature without delay, the House of Representatives passed H. R. 8573.[123] Three days later Senator Millard Tydings of Maryland successfully piloted the bill through the Senate[124] and on March 24, 1934 the bill received President Roosevelt's approval.[125] Thereupon Senate President Quezon, speaking for the Philippine Mission, announced that the Insular Legislature would ratify the new law on May 1, 1934. This date was selected in order to commemorate Admiral Dewey's destruction of the Spanish fleet in Manila Bay thirty-six years before.

On the subject of American-Philippine trade relations pending complete independence for the Islands, the provisions of the Tydings-McDuffie Act were identical with those provided for in the Hare-Hawes-Cutting Act. Laws affecting currency, coinage, imports, exports, immigration and the conduct of foreign affairs were left under the direct supervision and control of the United States.[126]

In Section 6 of both Acts it was provided that after the inauguration[127] of the government of the Commonwealth of the Philippine Islands trade relations between the Philippines and the United States should continue as now provided by law, subject, however, to the following exceptions:

1. That for every calendar year the free entry of Philippine sugar into the United States should be limited to 800,000 long tons for unrefined and 50,000 long tons for refined; for coconut oil the limitation was fixed at 200,000 long tons; and for yarn, twine, cord, cordage, rope and cable, tarred or untarred, wholly or in chief value of Manila hemp (abaca) or other hard fibers the collective total of 3,000,000 pounds was imposed.

2. In addition to the above quotas, it was provided that the Philippine government may levy an export tax on all articles, including the articles,

[122] *Cong. Record,* 73rd Cong., 2nd Sess., Part V, p. 4834.

[123] *Ibid.,* pp. 4831-43.

[124] *Ibid.,* p. 5164.

[125] *Public No. 127,* 73rd Cong., 2nd Sess.

[126] See Section 2, sub-paragraph (i) and (j) and (9) and (10) of the Hare-Hawes-Cutting Act and the Tydings-McDuffie Act respectively, *United States Statutes at Large,* Vol. 48, Part I.

[127] The government of the Philippine Commonwealth was inaugurated on November 15, 1935.

enumerated above, that may be exported to the United States free of duty. Provided, however, that during the sixth year after the inauguration of the government of the Commonwealth of the Philippine Islands there should be levied an export duty of five percent of the American tariff on products of the Islands exported to United States. On the seventh year this tax should be increased to ten percent, on the eighth year to fifteen percent and after the expiration of the ninth year this tax should be raised to twenty-five percent of the American tariff levied, collected, and paid on like articles imported from foreign countries. The proceeds of all these duties were to go into a sinking fund to help retire all bonded indebtedness of the Philippines.[128]

Finally, in Section 13 of both laws it was provided that at least one year before the granting of independence to the Philippine Islands "there shall be held a conference of representatives of the Government of the United States and the government of the Commonwealth of the Philippine Islands" to formulate "recommendations as to the future trade relations between the Government of the United States and the independent government of the Philippine Islands."[129]

The two laws regarding Philippine-American trade relations pending complete independence for the Islands were substantially alike. To the motivating factors behind the passage of the Hare-Hawes-Cutting Act—insofar as they were reflected in the Congress—our inquiry will now be directed.

We have noted that the movement to limit the free entry of Philippine products into the United States was not of recent origin. American agricultural interests which saw a menace in the unlimited free entry of Philippine products into the United States had been fighting hard for any change of policy from that which was originated with the Tariff Act of March 8, 1902, and concessions which had been written in the Tariff Act of August 5, 1909, were obtained only after President Taft had promised to maintain the quotas imposed upon Philippine sugar and tobacco imported into the United States.

During the Congressional hearings of 1921 upon the Fordney-McCumber tariff bill, the dairy and the cottonseed oil industries sent their representatives to plead for imposition of duties upon coconut oil and copra.[130] They urged the imposition of three cents a pound duty

[128] See *Appendix 1*, for a complete copy of Section 6 as it appears both in the Hare-Hawes-Cutting Act and in the Tydings-McDuffie Act.

[129] *Ibid.*

[130] See *Hearings* before the Senate Finance Committee on the Proposed Tariff Act of

on copra while five cents a pound duty was asked for coconut oil. Although the Philippines was not specifically mentioned, the result of granting their request would have been to curtail American importation from the Islands since the bulk of American imports of these products was supplied by the Philippines.[131]

The Fordney-McCumber Act of 1922 allowed copra to come into the United States free of duty while a duty of two cents a pound was levied on coconut oil and three and one-half cents a pound on coconut meat, shredded and dessicated, or similarly prepared, imported from foreign countries.[132] The free entry of similar articles from the Philippines into the United States would give an advantage to the products of the Islands equivalent to the amount of the duty.

Likewise the duty under the Fordney-McCumber Act levied on foreign sugar—raised to 2.206 cents from 1.256 cents a pound, the rate fixed in the Underwood-Simmons Act of October 1913[133]—would have meant a preferential advantage for Philippine sugar in the American market. In this case, however, the preference would have meant substantially equal to the duty on Cuban sugar.[134]

1921, *H. R. 7456* (67th Cong., 2nd Sess.), pp. 1164-1174. See also brief of A. M. Loomis, *Ibid.*, pp. 1181-1183.

131 United States Tariff Commission, *Philippine American Tariff and Trade Relations*, 1931, pp. 83, 85, Tables 13 (B) and 13 (D) respectively.

132 U. S. Tariff Commission, *Comparison of Tariff Acts, a comparison by paragraphs of the dutiable schedules and the free list of the Tariff Act of 1930 with the corresponding provisions of the Tariff Act of 1922*, (1934), p. 16, paragraphs 54 and 55; p. 85, paragraphs 756 and 758.

133 This Law was amended in 1916 repealing the free trade provision with regard to sugar, see *Supra*, p. 125, note 51.

134 The rates of duty in Tariff Acts of the United States, 1897-1930.

	Duty on 96 degrees centrifugal (cents per pound)		
Tariff Act effective	Full rate	Cuban rate (a)	Cuban rate refined (b)
July 24, 1909	1.685	1.6850	1.8631
August 6, 1909	1.685	1.3480	1.4425
March 1, 1914	1.256	1.0048	1.0752
May 28, 1921	2.000	1.6000	1.7121
September 22, 1922	2.206	1.7648	1.8885
June 18, 1930 (c)	2.500	2.000	2.1402

NOTE: (a) Under the terms of reciprocity treaty effective December 27, 1903, Cuba was given a 20 percent preference.

(b) Approximately 93.45 pounds of refined sugar are secured from 100 pounds of 96 degrees centrifugal sugar.

(c) Pursuant to President Hoover's proclamation of February 5, 1931, the rate on maple sugar was reduced from 8 cents per pound to 6 cents per pound and the rate on maple syrup was reduced from 5½ cents to 4 cents a pound.

Manila hemp (abaca) continues to come into the United States duty free. However, duties have been imposed on cordage, cables and other manufactures of hemp.

During the hearings before the Senate Finance Committee on the Fordney-McCumber Tariff bill, the cordage manufactures of the United States asked for a tariff protection against the "menace" of Philippine-made cordage.[135] Although Congress decided to raise the duties on cordage, cables, cords and twines and other products of which Manila hemp was the basic raw material[136] that body did not deem it proper to impose a tariff upon manufactured Manila hemp from the Philippines imported into the United States.

In the contest in 1929 over the tariff bill which finally became the Smoot-Hawley Act, the agricultural forces made another attempt to gain protection against Philippine products. An exception to the general demand for protection was the attitude of the tobacco producers and manufacturers who raised no serious opposition to continuing the advantage given to Philippine tobacco and its manufactures.[137] Their fear of a decade earlier had disappeared.

This change of attitude was aptly summarized by Mr. Nathan I. Bijur, the consistent defender of the home tobacco interest, in a rejoinder to the statement of Senator James E. Watson of Indiana to the effect that the Philippine people sent their tobacco to the United States just as the people from the state of Florida sent their tobacco to those Islands, said that had Philippine tobacco been just "a little better" it would have been able to replace American tobacco in their own home market. "Fortunately for the American farmer, it is not."[138]

The protection that tariff preferences had given to the principal export industries of the Philippines enabled these industries to continue their production at capacity in spite of the slump following the first World War. Hence, the war-boom productive expansion in Philippine industries coupled with the tariff preferences extended to them by the tariff Act of 1922, gave to the agriculture of the Islands a prosperity previously unequalled. During the decade of the twenties Philippine

[135] *Hearings* before the Senate Finance Committee on *H. R. 7456* (67th Cong., 2nd Sess.), statement of Mr. E. Heidrich, Vol. V, pp. 3477-3478.

[136] U. S. Tariff Commission, *Comparison of Tariff Acts 1922 and 1930*, schedule 10, paragraphs 1001-1005, pp. 100-102; schedule 15, paragraph 1504, p. 130, paragraph 1406, pp. 130-131.

[137] *Hearings* before the House Committee on Ways and Means on Tariff Readjustment, 1929 (70th Cong., 2nd Sess.), Vol. VI; also *Hearings* before a subcommittee of the Senate Finance Committee on *H. R. 2667* (71st Cong., 1st Sess.), Vol. VII.

[138] *Ibid.*, Vol. VII, pp. 6-7.

sugar export to the United States increased by about four hundred and fifty percent, coconut oil including copra in terms of coconut oil (oil content of copra is sixty-three percent) increased by two hundred and twenty-three percent, while hemp remained stationary.

Unhappily, however, this prosperity in Philippine agriculture was not shared by American agriculture. The Coolidge era seemed to have been merely one of industrial rather than agricultural prosperity in the United States. Henry A. Wallace, writing in 1925 in collaboration with his father, Henry C. Wallace (then Secretary of Agriculture in President Coolidge's Cabinet) emphasized the necessity of establishing "a relation of equality between agriculture and industry" in the United States.[139] Nine years later, as Secretary of Agriculture, Mr. Wallace described the plight of the American farmer in the following language: "The end of the World War had left the American farmer high and dry. Along with everybody else, but ten years ahead of most of them he was perched on the stilts of high prices, high labor costs, high land values and high debts."[140] In 1929, continued Secretary Wallace, at the peak of the "boom" the farmer was receiving only thirty-eight percent more for his products than he had received in 1913. On the other hand, for commodities used in his living and production, he paid fifty-two percent more than in 1913. For wages he paid seventy percent more while his taxes were one hundred and fifty percent higher.[141] While farm incomes which in 1920 had accounted for 14.9 percent of the national income, by 1929, this percentage had decreased to 7.8 percent or a drop of nearly fifty percent.[142]

As a result of this continued economic maladjustment, farm organizations became very active. Experienced lobbyists were employed to present their demands for aid in the Congress.[143] Under this increased pressure signs ominous to the Philippine interests began to appear in both

[139] Henry C. Wallace, *Our Debt and Duty to the Farmer*, 1925, pp. 214, 232.

[140] Henry A. Wallace, *New Frontiers*, 1934, p. 142.

[141] *Ibid.*, Appendix, p. 305.

[142] Henry A. Wallace, *op. cit.*, Appendix, p. 294. Professor Rexford G. Tugwell in an address delivered before the New York State Bankers' Association in Buffalo, on April 28, 1934 pointed out that the general deflation in 1921 caused the decline in prices of farm products "more extreme than the fall in general price level. Although farm land values, except in rare instances, never had been capitalized, on the basis of the extreme price levels of 1919, they collapsed and farm land became almost unsalable. Farm mortgages, contracted when prices were high, became frozen assets, causing the demise of thousands of rural banks. . . ." Quoted in his book, *The Battle for Democracy* 1935, pp. 222-40.

[143] For an interesting account regarding this matter, see G. L. Kirk, *Philippine Independence*, 1936, Chapters IV and V.

houses of Congress. Republican members of the farm bloc did not hesitate to sacrifice party lines by voting on any issue which in their minds would tend to alleviate their harrassed and depression-ridden constituents.

In the meantime, Dr. Orestes Ferrara, the Cuban Ambassador to the United States, in a statement printed in the *New York Journal of Commerce* of June 2, 1927, pointed out that the economic basis of the reciprocity treaty of 1903 between Cuba and the United States no longer responded to their "reciprocal interest." He maintained that this condition was due to the following causes: the imposition of a fairly high tariff rate on foreign sugar while maintaining the unlimited free entry of Philippine sugar into the United States.[144]

Nearly a month later, Dr. Ramon J. Martinez, President of the Cuban Association of Hacendados and Colonos not only endorsed strongly the Ambassador's stand but also indicated the advantage of stimulating a sugar industry which would always be available to the United States rather than of protecting the industry of an outlying possession from which the United States could be cut off easily in time of war.[145]

On December 12, 1927 the American Beet Sugar Association during its meeting in Chicago adopted a resolution urging Congress to re-impose the 300,000 ton limitation on Philippine sugar that might be admitted annually into the United States free of duty.[146] On February 23, 1928, Representative Charles B. Timberlake of Colorado introduced a joint resolution providing that only 500,000 tons of Philippine sugar might be admitted annually into the United States free of duty.[147] However, the House Committee on Ways and Means to which this resolution was referred decided not to alter the trade relations between the United States and the Philippines.[148] This campaign for limitation became acute when imported raw sugar slumped to the unparalleled low figure of 1.98 cents a pound in 1929.[149]

The farmers had not forgotten that the Republican Party, which they returned to office in 1928, had promised that "the home market, built up under the protective policy, belongs to the American farmer to the full extent of his capacity to supply it."[150] In view of this promise and believ-

[144] *New York Journal of Commerce*, June 2, 1927.

[145] *Facts about Sugar*, Vol. XXII, Part II, pp. 742, 743.

[146] *Ibid.*, p. 1225.

[147] *House Joint Resolution No. 214*, 70th Cong., 1st Sess.

[148] See *H. R. Report No. 2667*, 70th Cong., 1st Sess.

[149] L. S. Ellis, *op. cit.*, p. 104.

[150] Republican Party, *Campaign Textbook*, 1928, p. 87.

ing that prosperity of industry had been brought about by a high protective tariff, the farmers felt that better times for the farming industry could be brought about also by raising the rates on agricultural imports. This idea had been uppermost in the minds of the farm representatives during the hearings before the Senate Committee on Finance and the House Committee on Ways and Means on the general bill (H. R. 2667)[151] and on tariff readjustment respectively, in 1929.[152] This line of thought had been entertained also by a good many members of both houses of Congress during the debate on the general tariff bill which ultimately became the Tariff Act of June 17, 1930.

Farm leaders recognized at the outset that an increase in the tariff rates on agricultural products imported into the United States without a simultaneous limitation, or better still, the complete elimination of similar products from the Philippines admitted into the United States free of duty, would be a futile gesture and would not alleviate the condition of the farmers.[153] Hence, Congress was urged also to do something about the Philippine problem.

These farm groups as they appeared before the Congressional Committees during the hearings on tariff readjustment and on the general tariff bill, presented a formidable anti-Philippine bloc including all the dairy organizations, the cottonseed crushers' associations, the general farm organizations, the domestic sugar producers and the cordage manufacturer. Behind the scenes, of course, was the powerful Cuban sugar lobby.[154]

On the question of Philippine-Amercian trade relations all these organizations had a single aim in mind: the imposition of a strict limitation upon duty free imports from the Philippine Islands. On the other hand, these groups did not bother themselves about the equity of limiting Philippine exports to the United States while American exports to those Islands should continue to be admitted free of duty and unlimited. It was contended that this return to early trade relations

[151] *Cong. Record*, 71st Cong., 2nd Sess.

[152] *Hearings* before the Committee on Ways and Means of the House of Representatives on Tariff Readjustment, 1929 (70th Cong., 1st Sess.), Vols. I, V, VI, X and XVI. Also *Hearings* Before a subcommittee and the whole Committee on Finance of the U. S. Senate on *H. R. 2667* (71st Cong., 1st Sess.), Vols. V, VI, VII, XVI, XVII.

[153] *Hearings* before the Senate Committee on Philippine Independence, 71st Cong., 2nd Sess.), statement of Mr. Gray, p. 68.

[154] Regarding the Cuban interest in limiting the free entry of Philippine sugar into the United States see statement of Mr. Edwin P. Shattuck representing the United States Sugar Association and its Membership, the Cuban producers of raw sugar, *Ibid.*, Vol. V, p. 199 *et seq.*

between the two countries was not a violation of an established American policy.[155] The general attitude of the farm interests of the country was pointedly summarized by Chester H. Gray of the American Farm Bureau Federation when he added that the Senate Finance Committee, in deciding that question, should bear in mind "on the one hand, the producers in the Philippines who are on a low status of life, generally speaking, and the agricultural producers in America whom we wish to keep on as high a plane of life as at present. Do not consider the moral question without considering the moral question of the agricultural prosperity of the United States."[156]

The moral obligation of the United States to grant independence to the Philippines was also emphasized. It was pointed out that it had always been America's intention to give the Philippines its independence. The representative of the National Cooperative Milk Producers' Federation and other associated organizations maintained that America's "early tariff history with regard to taxing the Philippines was evidently strictly in line with that intention."[157] However, should the present free trade between the Philippines and the United States be maintained, it would "make it absolutely impossible in time for those people to desire independence, because all of the economic leading strings are to be a part of the corporated territory of the United States."[158]

The same attitude was entertained by a number of Senators when Section 301 relating to the American-Philippine trade relation in the general tariff bill[159] was finally debated on the floor of the Senate.

On October 9, 1929, Senator Edwin S. Broussard of Louisiana offered to amend the Philippine section of the general tariff bill (H. R. 2667) by providing for the imposition of the same rates of duty on Philippine products imported into the United States as are required to be levied upon like products imported from foreign countries. Until independence should have been granted, however, the revenues thus collected should be turned over to the Philippine government for the use and

[155] *Hearings* before a Subcommittee on Finance of the U. S. Senate on *H. R. 2667* Vol. VI, statement of Chester H. Gray, pp. 20-21.

[156] *Ibid. Hearings* before a Subcommittee on Finance of the U. S. Senate on *H. R. 2667* Vol. VI, pp. 20-21. See also his statement of July 15, 1929 in *Ibid.*, Vol. XVII, pp. 12-13.

[157] *Ibid.*, Vol. XVII, p. 215. Mr. Charles W. Holman represented also "The American Cotton Growers' Exchange" and "The National Livestock Association."

[158] *Hearings*, before the Senate Committee on *H. R. 2667* (71st Cong., 1st Sess.), Vol. XVII, p. 215.

[159] *H. R. 2667*, 71st Cong., 1st Sess.

benefit of the Islands. The Senator was not concerned how the Insular government should dispose of the money. His primary interest, according to him, was to give protection to American industries.

Senator William H. King of Utah offered to amend Senator Broussard's amendment by empowering the Philippine Legislature to call for a constitutional convention to prepare and formulate a constitution for an independent republican government of the Philippines. Immediately after the organization of this independent government it should be recognized by the President of the United States. However, this amendment provided for the right of intervention by the United States should the Philippines be unable to meet its bonded indebtedness. In that case the United States government should take hold of the customs collection in the Islands until such obligation had been met.[160]

Senator Burton K. Wheeler of Montana bluntly remarked that his primary interest in urging Philippine independence was based on the interest of the farmers of the United States. He looked at the Philippine problem merely as a question "whether or not we have the right to protect American industry and American labor, and one of the ways in which we can do it is to protect the sugar producers in my State. . . by giving the Philippines their independence."[161]

Senator Thomas J. Heflin of Alabama likened the Philippines to a millstone about the neck of the American cotton producers. He was especially anxious to exclude the "cheap and inferior vegetable oils" of the Philippines which compete with American "cottonseed oil, peanut oil, bean and corn oil." He urged independence for the Philippines as a measure of keeping "the home market for our American home people."[162]

Senator Arthur H. Vandenberg of Michigan, while agreeing that American sugar as well as many other farm commodities is exposed to Philippine competition, nevertheless was courageous enough to express his unwillingness "to discuss the propriety or the utility or the desirability of (Philippine) independence on the basis of our own domestic economic need."[163] He hastened to add, however, that the necessity for some type of protection existed.[164]

In no less patriotic mood, Representative O. H. Cross of Texas declared his intention of voting for Philippine independence, for doing

[160] *Cong. Record,* 71st Cong., 1st Sess., Part IV, p. 4377.
[161] *Ibid.,* p. 4381.
[162] *Ibid.,* p. 4395.
[163] *Ibid.,* 71st Cong., 2nd Sess., Part II, pp. 1307-1308.
[164] *Ibid.*

so would mean befriending agriculture, "the primary industry" of the United States. He referred to the Philippines as America's "queer" possession located in "such an outlandish quarter of the globe" which could be reached only after travelling "over devious, and checkered routes practically half around the world."[165]

Notwithstanding this pressure, the Administration remained firm in its opposition to a limitation of Philippine exports to the United States either by the imposition of tariff duties or by quota limitation. Hence, when the Smoot-Hawley tariff bill (H. R. 2667) was finally enacted into law on June 17, 1930 no provision was inserted in it regarding limitation on Philippine exports to the United States.[166] To the anti-Philippine coalition, therefore, there remained only one alternative—to marshall its forces and work for Philippine independence.

Back in the Philippines, in the meantime, Senate President Manuel L. Quezon, fully conscious of the significance of the new turn of events in Washington, urged the Philippine Legislature to send an independence Mission to the United States "to petition the Government and Congress of the United States for the early concession of independence to the Philippines."[167]

Senate President Quezon was not able to accompany the Independence Mission, which included such eminent Filipinos as Messrs. Sergio Osmeña (Pro-tempore President of the Senate) Ruperto Montinola (Senate Minority Floor Leader) Manuel Roxas (Speaker of the House of Representatives) and Pedro Sabido (House Minority Floor Leader). The two Resident Commissioners in Washington, Pedro Guevara and Camilo Osias, were *ex offcio* members of this Mission.[168]

That the Philippine Independence Mission made every effort to co-operate with the farm and labor groups of the United States was admitted by Resident Commissioner Osias who informs us that the Mission had "directed appeals to the American Federation of Labor and labor leaders and agencies, and to the various farm groups in the United States."[169] "Both in writing and in person," continued Mr. Osias, "we contacted Washington representatives of these organizations such as Messrs. Chester H. Gray of the American Farm Bureau Federation, Fred Brenckman of the National Grange, Chester W. Holman of the

[165] *Cong. Record,* 71st Cong., 2nd Sess., Part VIII, p. 8797.

[166] See U. S. Tariff Commission, *Comparison of Tariff Acts, 1922 and 1930.*

[167] *Official Gazette of the Philippine Islands,* Vol. XXIX, No. 154, p. 3855 for House concurrent Resolution No. 14, adopted Nov. 9, 1931.

[168] See *Ibid.,* for names of other members.

[169] Camilo Osias and Mauro Baradi, *The Philippine Charter of Liberty,* 1933, p. 8.

National Cooperative Milk Producers' Federation, A. M. Loomis of the National Dairy Union, and W. C. Husing of the American Federation of Labor."[170]

With such a formidable array of sponsors, coupled with the farm bloc in both Houses of Congress, Philippine independence legislation was well assured. Indeed, from December 2, 1929 to the enactment of the Hare-Hawes-Cutting Act (H. R. 7233) in January 1933 no less than thirty bills providing for Philippine independence had been considered in Congress.[171] The most important of all those bills was the first Hawes-Cutting bill (S. 3822) introduced in the Senate on January 6, 1930 under the joint sponsorship of Senators Harry B. Hawes of Missouri and Bronson Cutting of New Mexico.[172] This bill became the basis of bills subsequently introduced in the Congress providing for Philippine independence.

The basic plan of this bill appeared in the following provisions: first, a transitory or probationary period of five years; secondly, the gradual application of tariff duties by both governments during the second year of the transitory régime, starting at twenty-five percent of the regular tariff of the United States upon imports from the Philippines, and on all articles imported into the Islands from the United States, this duty to be increased by twenty-five percent each year thereafter. During the fifth year, full duties should be levied upon imports to both countries in the same manner as on all foreign imports. And finally, within the first six months of the fifth year the people of the Philippines should register their wishes in a plebiscite on independence. Should the Filipino people vote against independence, Philippine-American relations should continue to be governed as heretofore, and likewise trade relations between the two countries should be subject to the laws of the Congress.[173]

Aside from its assumption that a five-year period of preparation would be adequate, there were other reasons why the bill as constituted was considered unsatisfactory.[174] Then too, from the standpoint of the American exporters this idea of a two-way tariff was not acceptable. Finally, President Hoover and his entire cabinet did not hide their opposition to the idea of immediate independence or to any bill which offered independence for the Philippines on the basis of a plebiscite.

[170] *Ibid.*

[171] *Ibid.*, Chapters II-XI.

[172] *Cong. Record,* 71st Cong., 2nd Sess.

[173] See *Senate Report No. 781* (to accompany *S. 3822)* 71st Cong., 2nd Sess., Part I.

[174] The views of the minority regarding the provisions of this bill *(S. 3822)* were very critical. *Ibid.*, Part II.

The attitude of the Administration was summarized by both Secretary of State Henry L. Stimson and by Secretary of War Patrick J. Hurley as follows:[175]

(1) Economic reason alone ought to be sufficient to negative the proposal of immediate or early independence for the Philippines. In view of the general and financial preparedness of the Islands, immediate or early independence, according to Secretary of War Hurley, would be disastrous to the Filipinos themselves.

(2) The withdrawal of the United States from the Islands as provided for in the Hawes-Cutting bill (S. 3822) would be harmful to the interests of the United States both in the Philippines and in the Far East. Secretary of State Stimson told the Senate Committee that America's "future in the Far East turns upon our reputation for justice and fair dealing and justice."[176]

(3) The immediate withdrawal of American sovereignty or the granting of early independence to the Philippines by the United States without the expiration of sufficient time—a period of not less than thirty years—would inevitably be disastrous. It would create an unsettled condition in the Far East in connection with the present stablization of affairs in the different countries having interests in the Far East and exercising sovereignty there.

(4) It was deemed wise to increase gradually Philippine autonomy through administrative action under the Jones law. In return for this the Insular Legislature could be asked to curtail sugar production, limit Filipino emigration to continental United States and to increase the American preferential by raising the rates on all competitive imports from foreign countries.

Notwithstanding the favorable action of the Senate Committee on Territories and Insular Affairs the sponsors of the bill (S. 3822) did not get the bill before the Senate during the closing weeks of the session. This was due to two reasons, the open hostility of the Administration,

[175] See *Hearings* before the Committee on Territories and Insular Possessions of the United States Senate on Philippine Independence 71st Cong., 2nd Sess., pp. 657-694 for statement of Secretary Stimson; and 72nd Cong., 1st Sess., pp. 7-44, 113-145, for statement of Secretary Hurley.

See also Secretary Hurley's letter under date of May 15, 1930 to Senator Hiram Bingham, chairman of the Senate Committee on Territories and Insular Affairs including the memorandum for the Secretary of War concerning the political status of the Philippines submitted by General F. Le J. Parker, chief of the Bureau of Insular Affairs, under date of May 5, 1930.—Both documents are published as *Senate Document No. 150,* 71st Cong., 2nd Sess.

[176] See *Senate Hearings,* on *S. 3822,* 71st Cong., 2nd Sess., p. 659.

and the question of the usual pressure of business during the closing of weeks of the session. Nor was it brought to the Senate during the "lame duck" third session. This did not mean, however, that the movement to give the Philippines its independence was dead.

As a matter of fact, long before the first session of the 1931 Congress foes and friends alike of Philippine independence recognized that action on that matter could not be delayed further. This was due to two reasons. The country was plunging into one of the worst depressions in its history. The farm industries were clutching on to any panacea that promised relief. In such a receptive state of mind these interests were convinced that for their salvation the Philippines must be cut loose "to sink or swim for themselves." And finally, as a result of the 1930 election there was a shift in political control in Congress. To be sure the Democratic majority in the House was slim. The fact remains, however, that the reins of control were handed over to this Party. While the voting strength of the two major parties was evenly divided in the Senate, Republican members of the farm bloc tended to make inevitable action of some sort on the Philippine question.

It was in such a political atmosphere that the original Hawes-Cutting bill (S. 3822) was re-introduced in the Senate on January 7, 1932 as S. 2743.[177] On January 8, Representative Butler B. Hare of South Carolina, chairman of the House Committee on Insular Affairs, introduced the bill as H. R. 7233. Both the House and the Senate bills were identical in form and substance. It might be mentioned in passing that from December 7, 1931 to January 7, 1932 twelve bills and resolutions had been introduced both in the House and in the Senate. Some provided for immediate independence and the immediate application of American tariff and immigration laws. Others while favoring immediate independence for the Islands provided for the gradual application of the American tariff duties. Still others favored independence for the Philippines only at the end of a transition period ranging from fifteen to twenty years.[178] The bills that were considered by the respective committees of the House and of the Senate were the two bills above-noted.

The Senate bill (S. 2743) of January 7, 1932 was substantially the same as the original bill (S. 3822) of January 6, 1930 with the following exceptions:[179]

(1) It was provided that Philippine sugar admitted into the United

[177] *Cong. Record*, 72nd Cong., 1st Sess., Part II, pp. 1410-1411.
[178] For a list of these bills and resolutions, see Osias and Baradi, *op. cit.*, pp. 42-50.
[179] Osias and Baradi, *op. cit.*, p. 70.

States free of duty should not be "in excess of twenty percentum of the total sugar imported into the United States from Hawaii, Puerto Rico, the Virgin Islands, the Philippine Islands and from foreign countries during the previous calendar year."

(2) The annual quota of Philippine coconut oil to be admitted into the United States duty free was fixed in a novel way. It was provided that coconut oil from the Islands should not exceed "the amount of coconut oil brought into the United States in any one calendar year in the form of copra, such coconut oil to be determined on an oil content of copra of sixty-three percentum."

(3) The annual free entry of Philippine yarns, twines, cords, cordage, rope and cables, tarred or untarred wholly or in chief value of Manila hemp (abaca) or other hard fibers into the United States should not exceed a combined total of 7,600,000 pounds.

It is obvious that the above amendments were more liberal than the corresponding provisions of the original bill (S. 3822). This change of attitude may have been due to what Senator Hawes had seen and learned while in the Philippines during his visit there. However, the new bill as constituted did not please the farm interests. During the hearings before the Senate Committee on Territories and Insular Affairs they demanded more drastic action in limiting Philippine exports to the United States. They pointed out that the quotas for Philippine exports provided for in the bill (S. 2743) would be tantamount to the preservation of the *status quo*, and as such, would not offer them any substantial relief.[180] The position of the American Federation of Labor on the question of Philippine independence, according to Mr. W. C. Husing, the Federation's "legislative representative," could be summed up in two words: "keep faith."[181]

Opponents of Philippine independence, on the other hand, pointed out that the period of transition provided for in the bill would be inadequate to protect not only the Philippine economic interests but also those of the United States.[182] American interests doing business in the Islands were frankly skeptical. Their general attitude could be sum-

[180] *Hearings* before the Senate Committee on Territories and Insular Affairs on Philippine Independence (71st Cong., 2nd Sess.), Part I, p. 68, statement of Chester H. Gray representing the American Farm Bureau Federation. See also statement of A. M. Loomis, secretary of the National Dairy Union, *Ibid.*, pp. 104-105. Also statement of Frederick Brenckman of the National Grange, *Ibid.*, pp. 110-111.

[181] *Ibid.*, p. 113.

[182] *Ibid.*, Part VII, pp. 657-694, statement of Secretary of State Stimson. See also statement of Nicholas Roosevelt, *Ibid.*, Part IV, pp. 242-243.

med up in the following statement of Mr. D. F. Webster, vice President of the Pacific Commercial Company: the advocates of Philippine independence "frankly state that their purpose is to impose duties on the products of the Philippine Islands when imported into the United States. Attempts were made to do this during consideration of the Hawley-Smoot tariff bill. The sense of Congress was, however, that so long as the United States exercises sovereignty over the Philippine Islands and the products of the United States are admitted free of duty into the Philippine Islands, it is both inconsistent and morally unsound to tax the products of the Philippine Islands entering the United States. It is, therefore, now proposed that the United States relinquish sovereignty over the Philippine Islands that the products of the Islands may be taxed. The purpose of this proposal is purely selfish.... The adoption of this proposal so frankly avowed would mean a complete abandonment of the policy of the United States toward the Philippine Islands since they were ceded to the United States by Spain in 1899."[183]

Faced with this tangle of conflicting attitude, the Senate Committee on Territories and Insular Affairs thought it expedient to placate these interests on some of their demands. After a Senate subcommittee on Territories and Insular Affairs[184] redrafted the bill it was re-introduced by Senators Hawes and Cutting on January 26, 1932 as S. 3377 with the following limitations:[185]

1. Acts affecting currency, coinage, imports, exports and immigration should not become laws until approved by the President of the United States.[186]
2. The annual quota for Philippine sugar allowed duty free into the United States was fixed at 50,000 long tons for refined and 800,000 long tons for unrefined.
3. The annual quota for Philippine coconut oil was fixed at 200,000 long tons.
4. Cordage and other manufactured products wholly or in chief value of abaca or other hard fibers must not exceed a combined total of 3,000,000 pounds.

[183] *Hearings* before the Senate Committee on Territories and Insular Affairs on Philippine Independence (71st Cong., 2nd Sess.), Part III, pp. 251-252.

[184] This subcommittee was composed of Senators Cutting, Hawes, Johnson, Metcalf and Pittman.

[185] *Senate Report No. 354*, 72nd Cong., 1st Sess., pp. 7-9, 11, 12.

[186] Section 2, paragraph (I).

5. The probationary period was fixed at fifteen years, and Philippine immigration during the probationary period was limited to one hundred persons a year.

The Insular government was empowered to levy a graduated export tax on the principal exports of the Islands to the United States. This tax should begin on the eleventh year of the Commonwealth government and start at five percent of the American tariff levied upon similar products from foreign countries. In the twelfth year this tax should be increased by five percent and so on until twenty-five percent of the American tariff would be levied upon Philippine exports in the fifteenth year. The proceeds of this tax were to go into a special fund to be applied solely to the payment of the bonded indebtedness of the Islands.

7. Finally, should the Filipinos vote for independence during the plebiscite which should be held on the fifteenth year of the transition period, a conference of American and Filipino representatives would be called to formulate recommendations regarding the future trade relations between the two countries.

As above constituted S. 3377 was favorably reported to the Senate by the Senate Committee on Territories and Insular Affairs on February 24, 1932.[187]

As previously noted, on January 8, 1932, Mr. Hare, chairman of the House Committee on Insular Affairs, presented a bill (H. R. 7233) which was in form and substance analogous to the Senate bill (S. 2743) of January 7, 1932. On February 2, however, while hearings were being held on H. R. 7233 before the House Committee on Insular Affairs, Mr. Hare introduced a modified bill (H. R. 8758) entitled "a bill to enable the people of the Philippine Islands to adopt a constitution and form a government for the Philippine Islands, to provide for the independence of the same, and for other purposes."[188] This title was the same as that of the Senate bill (S. 3377) of January 26, 1932.[189] However, this modified bill (H. R. 8758) emerged from the House Committee on Insular Affairs as H. R. 7233 with its favorable report to the House that the bill as amended "do pass." The following were its pertinent provisions:[190]

[187] *Senate Report No. 354*, 72nd Cong., 1st Sess.

[188] *Cong. Record*, 72nd Cong., 1st Sess., Part III, p. 57; also *H. R. Report No. 806*, 72nd Cong., 1st Sess.

[189] See *Senate Report No. 354*, 72nd Cong., 1st Sess.

[190] *H. R. Report No. 806*, 72nd Cong., 1st Sess., pp. 13-15 and 17.

1. Acts affecting the currency or coinage laws should not become law until approved by the President of the United States.[191]

2. The annual quota for Philippine sugar admitted duty free into the United States was fixed at 50,000 long tons for refined and 800,000 long tons for unrefined sugar.

3. The annual quota for Philippine coconut oil was fixed at 200,000 long tons.

4. The combined total for cordage and other manufactured products of abaca or other hard fibers must not exceed 3,000,000 pounds annually.

5. The Islands were given a probationary period of eight years and Philippine immigration to the United States during this period was limited to fifty persons a year.

6. Finally, six months before the withdrawal of American sovereignty in the Islands a conference of American and Philippine representatives should be held to formulate recommendations regarding the future trade relations between the two countries.

It should be noted that both the House and the Senate bills as they emerged from their respective committees were identical in many of their provisions. Such differences as are important, were found (a) in the number of years for the probationary period provided for in the two bills, (b) the imposition of a graduated export tax and the provision for a plebiscite in the Senate bill, (c) the provisions in both bills regarding acts pertaining to currency, imports, exports and immigration, and (d) the number of Philippine immigrants a year allowed into continental United States.

In one respect, it can be said that the House bill was more liberal than the Senate bill. Providing only that acts of the Philippine government "affecting the currency or the coinage laws shall not become law until approved by the President of the United States" makes it possible for the government of the Philippine Commonwealth to make some commercial arrangements with other countries during the transition period. Such a step was necessary, according to the House Committee, because "the backbone of the Philippine economic system is the present reciprocal free trade with the United States."[192] It was recognized also that a sudden disruption of this relationship would injure both American and Philippine economic interests.

We can not justify the termination of this relationship [continued the House

[191] Section 2, paragraph (I); See *Appendix I*.

[192] *H. R. Report No. 806*, p. 10.

Committee] without allowing the interests concerned an opportunity to prepare themselves to meet the new conditions which will obtain after independence, when the Philippine Islands will have been placed outside the tariff wall of the United States. More particularly we owe a duty to Philippine industries which have been built up on the basis of free trade and to the people who depend for their livelihood on such industries. It is our duty to give them an opportunity to place themselves on a competitive basis before a radical change is forced upon them.[193]

It was, however, on April 4, 1932, when in the course of his analysis of the bill (H. R. 7233) in the House, that Mr. Hare made a specific statement regarding the necessity of allowing the Islands to make commercial arrangements with foreign countries during the transition period. He said: "We try to keep from shutting them off immediately by giving them time and opportunity to make trade agreements and commercial treaties with other countries, so that when we finally withdraw our sovereignty they will be able to continue successfully."[194]

During the lengthy hearings that were held in the Congressional Committees with regard to the general question of Philippine independence, representatives of farm and labor interests had little in common with the point of view expressed by Secretary of State Stimson and Secretary of War Hurley that the political and social institutions of the Filipino people "have not yet developed to a point where the stability of an independent government would be reasonably assured."[195] Instead, the farm and labor interests joined hands with the Filipino leaders in demanding early independence for the Philippines. The farm interests even insisted that the independence plebiscite should come at the beginning rather than at the end of the transition period. They were certain that that plebiscite would be acted upon favorably at the beginning of the period.

A summary of the general attitude of the farm groups was expressed by Fred Cummings, President of the National Beet Growers' Association, in the following words: "I believe it is time for the United States to stop acting as a good cousin or good brother to the whole world, and that the United States ought to stay at home and attend to its business. . . . I want their [the Philippines] independence to be just as quick as it can be legally arranged, and I want it to be definite and certain when the bill is passed. . . . I do not agree that at the end of this five-year

[193] *Ibid.*, p. 11.

[194] *Cong. Record,* 72nd Cong., 1st Sess., Part VII, p. 7401.

[195] *Hearings* before the House Committee on Insular Affairs (72nd Cong., 1st Sess.) statement of Secretary Hurley, p. 385; also *Hearings* before the Senate Committee on Territories and Insular Possessions, (71st Cong., 2nd Sess.) statement of Secretary Stimson, p. 659. *et seq.*

period they be allowed to vote for independence, because when they are paying one hundred percent tariff rates, they might change their ideas. I want to have it so that if they do get a change of heart—well, they have made their choice and they should keep it."[196]

When H. R. 7233 was finally brought to the House on April 4, 1932 for consideration, Mr. Hare asked the suspension of the rules of the House, and debate on the proposed measure was limited to forty minutes. In this instance two-thirds majority was required to pass the bill. When the roll was called 306 answered aye, 47 answered nay, 79 not voting. Certainly, this demonstration showed the determination of the House "to do something" for the American farmer.[197]

This bill was immediately sent to the Senate which referred it to the Committee on Territories and Insular Affairs. The Senate reported it back by striking out substantially everything after the enacting clause and substituted the Hawes-Cutting bill (S. 3377) which the Committee had reported to the Senate almost two months earlier.[198]

The debate in the Senate on this measure was listless. It was a sort of a "running fight" between those who were in favor and those who were against the proposed legislation. Senator Royal S. Copeland of New York questioned the constitutional right of Congress "to alienate sovereignty" over any section of the United States.[199]

Senator Vandenberg stated that while he agreed with the theory of the proposed measure of "progressive economic preparation for ultimate economic self sufficiency," he did not approve of a too long postponement of this economic preparation.[200] To his mind, the high export tax should begin earlier rather than end precipitously to conclude within five subsequent years. This would be "almost suicidal" to the "export structure and practice of the Commonwealth."[201] He doubted whether the Senate could "take intelligent and deliberate action upon a problem involving the destinies of 13,000,000 people and the responsibilities of the United States and its honor in the Far East when all through six hours of debate today there has not been an average of over six Senators on the floor of the Senate at any one time."[202]

[196] *Hearings* before the House Committee on Insular Affairs (72nd Cong., 1st Sess.), pp. 158-159.

[197] See *Cong. Record,* 72nd Cong., 1st Sess., Part VII, p. 7411.

[198] *Cong. Record,* 72nd Cong., 1st Sess., Part XIII, pp. 14256-14259 for the copy of this bill.

[199] *Ibid.,* p. 14262.

[200] *Ibid.,* p. 14275.

[201] *Ibid.*

[202] *Ibid.,* p. 14277.

To this remark Senator Arthur R. Robinson of Indiana answered by saying that he would not mind being publicly accused of favoring first the interest of the 120,000,000 Americans.[203]

The brilliant Senator from Michigan, Mr. Vandenberg, reminded his colleagues that while he was insisting that "we have an obligation to the Philippine Islands and to our stewardship, which rises far above a mere contemplation of beet sugar or immigration or cane sugar or cordage or coconut oil or any other kindred domestic commodity, I have said time and again that with the balance of trade against us in a ratio of four to one as between the Philippine Islands and the United States, we most emphatically are entitled to consult that equation for the purpose, at least, of obtaining an equality of right and consideration for ourselves."[204] The proposed measure, he maintained, failed to provide this. Concluding his remarks, Senator Vandenberg emphasized that he was in favor of Philippine independence provided "it has a reasonable chance to succeed permanently. I favor progressive economic preparation of the Philippines for this triumphant climax. Meanwhile, so long as the United States has responsibilities in Manila and the Far East I insist that the United States shall have authority commensurate with these responsibilities."[205]

As an answer to Senator Copeland's remark that there was nothing back of the Philippine independence bill except "sordid selfishness" Senator Pittman of Nevada corrected him by saying that it was "a very modulated selfishness" since "we tried to meet the wishes of both sides."[206]

On July 1, 1932 on the motion of Senator Joseph T. Robinson of Arkansas the Senate agreed to postpone further consideration of the Philippine independence bill until the 8th day of the following December.[207]

During the Presidential campaign there was little discussion regarding the Philippine issue. No mention of the Philippines was made in the Republican platform. The Democratic platform merely reiterated the old statement of the Party that it favored Philippine independence.[208] In only one instance during the campaign did President Hoover refer

[203] *Ibid.*
[204] *Ibid.*, p. 14278.
[205] *Ibid.*
[206] *Ibid.*, p. 14363.
[207] *Ibid.*, p. 14441.
[208] For a comparison of the Democratic and Republican Platforms, see Republican Party, *Campaign Textbook*, 1932, Chapter IX.

to the Philippine issue. That was a speech delivered at Denver, Colorado, and hence a sugarbeet audience, in which he criticized the Philippine sugar quota provided for in the Hawes-Cutting bill as too high, not giving an adequate protection to the American domestic producers. Governor Roosevelt only made a passing reference to the Philippine issue when he said at Salt Lake City that "the American people are interested in Philippine independence which the Democratic party favorably endorses."[209]

When the election was over, the question of Philippine independence was considered according to schedule. More drastic action was demanded. The Senate, in spite of the remonstrances of Senator Hawes that to reduce the sugar quota "below that fixed in the bill will ruin the Philippine Islands; it will crush them; they cannot exist without a period of reconstruction,"[210] approved the amendment of Senators Huey P. Long of Louisiana and Reed Smoot of Utah. This amendment called for further reduction of the sugar quota from the Islands to 585,000 tons. This amendment was adopted in the face of Representative Hare's public recommendation—Mr. Hare had just returned from his trip to the Philippines—that "it is with a keen sense of our obligation to be absolutely fair to the people of the Philippine Islands" that their duty free sugar quota should be raised to 1,100,000 tons.[211]

The Senate agreed also to shorten the transition period from fifteen to twelve years and eliminated all Filipino immigration. To appease the sugar interests and the general farm group, the Senate agreed further to amend the bill by striking out the provision regarding the plebiscite during the final year of the transition period, and in its place was inserted a provision that should the Philippine electorate ratify the constitution which should be submitted by the constitutional convention, such ratification "shall be deemed an expression of the will of the people of the Philippine Islands in favor of Phillippine independence."[212]

Senator Robert M. LaFollette of Wisconsin termed that amendment "absolutely indefensible." For the Senate to insist upon that amendment, he continued, was to become a party with those who would force the Philippine people "to accept perchance a constitution which would violate the entire conception of the type of government which they

[209] G. L. Kirk, *op. cit.*, p. 117.

[210] *Cong. Record*, 72nd Cong., 2nd Sess., Part I, p. 267.

[211] For a copy of Mr. Hare's letter to Senator Hawes under date of December 6, 1932 see *Cong. Record*, 72nd Cong., 2nd Sess., Part I, pp. 180-181.

[212] *Cong. Record*, 72nd Cong., 2nd Sess., Part I, p. 612.

wished to see set up in the Islands in order that they may achieve their desire for independence."[213]

The American farm interests demanded the change[214] and the Senate by a vote of 44 to 29 (23 not voting) agreed to incorporate this amendment in the proposed measure.[215] Finally, on December 17, 1932 the Senate approved the House bill (H. R. 7233) as amended without a record vote.[216]

However, the House did not accept the bill passed by the Senate. It preferred its own bill of April 3, 1932. Consequently, a conference was called. On December 28 the conferees agreed on the following pertinent provisions which were subsequently approved by the House and the Senate.[217]

1. The probationary period was fixed at ten years.
2. Annual quotas on Philippine imports as provided for in both bills were maintained.
3. Filipino immigration into the continental United States was limited to fifty persons a year.
4. The application of a graduated export tax during the sixth year of the transition period was provided for. Revenues derived therefrom to be placed in a special fund to help pay the bonded indebtedness of the Philippine Islands.
5. The Senate provision regarding laws pertaining to the currency, imports, exports, and so forth, was adopted.
6. Finally, the provision in both bills regarding trade conference was maintained.

On January 3, 1933, the bill (H. R. 7233) as amended and approved was sent to President Hoover for his signature. On January 13, the President sent the bill back to Congress without his approval. In a scathing indictment he denounced the bill as having completely failed to discharge America's "triple responsibility": (a) responsibility to the Philip-

[213] *Ibid.*, p. 616.

[214] See the letter of the Secretary of the Farm Bureau Federation to Senator L. I. Dickinson of Iowa under date of December 14, 1932 in *Cong. Record*, 72nd Cong., 2nd Sess., Part I, pp. 426-427.

[215] See Section 4, Hare-Hawes-Cutting Act (*H. R. 7233*) in *House Document No. 524*, 72nd Cong., 2nd Sess.; also see Section 4 of *Public No. 127*, 73rd Cong. (commonly known as the Tydings-McDuffie Act).

[216] *Cong. Record*, 72nd Cong., 2nd Sess., Part I, p. 636.

[217] *H. R. Report No. 1811* (Conference Report to accompany *H. R. 7233*), 72nd Cong., 2nd Sess. See also *Supra*, pp. 151-155.

pine people (b) responsibility to the American people and (c) responsibility to the world at large.

We are responsible to the Filipino people, he said, "in finding a method by which we consummate their aspiration" without projecting them "into economic and social chaos, with the probability of break-down in government." "Our responsibility to the American people," he continued, lies in our seeing "the fact of Philippine separation accomplished without endangering ourselves in military action hereafter to maintain internal order or to protect the Philippines from encroachment by others." Finally, President Hoover pointed out that America's responsibility to the world lay in the fact that "having undertaken to develop and perfect freedom" for the Filipino people "we shall not by our course project more chaos into a world already sorely beset by instability."[218]

The ten-year period of readjustment, according to President Hoover, was "too short, too violent"; it would inevitably bring the Philippine Islands to a state of chaos. Many of the Philippine industries, he continued, "can not compete with the lower standards of living and costs in other tropical and sub-tropical countries, except by virtue of their favored entrance to our markets."[219] The inevitable consequence of this provision could hardly be exaggerated.

The President was especially critical about the question of domestic relief which would result from the passage of the bill. He reminded Congress that "we are trustees" for the Philippine people and "we must not let our selfish interest dominate that trust." He maintained that the bill offered "no effective protection" to the American farmer, and sugar benefits were certain to inure "more largely to foreign producers than to our own farmers." "If we are to predicate the fate of 13,000,000 people upon this motive," he continued "we should at least not mislead our farmers about it."[220]

President Hoover, while sharing in the concern of his cabinet members about promising independence to the Philippines at a time when there was political instability in the Orient, was not unmindful of the possible effect of that independence upon "the development of our own economic life and trade" in the Far East.[221]

The President asked Congresss that "before any plebiscite is held we

[218] *House Document No. 524*, pp. 1-2.
[219] *Ibid.*, p. 3.
[220] *Ibid.*
[221] *Ibid.*

should honestly and plainly declare our intentions." He reminded that body that "in the discharge of the moral responsibilities of our country we have no right to force an irrevocable decision on their part . . . at a moment in history when the outlook in the world and their surrounding is at best unfavorable to their permanent independence."[222] Concluding his message, President Hoover said: "Neither our successors nor history will discharge us of responsibility for action which diminish the liberty we seek to confer nor for dangers which we create for ourselves as a consequence of our acts."[223]

Hardly had the echo of the President's words died away when the House by a vote of 274 to 94 overrode the President's veto and the Senate four days later followed suit by a vote of 66 to 26. Thus H. R. 7233 commonly known as the Hare-Hawes-Cutting bill became law on January 17, 1933.

[222] *House Document No. 524*, p. 3.
[223] *Ibid.*, p. 4.

5: *The Approach to Independence*

May 1934 to July 1946

On May 1, 1934, the Philippine legislature accepted the Tydings-McDuffie Act, commonly known as the Philippine Independence Law. This acceptance carried with it the hope and prayer of the Filipino people that the Congress of the United States would soon amend the economic provisions of the law in a manner previously outlined in President Roosevelt's message of March 2, 1934. In this message, be it recalled, the President recommended the passage of the Tydings-McDuffie bill in lieu of the Hare-Hawes-Cutting Act which the Philippine legislature did not accept. He was confident that whatever "imperfections or inequalities" there were in the original act could be corrected later "after proper hearing and in fairness to both peoples."[1] This message was generally interpreted in the Islands as an assurance of further consideration of American-Philippine trade relations. It was felt that prompt action in this respect would mean that much time could be saved which the Filipino people might utilize to institute proper and adequate measures to safeguard and maintain their independence.

In its resolution[2] accepting the Independence Law, the Philippine legislature addressed also an appeal to President Roosevelt requesting the creation of a Congressional committee, whose expenses would be borne by the Insular treasury, to investigate conditions in the Islands in the light of the economic provisions of the law. Pursuant to this request, the President, under date of July 16, addressed two identical letters[3] to Vice President John N. Garner, for the Senate, and to the Honorable Henry T. Rainey, Speaker of the House of Representatives. A copy of this resolution was inserted in each letter.

While President Roosevelt questioned the propriety of the resolution having been addressed to him, he was of the opinion that it would be "useful and opportune at this moment" for the Senate and House of Representatives "to appoint a committee for the purpose of

[1] *Cong. Record*, 73rd Cong., 2nd Sess., Part IV, p. 3580.
[2] *Cong. Record*, 73rd Cong., 2nd Sess., Part VIII, p. 8040.
[3] *Ibid.*, Part II, pp. 12076, 12567-12568.

investigating conditions in the Philippines and reporting to Congress thereon."[4] This step was favorably acted upon and a committee of eight was subsequently created with equal representation for each House.[5]

The findings of the Congressional committee were practically a restatement of the well-noted unbalanced economic development of the Philippine Islands.[6] The economy of the country has been wholly dependent upon a few staple products—sugar, coconut products, manila hemp (abaca), and tobacco. Except for hemp, these products find an exclusive market in the United States where a preferential treatment is extended to them. Without this protection it would seem doubtful whether they could withstand foreign competition. On the other hand, hemp has a world market and gets no preference in the United States tariff. Consequently, Philippine economy must be reorganized if the country can be expected to weather the economic shocks that would follow the application of the quota and tariff provisions of the Tydings-McDuffie Act. The creation of the fact-finding commission contemplated in the provisions of section 13 of the law was considered and its immediate establishment was favorably indorsed by the Congressional committee.

As early as December 31, 1934, Senators Millard E. Tydings, Kenneth McKellar and others, members of the Congressional committee, sent from Manila a joint cablegram to President Roosevelt recommending the creation of a committee on Philippine affairs.[7] Acting upon this recommendation, an Interdepartmental Committee on Philippine Affairs was set up and began in January, 1935, a study of American-Philippine trade relations. From that time until its reorganization in the Spring of 1937, this Interdepartmental Committee was engaged in studying Philippine problems and coordinating the activities of the

[4] *Cong. Record,* 73rd Cong., 2nd Sess., Part II, pp. 12075, 12567-12568.

[5] *Ibid.*

The following were the Senators and Representatives who were appointed to this special committee: Senators Millard E. Tydings of Maryland, Carl Hayden of Arizona, Kenneth McKellar of Tennessee, Ernest W. Gibson of Vermont and Representatives John McDuffie of Alabama, Joe L. Smith of West Virginia, Ralph L. Lozier of Missouri, Carroll L. Beedy of Maine.

[6] *Cong. Record,* 74th Cong., 1st Sess., Part VI, pp. 6842-6848; *Ibid.,* Part VII, pp. 7199-7202; also *Sen. Doc. No. 57* Parts I and II (74th Cong., 1st Sess.)

[7] See *Cong. Record,* 75th Cong., 1st Sess., Part V, pp. 5049-5050 for the letter of Assistant Secretary of State Francis B. Sayre to Senator Millard E. Tydings, dated Washington, May 24, 1937; also Joint Preparatory Committee on Philippine Affairs *Report* of May 20, 1938, Volume I, Appendix II, pp. 189-192.

various administrative departments and agencies of the United States government concerned with Philippine affairs.[8]

In the meantime, on April 8, 1935, Senator Tydings introduced a bill (S. 2530) to amend the cordage provision of section 6 of the Tydings-McDuffie Act, "to protect American and Philippine labor and to preserve an essential industry, etc."[9] Two days later, the Senate Committee on Territories and Insular Affairs of which Mr. Tydings was the chairman reported this bill favorably and recommended its adoption.[10] On May 1, with hardly any debate, the bill was passed and it was immediately dispatched to the House.[11] On June 3, the House approved the proposed legislation in lieu of its own bill (H. R. 7348) for the same purpose,[12] and on June 5, it was sent back to the Senate with its approval.[13] Nine days later, with the signature of President Roosevelt this bill became law.[14] Briefly summarized this law provides that:

1. Beginning January 1, 1935, and for three years thereafter, an absolute quota of 6,000,000 pounds annually was provided for all yarns, twines (now including binding twines), cords, cordage, rope, and cable tarred or untarred wholly or in chief value of manila hemp (abaca) or other hard fiber, produced or manufactured in the Philippines, to be allowed free entry into the United States.

2. Exportation to the United States of said products was to be allocated under export permits to be issued by the Philippine government.

3. Before independence was granted to the Islands and at least ninety days before the expiration of the three-year period, the President of the United States, by proclamation, might extend this law for an additional period of three years or more provided such extension was accepted by the President of the Commonwealth of the Philippines.[15]

4. Provision was made to incorporate this legislation into the revenue laws of the United States; and the Secretary of the Treasury was

[8] See *Cong. Record,* 75th Cong., 1st Sess., Part V, pp. 5049-5050 for the letter of Assistant Secretary of State Francis B. Sayre to Senator Millard E. Tydings *Op. Cit.;* also Joint Preparatory Committee on Philippine Affairs *Report, Op. Cit.,* pp. 189-192.

[9] *Cong. Record,* 74th Cong., 1st Sess., Part V, p. 5210.

[10] *Ibid.,* p. 5410.

[11] *Ibid.,* Part VI, pp. 6692, 6704.

[12] *Ibid.,* Part VIII, pp. 8595-8599.

[13] *Ibid.,* p. 8664.

[14] *Ibid.,* Part IX, p. 9351; *Public, No. 137.*

[15] Extended to May 1, 1941 by virtue of President Roosevelt's proclamation dated January 26, 1938—see *Infra,* p.

authorized to promulgate needful rules and regulations to make effective its provisions and to see that nothing in this law, unless specifically provided, should be construed to modify or repeal the provisions of the Tydings-McDuffie Act.

5. This law was not to affect the free entry of manila hemp (abaca) which had been allowed from all sources since 1890.

In urging the immediate approval of this proposed measure, Representatives Bennett Champ Clark of Missouri and William A. Ashbrook of Ohio reassured their colleagues that the pending legislation was previously agreed upon by both the American and Philippine cordage interests. Furthermore, they emphasized that the provisions of the bill were designed primarily to give added protection to American cordage manufacturers.[16] They were alive to the consequences to domestic cordage manufacturers of the steady increase of Philippine exportation of cordage to the United States. They noted that in 1931 Philippine export of this product was only 4,599,113 pounds, but in 1933 this figure reached 6,876,227 pounds, and in 1934 it reached over 8,943,167 pounds.[17] These figures tend to show that Philippine cordage manufacturers could send more of their products to the United States and still pay the tariff.

Representative Carl Stefan of Nebraska gave a more pointed argument for the adoption of the bill without delay. He explained that under the program of hours and wages set forth by the National Industrial Recovery Act, commonly known as the N.R.A., workers in American cordage mills were paid an average of forty-five cents an hour while similar laborers in the Philippines were paid an average of only sixteen cents an hour. He indicated furthermore that most of the cordage coming from the Islands goes to big chain stores such as Sears, Roebuck and Company, and Montgomery Ward. These stores, he continued, "compete with the independent merchant, who cannot buy at wholesale at the price for which this cheap imported cordage is retailed by the chain organizations. In this way, these big chain stores throttle the independent merchant by using this cheaply manufactured cordage."[18] He admitted that the proposed measure was written primarily for "the protection of American cordage industry as against the cheap manufactured cordage of the Orient."[19]

[16] *Cong. Record*, 74th Cong., 1st Sess., Part VI, p. 6704, for statement of Representative Bennet Champ Clark; For statement of Representative William A. Ashbrook see *Ibid.*, Part VIII, p. 8596.

[17] *Annual Report*, Insular Collector of Customs, 1937, Table 16; see also United States Department of Commerce, *Statistical Abstract of the United States*, 1943, p. 552.

[18] *Cong. Record*, 74th Cong., 1st Sess., Part VIII, p. 8598.

[19] *Ibid.*

The official attitude of the Insular government regarding this proposed measure was expressed by Mr. Francisco Delgado, one of the Philippine Resident Commissioners in Washington. He pointed out that representatives of the Islands gave their approval of this bill not only "by reason of the mutual concessions made in its provisions" but also "to show the American people that the Filipinos are, and always have been, willing to meet the requirements of this country at least half way."[20]

On the basis of the above assurances this proposed measure was approved by the House of Representatives and subsequently became a law in spite of the claims raised by Messrs. Fred L. Crawford of Michigan and George H. Mahon of Texas that this bill might later serve as "an opening wedge" for the upward revision of quotas on Philippine sugar and for allowing coconut oil free entry into the United States.[21]

The restrictions placed on Philippine cordage as provided for in the act under review (Cordage Act of June 14, 1935) differ fundamentally from those imposed by the original law. Whereas that law permitted free entry of 3,000,000 pounds of manufactured products of manila hemp (abaca) and did not limit the amount which could be imported in excess of this free quota, provided full duty was paid on it, the cordage act fixed an absolute quota which could not be exceeded. Furthermore, under the present act binder twine was included in the absolute quota. However, only negligible quantities of binder twine have at any time been exported by the Philippines to the United States.[22]

There was another factor which affected shipment of Philippine cordage to the United States. That was the so-called "spread" in the freight rates on baled abaca and on finished rope. According to the Trans-Pacific Conference contract rates on ropes and abaca were as follows: (1) beginning April 1, 1938, the rate on Philippine rope to Atlantic and Gulf ports was $40 per 20 cwt.; (2) on abaca, effective February 1, 1938, the rate of $4 per bale of 278.3 pounds for the same ports was provided. In view of the fact that one pound of abaca is required to produce one pound of rope, the freight differential which was approximately one cent per pound tended to favor the movement of abaca rather than of rope.[23]

[20] *Ibid.*

[21] *Ibid.*, pp. 8597, 8599.

[22] See statement of Assistant Secretary of State Francis B. Sayre before the Senate Committee on Territories and Insular Affairs during the hearings on S.1028 held on February 16, 1939, published as Appendix F in the Report *of the Special Mission to the United States*, 1938-1939, pp. 109-126.

[23] See Joint Preparatory Committee on Philippine Affairs *Report, Op. Cit.*, pp. 67-74.

On January 26, 1938, President Roosevelt issued a proclamation extending the Cordage Act to May 1, 1941. This extension, according to the press release of the White House, "was intended merely as a stopgap measure to maintain, without prejudice, the *status quo* with respect to the importation of Philippine cordage to the United States" until the President "may have occasion to make such recommendations . . . as he may find appropriate after consideration of the report to be rendered by the Joint Preparatory Committee on Philippine Affairs."[24] However, the cordage provisions of the Tydings-Kocialkowski Act of August 7, 1939, which will be discussed presently, merely extended the operation of the law to July 4, 1946. These were likewise continued in effect to 1974 in the provisions of the Philippine Trade Act of 1946.[25]

Meanwhile, Governor General Frank Murphy, pursuant to the letter of President Roosevelt under date of April 10, 1935,[26] issued Executive Order No. 780 under date of July 9, 1935 creating two committees, namely, a technical trade committee and a Phillippine interdepartmental committee.[27] The former was entrusted with the functions of collecting, arranging and interpreting "available statistics," and of submitting to the Governor General reports thereon. The latter, which consisted of the Secretary of Finance, Secretary of Agriculture and Commerce, and the Secretary of Public Works and Communications, was authorized "to review the work and reports of the technical trade committee and to advise the Governor General in respect to major economic policies."[28]

The avowed purpose of Governor General Murphy in creating these committees was to help facilitate the speedy readjustment of the national economy of the Philippines in line with the aims of the Interdepartmental Committee on Philippine Affairs previously outlined. It was also recognized that readjustment of the national economy of the Islands independent of preferences in the United States market would mean inversely the readjustment of American export trade to the Philippines to a non-preferential position in that market. It was apparent therefore that solution of the problems posed by the readjustment of American-Philippine trade relations could be best achieved by a joint committee of American and Filipino experts authorized to explore

[24] Joint Preparatory Committee on Philippine Affairs, *Op. Cit.*, p. 72, footnote no. 63 for the text of this release.

[25] See *Infra*, pp. 192-193.

[26] Joint Preparatory Committee on Philippine Affairs, *Op. Cit.*, p. 10.

[27] *Cong. Record*, 74th Cong., 1st Sess., Part XII, p. 12911.

[28] *Ibid.*

into the problems and recommend a possible approach for their solution.

President Franklin D. Roosevelt and Commonwealth President Manuel L. Quezon were agreed on this joint inquiry and consequently on April 14, 1937, a Joint Preparatory Committee on Philippine Affairs was created and entrusted with a general function "to consider proposals which have been made for changing the political and economic relations of the United States with the Philippines; to hold public hearings for interested parties both in the United States and in the Philippines; to study the problem of making adjustments in Philippine national economy; to prepare the way for a trade conference; and to make recommendations."[29]

After months of public hearings held in the United States and in the Philippines, the Joint Preparatory Committee on Philippine Affairs submitted its recommendations[30] and these became the basis of amendatory legislation approved on August 7, 1939, commonly known as the Tydings-Kocialkowski Act. These recommendations may be roughly divided into three parts, namely, trade relations during the Commonwealth period (November 15, 1935 to July 3, 1946), trade preferences after independence (July 4, 1946 through December 31, 1960), and necessary steps to be taken by both the American and the Philippine governments to make effective the committee's recommendations.

The pertinent points of these recommendations may now be briefly summarized.

1. During the Commonwealth period, or to be exact, during the remaining years of the Commonwealth period (1940-1946), Philippine exports to the United States were placed under the following classifications:

(a) Those products with specific quotas not subject to export tax but subject to annually declining duty free quotas. Under this provision, cigars were given a quota of 200,000,000 cigars; scrap tobacco, cigar-ends and stripped filler tobacco were given a combined total of 4,500,000 pounds; coconut oil, a quota of 200,000 long tons; and pearl buttons, 850,000 gross. These quotas were to be progressively diminished by five percent for each succeeding calendar year until December 31, 1945. For the period January 1, 1946 through July 3, 1946, the quota for each of the above-named products was one-half of the quota for the preceding year. Thus, taking the case of coconut oil as illustra-

[29] *Cong. Record*, 75th Cong., 1st Sess., Part V, p. 5050.

[30] For a complete copy of these recommendations see Joint Preparatory Committee on Philippine Affairs *Report, Op. Cit.*, pp. 161-173.

tion, the Philippine quota at the end of the calendar year 1945 would be 150,000 long tons. For the period January 1, 1946 through July 3, 1946, this quota was to be reduced to 75,000 long tons. The same formula would apply to the rest of the products of the Philippines under this classification. It was provided, further, that shipments in excess of the above quotas were to be subject to the prevailing duties in the United States. The Insular government was not to levy export taxes on these products.

(b) Products whose quotas would remain the same throughout this period but upon which export taxes would be collected. Sugar and manufactured products of manila hemp (abaca), exclusive of binder twine, were placed under this classification. For sugar a quota of 850,000 long tons was provided, of which not more than 50,000 long tons was to be refined sugar. For the manufactured products of manila hemp (abaca), exclusive of binder twine, a combined total of 6,000,000 pounds was provided. Shipments of these products in excess of the above quotas, while free from Philippine export taxes, would have to pay the prevailing duties in the United States. Beginning January 1, 1941, export taxes equal to five percent of the prevailing duties in the United States were to be collected on these products. These export taxes were to be increased progressively by an additional five percent on January 1, 1942, and on January 1, thereafter, until January 1, 1945, these export taxes were to equal twenty-five percent of the then prevailing duties in the United States. During the period January 1, 1946 through July 3, 1946, however, the export taxes would remain at twenty-five percent of the United States duty.

(c) Finally, embroideries, manila hemp (abaca) fiber, copra and other products of the Philippines not mentioned in the above provisions were placed under special provisions when exported to the United States. In collecting an export tax on embroideries exported to the United States, it was provided that the tax should be computed on the basis of the dutiable value of any such article, less the cost (c.i.f. the Philippines) of any cloth of United States origin used in the production thereof. Copra and manila hemp (abaca) fiber, and other products not mentioned in the above classifications, were to be allowed free entry into the United States.

The products for which quotas were provided were to be allocated among manufacturers or producers whose products were exported in 1937, on the basis of the production which each manufacturer's maximum production shipped to the United States (either directly or through others) in any calendar year during the five year period, 1933-

1937, bore to the total of such maximum shipments of all manufacturers. The Commonwealth government was authorized to provide rules and regulations for the allocation of these quotas.

In consideration for these trade privileges extended to the Philippines all products of the United States imported into the Islands during the Commonwealth period were allowed free entry. Furthermore, the Philippine government agreed to raise its tariff duties on evaporated milk, canned fish, and cotton textiles imported into the Islands from foreign countries in order to extend reciprocal protection to like products of the United States exported to the Philippines.[31]

2. During the post independence period (July 4, 1946 through December 31, 1960) Philippine products exported to the United States were placed under the following classifications: (a) those under declining duty free quotas and (b) those whose quotas would not be decreased but whose tariff preferences would be gradually diminished.

Philippine products with declining quotas were cigars, coconut oil, scrap tobacco, cigar-ends and stripped filler tobacco, and pearl buttons. On the other hand, sugar and manufactured products of manila hemp (abaca) would not have their quotas decreased but their tariff preferences diminished.

Specifically, it was provided that for the period July 4, 1946 through December 31, 1946, 75,000,000 cigars could be imported duty free into the United States. The duty free quota of 150,000,000 cigars for the calendar year 1945 would be reduced by 10,000,000 (that is, five percent of the initial quota of 200,000,000 cigars) for the calendar year 1947 and by the same amount for each succeeding calendar year, until 1961.

With reference to scrap tobacco, cigar-ends and stripped filler tobacco exported to the United States, these products were given a combined duty free total of 1,687,500 pounds for July 4, 1946 through December 31, 1946. The duty free quota for the calendar year 1945, which was 3,375,000 pounds, would be reduced by 225,000 pounds (that is, five percent of the initial quota of 4,500,000 pounds) for the calendar year 1947, and by the same amount for each succeeding calendar year, until 1961.

Shipments of the above products to the United States in excess of their respective quotas would be subject to whatever duty was then existing.

Inversely, for the period July 4, 1946 through December 31, 1946,

[31] Joint Preparatory Committee on Philippine Affairs, *Op. Cit.*, pp. 193-195.

American cigarettes were given to enter the Philippines a duty free quota of 1,125,000,000. For the calendar year 1947 a duty free quota of 2,100,000,000 cigarettes was given to the United States. This quota would be reduced by 150,000,000 (that is, five percent of 3,000,000,000 cigarettes which was the approximate number shipped to the Philippines in 1937) for each succeeding calendar year, until 1961. As in the case of Philippine products exported to the United States, shipments in excess would be subject to the full existing duty in the Philippines.

Under these recommendations, the sugar quota for the Philippines remained the same, that is, 850,000 long tons. On or after July 4, 1946, sugar exports from the Islands to the United States would pay a duty equivalent to twenty-five percent of whatever the then existing duty levied on this product by the United States. This rate would be increased by five percent of the duty on each succeeding January 1, until January 1, 1961 when the full United States duty would be collected and all preferences ended. Shipments in excess of the quota would be subject to the full duty in force at the time.

Upon the termination of the Cordage Act on May 1, 1941, the annual quota of 6,000,000 pounds, exclusive of binder twine, which was to be allowed free entry was maintained, and made into a customs quota. It was provided further that shipment within the quota was subject to Philippine export taxes and shipment in excess of this quota would be permitted to enter the United States upon payment of the full United States duty. The export tax collected was to be equivalent to five percent of the then existing duties in the United States subject to certain exceptions and qualifications.[32] This tax was to be increased by an additional five percent on January 1, 1942, and on each succeeding January 1, until January 1, 1945, when the tax would be equal to twenty-five percent of the then existing duties of the United States.

After July 4, 1946, the quota on cordage would be retained but it would be subject to graduated import duties beginning with twenty-five percent of the then United States duties, later to be increased by five percent on each succeeding January 1, until January 1, 1961, when the full United States duties would be collected and all preferences ended.

On and after July 4, 1946, the Philippine government was to impose duties on all American products, except cigarettes, equivalent to twenty-five percent of the then existing duties in the Philippines col-

[32] Joint Preparatory Committee on Philippine Affairs, *Op. Cit.*, pp. 161-163.

lected on like products from foreign countries. This rate would be increased by five percent on each succeeding January 1, until January 1, 1961 when the full Philippine duties would be collected and all preferences extended to American products in the Islands would be terminated.

Under the heading of special provisions were the following pertinent recommendations. It was provided that in the assessment of taxes the dutiable value of imports into the United States of Philippine embroideries made of cloth which is the product of the United States, the tax should be computed on the basis of the value of such article, less the cost (c.i.f. the Philippines) of any cloth of United States origin used in the manufacture thereof. It was specifically provided that the term "American article" means an article which is the growth, product, or manufacture of the United States, in the manufacture of which no materials of other than Philippine or United States origin valued in excess of twenty percent of the total value of such article was used and which was brought into the Philippine Islands from the United States. The same principle governed also the definition of "Philippine article" shipped to the United States.

It was provided also that the rate of excise tax imposed on coconut oil should be no higher than the rate applicable to palm oil (except for use in making tin plate) or to palm-kernel oil. Provisions for the allocation of quotas were maintained. Furthermore, products of the United States shipped to the Philippines and manufactured into articles which were exported later to the United States should be entitled to a drawback of the Philippine preferential duty paid on such products of the United States, without thereby becoming subject to the existing full duties in the United States. This provision applied also to Philippine products similarly prepared for export to the United States.

3. And finally, the Joint Preparatory Committee on Philippine Affairs urged the incorporation of the above recommendations into a treaty between the two countries to become effective on July 4, 1946, and to continue in effect through December 31, 1960. The same treaty might be terminated on two years' notice at any time after July 4, 1953. The Committee believed that determining the future trade relations of the Philippines with the United States well in advance would insure an orderly transition and a better opportunity for the adjustment of the Philippine national economy.

Aside from the above-noted recommendations, the Committee suggested the continuance of certain provisions during the Commonwealth period for setting aside certain sums of money to safeguard the orderly liquidation of the bonded indebtedness of the Philippines. The continuance of the existing dollar exchange standard was also recommended. And lastly, rights and privileges enjoyed by American citizens in the Philippines before the inauguration of the Commonwealth government for the Islands and likewise those enjoyed in the United States by the citizens of the Philippine Islands, were not curtailed.

While the above recommendations were aimed at assuring the fairest possible treatment for the Philippines, they were equally fair to the United States. During the transition period, Philippine exports to the United States were subject to quota restrictions and to a decreasing tariff preference. On the other hand, throughout the same period no limitation in quantity was placed on American products exported to the Philippines. Nor were tariff preferences extended to American products exported to the Islands, as provided for in the Philippine tariff act, decreased. In certain cases, as a matter of fact, Philippine tariff rates were to be raised to meet the wishes of certain American interests. During the post-independence period, products of the two countries would enjoy equal tariff preferences, but quota restrictions were imposed on four Philippine products to only one American product.

The primary aim of these recommendations was to complement the provisions of the Tydings-McDuffie Act in order to give a chance of survival to a number of Philippine industries which would otherwise be forced to liquidate before the transition period ended. After independence, provisions were also to be made to enable business interests in both the Philippines and the United States an opportunity to adjust themselves or liquidate. It was felt that only through the adoption of these recommendations would it be possible to make the Philippines effectively free under conditions which would give the Filipino people a fair chance to work out a program which would assure the economic and political stability of the Republic.

These recommendations, as previously noted, were embodied in a bill (S. 1028) which Senator Tydings of Maryland introduced, by request, on January 26, 1939. Mr. Tydings explained that "in introducing the bill at their request I do not want to assume the responsibility for it as my own."[33] He believed, however, that it was "a subject upon which a bill ought to be framed and that the bill as presented will

[33] *Cong. Record*, 76th Cong., 1st Sess., Part I, p. 810.

furnish a very fair basis for consideration."[34] Representative Kocialkowski of Illinois, chairman of the House Committee on Insular Affairs, introduced a similar bill (H.R. 3330) on the same date.[35]

During the hearings on this bill (S. 1028) which were started on February 16, 1939, and concluded on March 15, the Senate Committee on Territories and Insular Affairs heard the testimony of Assistant Secretary of State Francis B. Sayre, in his capacity as chairman of the Interdepartmental Committee on Philippine Affairs, Brigadier General Charles Burnett, Chief of the Bureau of Insular Affairs, Vice President Sergio Osmeña of the Commonwealth of the Philippines then in Washington as head of a special mission in connection with the execution of the recommendations of the Joint Committee on Philippine Affairs,[36] and the Resident Commissioner of the Philippines to the United States, Joaquin M. Elizalde. There were also private individuals, both American and Filipinos, representing diverse interests.[37]

Secretary Sayre explained the background of the proposed legislation, its specific provisions and stressed the point that the bill was confined to economic and commercial arrangements and did not touch upon the political issues connected with Philippine independence. He concluded with the hope that the Filipino people be given every chance to make their independence secure and continuing. This, according to him, was the purpose of the bill.

General Burnett, in behalf of the War Department and the Bureau of Insular Affairs, expressed unqualified support of the bill. Vice President Osmeña and Commissioner Elizalde emphasized the point that the bill aimed to complement the Tydings-McDuffie Act by enabling a number of Philippine industries to survive. Furthermore, the bill provided an opportunity for business interests both in the Philippines and in the United States to adjust or liquidate during the post independence period.

Representatives of American domestic interests, on the other hand, were equally insistent against giving any advantage to Philippine products which competed with those in the United States. Mr. A. M. Loomis, representing the Domestic Fats and Oils Conference and Mr. H. Beach Carpenter a representative of the United States Cane Sugar

[34] *Ibid.*

[35] *Ibid.*, p. 859.

[36] *Report of the Special Mission to the United States, Op. Cit.*, p. 55.

[37] See *hearings* before the Senate Committee on Territories and Insular Affairs held in Washington from February 18 to March 15, 1939.

Refiners' Association were on hand to voice the demands of their respective interests. Messrs. Vicente Villamin and Luis Sarmiento registered their opposition to the bill on the ground that it not only restricted the treaty making power of the Philippine government after independence but also that it failed to provide adequate protection to Filipino seamen in the American Merchant Marine. Mr. Salvador Araneta advocated a substitute program consisting of freezing the mutual tariff preferences as soon as they reached forty percent of the scheduled rates.

Among other proponents of this proposed legislation were Mr. J. S. MacDaniel, chairman of the Cordage Institute, New York City, Mr. J. M. Crawford of the Philippine Packing Corporation, Mr. J. J. Underwood of the Seattle Chamber of Commerce, Mr. Herman Fakler of the Millers' National Federation who supported the bill on behalf of the North Pacific Coast Millers' Association; Attorney Cheswell M. Micou, counsel for the National Foreign Trade Council, Inc., who made a lengthy statement in favor of indefinite continuance of trade preference between the United States and the Philippines; Mr. E. P. Thomas, President of the National Foreign Trade Council, Inc., of New York, who advocated the continuance of the two-way free trade arrangement as beneficial to both countries; Mr. John B. Gordon, Secretary of the Bureau of Raw Materials for American Vegetable Oils and Fats Industries, who based his support of the bill on the ground that it would help the coconut crushing industry in the Islands; and former Senator Harry B. Hawes who argued for preferential treatment for sugar of the Philippines to the United States. The former Senator even advocated the revision of the Joint Commission feature of the Tydings-McDuffie Act with Congressional representation in the American membership, pointed out America's moral obligation toward the Philippines and stressed the importance of Philippine trade to the United States and the need for orderly adjustment in the Islands.

At the closing session on March 15, the Association of Sugar Producers of Puerto Rico filed a brief opposing the sugar provision of the pending legislation on the ground that it gave a long term guaranty of sugar quotas to the Philippine Islands and was prejudicial to domestic producing areas.

At the outset of the hearings it was noted that some members of the Senate Committee were not inclined to concede that a valid commitment existed in favor of granting the Philippines new legislation on the basis of the alleged "imperfection or inequalities" in the Tydings-

McDuffie Act as indicated in President Roosevelt's message of March 2, 1934 without the sanction of Congress. In addition to this, there developed a strong opposition to the proposed legislation especially with reference to trade preferences after 1946. Isolationists both in the Committee and in the general membership in Congress were apprehensive of the results of prolonging American responsibility in the Philippine Islands. These were further complicated by the impression that some Senators had that the Filipinos were not in earnest on obtaining approval of the pending legislation. To counteract this impression and to assure Congress of the Filipino attitude on the matter, President Manuel L. Quezon sent cablegrams to Senator Tydings and Representative Kocialkowski strongly indorsing the pending measure.[38]

The Senate Committee thought it advisable, however, to postpone further action on the bill. It authorized the publication of a statement to the effect that in view of the prospective visit of President Quezon, it would be wise to await his arrival and to acquaint him with the views of the American people and various interests in line with the point of view of the Filipino people and interests relative to the economic phases of Philippine independence.[39]

Meanwhile it became apparent to the members of the Philippine mission and to those who were friendly to the cause of the Islands both in Congressional and Administrative circles that the proposed legislation as constituted would be defeated in Congress. It was felt advisable therefore that the bill should deal only with the balance of the transition period, that is, the period from 1940 to 1946. This shift had the approval of President Quezon. The plan was relayed also to Assistant Secretary of State Sayre, who, after consultation with President Roosevelt, expressed conformity with the idea.

At this juncture, it was realized that the personal intervention of President Roosevelt was necessary if action on Philippine matters was to be had during this session of Congress. Ever solicitous to do something to alleviate conditions in the Islands, President Roosevelt personally called Senator Tydings and other members of the Senate Committee on Territories and Insular Affairs to the White House for conference on May 9. This conference proved to be most harmonious. Despite previous differences between President Roosevelt and Senator Tydings, an agreement was reached to formulate a bill that would prevent the disruption or dislocation of some of the Philippine industries

[38] *Report of the Special Mission to the United States, Op. Cit.*, p. 143.
[39] *Ibid.*, p. 28.

at least until 1946. It was in accordance with this agreement that a new bill was introduced simultaneously in the Senate (S. 2390)[40] and in the House of Representatives (H.R. 6262)[41] on May 10, 1939 by Senator Tydings and Representative Kocialkowski respectively.

In introducing this new bill (S. 2390), Senator Tydings made the following explanations. The present bill did not go beyond 1946. With respect to Philippine embroideries and pearl buttons exported to the United States, it was found necessary to substitute "a five percent reduction in the quota each year for a five percent tariff, as was originally incorporated in the independence bill itself. Outside of that it practically deals with no other feature of the Philippine question."[42]

In the meantime, the House Committee on Insular Affairs postponed action on H.R. 6262 pending the outcome in the Senate Committee and in the Senate itself of the Tydings' bill (S. 2390).

Under the proposed measure (S. 2390), Philippine exports to the United States allowed to enter therein free of duty were classified under the following catgeories: (1) those placed under a quota upon which no export taxes would be collected were to be subject to a progressively declining annual quota; (2) those with specific quotas, either a customs quota or an absolute quota, and which were not to be subject to export taxes; (3) those not placed under quotas but upon which export taxes would be collected based on a special formula and (4) those whose free entry would not be subject to any limitation.

Under the first classification were listed the following goods with their respective original quotas as of the calendar year 1940.

(a) cigars (exclusive of cigarettes, cheroots of all kinds, and paper cigars and cigarettes, including wrappers), 200,000,000 cigars;

(b) scrap tobacco, and stemmed and unstemmed filler tobacco described in paragraph 602 of the Tariff Act of 1930, 4,500,000 pounds;

(c) coconut oil, 200,000 long tons;

(d) buttons of pearl or shell, 850,000 gross.

Under this classification it was provided further that beginning with the calendar year 1941 through the calendar year 1945, each of the said quotas would be progressively decreased by five percent of the corresponding original quotas. However, for the period January 1, 1946 through July 3, 1946, each of the said quotas should be one-half of the corresponding quota specified in the calendar year 1945.

[40] *Cong. Record,* 76th Cong., 1st Sess., Part V, pp. 5343-5344.
[41] *Ibid.,* p. 5408.
[42] *Ibid.,* Part I, p. 810.

Manufactured products of manila hemp (abaca) and sugar were placed under the second classification. The former was given an absolute quota of 6,000,000 pounds annually, while sugar was given an annual quota of 850,000 long tons with the proviso that not more than 50,000 long tons might be refined sugar. It was provided furthermore that the quota for sugar during the period January 1, 1946, through July 3, 1946, would be 425,000 long tons of which not more than 25,000 long tons was to be refined sugar. During the same period the quota for manufactured products of manila hemp (abaca) was not to exceed 3,000,000 pounds.

Philippine embroideries were placed under the third classification. In imposing export taxes on these products, the Philippine government was directed to give allowance to the cost—cost, insurance and freight to the Philippines—of any cloth of United States origin used in their manufacture.

Copra, and manila hemp (abaca) not dressed or manufactured in any manner, belonged to the fourth classification and, as such, were allowed unlimited free entry into the United States. The Philippine government was forbidden to levy export taxes on these products.

Under the proposed legislation, the Philippines could export sugar to the United States in excess of its duty free quota—not exceeding, of course, the taxable quota which the Philippines were allowed annually—upon payment of the then existing duty. On these shipments the Philippine government was to impose export taxes which would be equivalent to five percent of the existing duty in the United States beginning 1941. On each succeeding calendar year thereafter, this tax would be increased progressively by an additional five percent of the duty. During the period January 1, 1946 through July 3, 1946, however, the export tax was to remain at twenty-five percent of the existing duty. Money collected from these taxes would be refunded by the Philippine government and deposited with the United States Secretary of the Treasury for the bonded indebtedness of the Philippine Islands.

Provisions were made for the allocation of the above quotas among producers and manufacturers of these products of the Islands; Philippine citizens and corporations in the United States and all places subject to its jurisdiction would continue to exercise the same rights and privileges until after the withdrawal of American sovereignty in the Philippines; and the President of the United States was authorized to make arrangements for the retention, or for securing in the Islands, of properties which could be used for future American diplomatic and consular establishments in the Philippines.

It will be noted that the provisions of this new Philippine bill were quite different from the recommendations of the Joint Preparatory Committee on Philippine Affairs. It is noteworthy, however, that the principle of declining quotas was substituted for that of increasing tariffs. Such arrangement, according to Senator Tydings, would be better for the Filipinos in that they would know how much they might produce and export to the United States and thereby readjust their economy. He emphasized also that this arrangement would safeguard the best interests of the American people.[43] At best, this bill was a compromise measure and was the best legislation obtainable at the time. Its provisions were designed to give the Filipinos an opportunity to adjust themselves gradually to changed conditions rather than be subjected to a drastic and violent change in their economic status in July 1946.

On May 18, 1939, the Senate Committee on Territories and Insular Affairs reported this bill favorably with some amendments. The most important of these were those dealing with the definition of "refined sugar," the removal of the excise tax on coconut oil when used for a specific industrial purpose as in the manufacture of soap, and the imposition of export taxes on Philippine cordage imported into the United States.[44]

It was not until May 31, however, that general debate on this bill took place in the Senate. Senator Tydings explained that the proposed legislation (S. 2390) dealt only with the time up to independence, and was concerned only with the economic and trade relations between the United States and the Philippines for the duration of the transition period.

Senator Tydings explained further that certain changes were made in the provisions of the existing law to meet the requests of Americans and Filipinos alike. These changes dealt with the application of tariffs on certain products of the Philippines exported to the United States. The law provided, continued the Senator, that "commencing 1941 and extending to the year 1946, tariffs should be levied on products coming from the Philippine Islands into the United States starting with five percent of the existing tariff in 1941, ten percent of the existing tariff in 1942, and increasing five percent each year until 1946, when one hundred percent of the tariff would fall upon products

[43] *Cong. Record,* 76th Cong., 1st Sess., Part VI, p. 6332.
[44] *Senate Report No. 453* to accompany S.2390 (76th Cong., 1st Sess.)

coming from the Philippine Islands to the United States."[45] It was clearly established during the public hearing[46] that application of these taxes on Philippine cigars, scrap tobacco, cigar-ends, stripped filler tobacco, coconut oil, pearl buttons and embroideries would tend to destroy these industries even before the end of the transition period in 1946. Since these articles (excluding sugar) constituted almost forty percent of the total value of all Philippine exports to the United States,[47] their virtual elimination from that market would not only result in retarding the economic readjustment of the Philippines but also would curtail the purchasing power of the Filipino people in the American market. Philippine purchases in the United States in 1938 was almost $91,000,000[48]—a figure that must have "helped" Mr. Tydings to decide that "we do not want to destroy that buying power, particularly at this time of unemployment."[49] Consequently, a formula previously recommended by the Joint Preparatory Committee on Philippine Affairs of a constantly decreasing quota for constantly increasing tariffs was substituted for the above provisions. As Senator Tydings cogently put it, the shift would be beneficial to the Filipinos but more so would it work out to the satisfaction of American interests concerned.

One of the amendments proposed by the Senate Committee was the elimination of "direct consumption sugar" from the definition of "refined sugar" as used in the Sugar Act of 1937.[50] The Committee pointed out that if this should be the case it might alter the Philippine quota for "refined sugar." As a matter of fact, under the Sugar Act of 1937 the Philippines were accorded a quota for direct consumption sugar of 80,214 short tons, an amount which was very much higher than 50,000 long tons as specifically provided in the Tydings-McDuffie Act.[51] Two days before the bill came up to the Senate for discussion, an agreement was reached with the Philippine government making the above amendment unnecessary.[52]

[45] *Cong. Record,* 78th Cong., 1st Sess., Part VI, p. 6332.

[46] See *Hearings* before the Senate Committee on Territories and Insular Affairs held in Washington from February 16 to March 15, 1939.

[47] United States Department of Commerce, *Statistical Abstract of the United States,* 1943, pp. 557, 591.

[48] *Ibid.,* p. 550.

[49] *Cong. Record,* 76th Cong., 1st Sess., Part VI, p. 6334.

[50] See section 101 of the *Sugar Act of 1937 (Public, No. 414)*; see also supplementary statement of Hon. Sergio Osmena before the Senate Committee on Territories and Insular Affairs on S.1028 in *Report of the Special Mission to the United States, Op. Cit.,* pp. 157-160.

[51] *Senate Report No. 453* to accompany S.2390 (76th Cong., 1st Sess.)

[52] *Cong. Record,* 76th Cong., 1st Sess., Part VI, p. 6333.

In answer to the question of Senator Alben W. Barkley of Kentucky whether in the pending bill the Philippines could send their sugar quota all in raw form, Senator Tydings answered in the affirmative. He even confided that "the attitude of Congress has been to permit the importation of raw sugar and have it refined in this country rather than to have them develop the refined sugar business in the Islands. To speak frankly, that is what Congress, and particularly those interested in sugar legislation, wanted. We thought we were meeting that view by putting the possibility of cutting out the exportation of refined sugar up to them, and having it all in raw state, and they were satisfied to proceed in that way. . . . This, concluded Senator Tydings, "will provide employment in this country which would not otherwise exist."[53]

The Cordage Act of June 14, 1935 which was extended to May 1, 1941 by President Roosevelt's proclamation of January 26, 1938, was extended by the present bill to July 4, 1946. After May 1, 1941, by virtue of the Senate Committee amendment, Philippine cordage shipped to the United States would be subject to the export tax.

An effort was made during the debate in the Senate to amend the processing tax on coconut oil in order to exempt it from the three-cent tax when used in manufactures. However, certain Senators objected to this proposal on the ground that American producers of commodities competing with coconut oil would be affected, since coconut oil would be much cheapened. It was said that the principal beneficiaries of the change would be the soap manufacturers. It was pointed out that the price of soap had remained constant during the period 1930 through 1938 when the price of oil had varied, so the point was made that the price of soap would be constant and the profit from striking out the tax would go to the soap manufacturers. Defenders of domestic vegetable oil industries believed that if the tax were removed, more oil would be used by the manufacturers and thus cut into the sale of competing products. If this were true, the amendment would benefit the Philippines, since there would be a larger importation of coconut oil and as the discriminatory tax on non-Philippine coconut oil and copra was maintained, the increase would come wholly from the Islands. However, the amendment was stricken out in the Senate on a point of order as a revenue measure.[54]

[53] *Ibid.*, p. 6334.
[54] *Ibid.*, pp. 6339-6350.

There were two amendments presented on the floor, namely, the amendment presented by Senator Bennett Champ Clark of Missouri and that of Senator John E. Miller of Arkansas.

Senator Bennett Champ Clark introduced an amendment to section 13 of the Tydings-McDuffie Act. Briefly stated this change involved the following points, namely, (1) the time limit was changed from one to two years, (2) the holding of the conference was made mandatory rather than permissive, (3) former Senator Hawes' suggestion was adopted concerning Congressional representation in the American membership[55] while Philippine representatives were to be appointed by the President of the Philippines with the approval of the Commission on Appointments, and (4) a provision for the filling of vacancy should it occur.[56]

While Senator Norris of Nebraska seemed to have aptly summarized the general attitude of the Senate toward Senator Clark's amendment "as a great improvement" and therefore to be adopted,[57] he concurred with Senator Tydings in the inadvisability of making the conference mandatory. At any rate, the Senator from Nebraska did not wholly subscribe to the "implications" advanced by Senator Tydings.

Senator Tydings pointed out at the outset that he was not against the amendment, and that he was merely presenting his observations on the "implications" of the mandatory aspects of the conference as constituted in the amendment. He was fearful that this projected conference might be "used as a vehicle to bring up the whole question all over again." Continuing, he pointed out that "there are a good many people interested in the Philippine problem in this country and in the Philippines who are looking for the day when this particular act will be used as a means of translating what we assume now is going to be an ultimate independence of the Philippines into a dominion status of the Philippines similar to that of Canada with relation to Great Britain."[58]

To allay the fears of Senator Tydings, Senator Clark reminded him and the Senate in general that the amendment would not in the least affect the original portion of section 13 of the law which specifically provides that "nothing in this proviso shall be construed to modify or affect in any way any provision of this act relating to the procedure

[55] See *Supra*, p. 176.
[56] *Cong. Record*, 76th Cong., 1st Sess., Part VI, p. 6352.
[57] *Ibid.*
[58] *Ibid.*, p. 6353.

leading up to Philippine independence or the date upon which the Philippine Islands shall become independent."[59]

After a short debate, and after that part of the amendment objected to by Senator Connally as dealing with revenue matters—although it was merely a repetition of that part of section 13—was removed, the amendment was approved.

Another amendment which was presented on the floor and approved by the Senate was that of Senator John E. Miller of Arkansas. The purpose of this amendment, as the Senator explained it, was to reallocate cordage shipments from the Philippines to the United States. The formulae under which reallocation should be made were: (1) the number of spindles installed as of February 1, 1939, (2) the average annual production of each manufacturer for the calendar years 1931, 1932 and 1933, and (3) the amount or quantity shipped by each manufacturer in the 12-month period immediately preceding the inauguration of the Philippine Commonwealth.[60]

It was conceded that one of the objectives of the amendment was to assure fair distribution of the business among the different cordage firms in the Philippines. On the other hand, it was also recognized that the provision for allocation on the number of spindles would be unfair. The fundamental objection to this amendment hinged on the fact that it would limit the power hitherto conferred upon the Philippine government by paragraph 2 of section 1 of the Cordage Act of June 14, 1935.[61] Senator Tydings observed that the amendment "might have to be dropped or altered in conference."[62] As a matter of fact, in presenting his amendment Senator Miller frankly stated that his purpose was "to have the question go to conference."[63]

After Senator Miller's amendment was ultimately approved, the bill (S. 2390) was engrossed for third reading, read the third time and approved without a record vote.[64] This amendatory legislation was then dispatched to the House of Representatives which in turn referred it to the House Committee on Insular Affairs.[65]

Be it recalled that on May 10, 1939 Representative Leo Kocialkowski of Illinois introduced a bill (H.R. 6262) to amend section 6 of the Tydings-McDuffie Act. Action on this bill was postponed pending the

[59] *Ibid.*, pp. 6353-6354.
[60] *Ibid.*, p. 6355.
[61] *Public, No. 137,* section 1, paragraph 2.
[62] *Cong. Record,* 76th Cong., 1st Sess., Part VI, p. 6333.
[63] *Ibid.*
[64] *Ibid.*
[65] *Ibid.*, p. 6550.

final outcome of the identical bill in the Senate (S. 2390) introduced on the same day by Senator Tydings. The passage of this bill in the Senate gave added impetus for its adoption in the House. There were some difficulties, however, which had to be cleared first before favorable action on it could be had. This involved numerous conferences and detailed explanation of the provisions of the Senate bill. To obviate parliamentary and constitutional difficulties which might have cropped up, and to meet the wishes of varied interests, it was agreed ultimately that a new bill should be introduced whose provisions would be identical with the bill approved by the Senate, without the Miller amendment.[66] Thus, on July 7, Representative Kocialkowski introduced a new bill (H.R. 7096) in lieu of his former bill (H.R. 6262). Three days later the House Committee on Insular Affairs reported this bill favorably without amendment.[67]

In recommending the immediate approval of the bill, the House Committee on Insular Affairs went further than the Senate when it called attention to the "disturbed political and economic conditions of the world today." Furthermore, immediate and favorable action on the pending legislation was also urged in order "that those directly interested, as well as the world at large, may know the attitude of the United States toward those phases of United States-Philippine relationships which are dealt with in this bill, and so that the Filipinos themselves may be in position to make those readjustments in their economy which are essential to a constructive preparation for independence."[68]

The difficulties which the pending bill would have encountered having been ironed out previously and satisfactorily,[69] subsequent consideration in the House on July 31 regarding its adoption evoked very little debate.[70] Aside from the futile protests of Representative Fred L. Crawford of Michigan, one of the consistent defenders of the domestic sugar industry, that the Congress "have legislated carelessly in connection with Philippine-American affairs,"[71] the House moved with the precision of a well-oiled machine. The bill as constituted was approved and was sent immediately to the Senate which adopted the same in lieu of its own bill (S. 2390) on the assurance of Senator Tyd-

[66] For an account of these conferences, see *Report of the Special Mission to the United States, Op. Cit.*, pp. 37-44.

[67] *House Report No. 1058* to accompany H.R. 7096 (76th Cong., 1st Sess.)

[68] *Ibid.*

[69] See *Report of the Special Mission to the United States, Op. Cit.*, pp. 37-44.

[70] *Cong. Record*, 76th Cong., 1st Sess., Part X, pp. 10591-10601.

[71] *Ibid.*, p. 10597.

ings that both bills were substantially the same.[72] On August 7, 1939, upon signature of the President it became law.[73]

Hardly had two years elapsed since the enactment of the Tydings-Kocialkowski Act when the Philippine economy was in a precarious state. On behalf of the Insular government therefore, Commissioner Elizalde requested the suspension for a year of the collection of export taxes on Philippine products imported into the United States as provided for in the law. This request was made in a letter addressed to Senator Tydings under date of June 10, 1941.[74] The reasons given to support this request were: (1) the war then current in Europe and the unsettled conditions in the Far East which disrupted the economic readjustment program of the Philippines; (2) the war in Europe and the fact that the resultant loss to the Philippines of European markets had accentuated the dependence of the Islands on the American market; (3) the extension to the Philippines of the export-control law which dealt a death blow to trade with Japan; (4) the acute shortage of ships in the Pacific, which raised freight rates and insurance charges to prohibitive proportions thereby threatening Philippine trade with the United States, the very life-blood of the Islands and (5) the fact that the money originally intended to fortify the economic structure of the country was diverted to other channels.

Immediate action on this request was urged by Commissioner Elizalde in order to reduce the possibility of "widespread unemployment, social unrest, and human sufferings" in the Islands.[75] And to avoid "any misconception on the motives and purpose" of the legislation requested by the Philippine government, the Commissioner categorically affirmed that the request for a year's suspension of the tax "in no way contemplates any alteration in the program of ultimate independence for the Philippines in 1946, nor even a change in the philosophy underlying the ten-year economic-adjustment plan charted for the Commonwealth by law."[76]

This request took substance in a bill (S. 1623) introduced by Senator Tydings on the following day (June 11), the primary aims of which were to suspend for a year (1) progressive reduction of quotas on cigars, scrap tobacco including stemmed and unstemmed filler to-

[72] *Cong. Record*, 76th Cong., 1st Sess., Part.
[73] *Ibid.*
[74] For a copy of this letter, see *Cong. Record*, 77th Cong., 1st Sess., Part V, pp. 4995-4996.
[75] *Ibid.*
[76] *Ibid.*

bacco, coconut oil and buttons of pearl or shell, and (2) collection of export taxes on Philippine products imported into the United States specifically provided for in subsection (b) of section 6 of the Tydings-Kocialkowski Act. In line with the assurances of Commissioner Elizalde, it was provided in section 3 of this bill that "nothing in this act shall change in any respect not herein expressly provided for the provision of the act of March 24, 1934, as amended."[77]

In spite of the request for immediate action on this bill, it took the Senate Committee on Territories and Insular Affairs five months to act on it. It was not until November 13 that the Committee acted on this bill and, with only slight amendment on its title, recommended its adoption.[78] When the bill came up ultimately for debate in the Senate on November 19, Senator Vandenberg, in a caustic remark pointed out that the bill could be taken as "a precedent for the progressive disintegration of the Tydings-McDuffie Act" and a "piecemeal revision of the Philippine independence formula."[79] As an answer to this observation Senator Bennett Champ Clark assured him that that was not the aim of the Committee. It was to preclude that possibility, according to Mr. Clark, that the provisions in section 3 were inserted in the bill. The proposed measure, he continued, "was occasioned simply and solely because the original policy for a progressive severing of the economic ties between the people of the Philippines and the people of the United States was based on a contemplation of normal economic conditions. . . . The very great dislocation in their economic structure," he pointed out, "has been brought about, first, because they have not been able to secure bottoms; and, secondly, because such sugar and other commodities as they have been able to export bear much higher freight rates than they formerly did."[80] He urged therefore that immediate and favorable action be given to this bill in order to extend the needed relief for the Philippine Islands.

The Senate approved the bill on the same day[81] and on November 21, it was sent to the House for its consideration. It was not until December 3, however, that this bill finally emerged from the House Committee on Insular Affairs with its indorsement.[82] This bill was scheduled to be considered on the floor of the House the day it obtained

[77] *Ibid.*
[78] *Senate Report No. 828* to accompany S.1623 (77th Cong., 1st Sess.).
[79] *Cong. Record,* 77 Cong., 1st Sess., Part VIII, p. 9002.
[80] *Ibid.*, p. 9003.
[81] *Ibid.*
[82] *House Report No. 1460* to accompany S.1623 (77th Cong., 1st Sess.).

the approval of the House Committee. But Representative John Taber of New York requested postponement on the ground that "the bill is of such a character and of such importance" that it deserved to be fully considered.[83] Discussion on it was finally had on December 12 and, with hardly any debate except for the specter of fear constantly dragged in by Representative Fred L. Crawford of Michigan on behalf of the domestic sugar interests, the bill passed.[84] Ten days later upon the signature of President Roosevelt it became a law.[85]

It may be said in passing that final approval of the bill was made when the promised relief would no longer be useful. Japan struck on the morning of December 7, 1941 with brutal suddeness which, to the Filipinos in particular, was both stunning and unnerving. Material distress and spiritual depression became the lot of the rank and file of the people and, for the moment, they felt lost and alone in their misfortune. However, in the midst of this feeling of frustration and loneliness they found refuge in the sustaining thought of their faith in America. And the ugly realities engendered by the so-called "Co-Prosperity Sphere" shook them from their mood of helpless resignation. They fought the invaders with tenacity—more often to the extent of foolish abandon—to help preserve and maintain, in their own crude way and without any lend-lease, the democratic way of life—the only remaining and tangible thing with which to remember the America they knew. The epic of their struggle is now a matter of history. They did their part.

In a message to Congress under date of October 6, 1943,[86] President Roosevelt intimated that on several occasions he had addressed messages on behalf of the American people "to the courageous people of the Philippines expressing our admiration for their heroism and loyalty," and assuring them that "the Government of the United States of America will see to it that their independence will be promptly established and—still more important—that it will be protected." He was sure that the American people shared with him the belief that the Filipino people "have earned the right juridically to be free and independent." He requested that Congress should give him the authority, after consultation with the President of the Commonwealth of the

[83] *Cong. Record,* 77th Cong., 1st Sess., Part IX, p. 9498.

[84] *Ibid.,* p. 9743.

[85] *Ibid.,* p. 10090 (*Public, No. 367*).

[86] For a copy of this message see *Sen. Doc. No. 101* (78th Cong., 1st Sess.); see also *Cong. Record,* 78th Cong., 1st Sess., Part VI, p. 8121.

Philippines, to advance the date of Philippine independence. He maintained that in order "to make good our pledge that the independence of the Philippines will be protected in the future," and to give the Filipinos "the opportunity of economic rehabilitation which is their due," it would be necessary that the Congress should (1) authorize the President of the United States and the President of the Commonwealth of the Philippines to enter immediately into negotiations to provide for full security for the Philippines, for the mutual protection of the United States and the Islands, and for the future maintenance of peace in the Pacific; (2) adjust the economic relations between the two countries and assuring for the Philippines economic stability; and (3) provide for the Islands physical and economic rehabilitation. To the President's mind, these were due to the Filipino people "in recognition of their heroic role in this war, the political ties which have bound us together, and the bonds of friendship which will join us together in the future."[87]

In line with the recommendations of President Roosevelt, Senator Tydings introduced two joint resolutions (S. J. Res. 93 and S. J. Res. 94) on November 3, 1943.[88] Senate Joint Resolution 93 dealt with the question of when the Philippine independence should take place, in the light of current conditions in the Islands. Ultimately, however, it was thought advisable that the date originally provided for in the Tydings-McDuffie Act for the independence of the Philippines be maintained. On the other hand, Senate Joint Resolution 94 provided for the creation of a Filipino Rehabilitation Commission which was authorized (1) to inquire into "all matters affecting post-war economy, trade, finance, economic stability and rehabilitation of the Philippine Islands," (2) to formulate recommendations for the future trade relations between the United States and the Republic of the Philippines and, (3) to consider the extension of the present trade relations between the two countries for a period of years to correspond with "the period of occupancy by the Japanese, and to consider if in addition thereto other time for trade adjustments is required for the reestablishment of trade relations as provided for in the original Independence Act."[89]

[87] *Sen. Doc. No. 101* (78th Cong., 1st Sess.).

[88] See *Public, No. 380* and *Public, No. 381* (78th Cong., 2nd Sess.).

[89] *Public, No. 381;* For the debate on S. J. Res. 94 see *Cong. Record,* 78th Cong., 2nd Sess., pp. 6286-6289, 6328.

Manifestly, these inquiries took substance in the two bills passed by Congress, namely, the bill (S. 1610) to provide for the rehabilitation of the Philippines which became known subsequently as the Philippine Rehabilitation Act of 1946, and the bill (H.R. 5856) to provide for trade relations between the United States and the Philippine Islands, which was ultimately known as the Philippine Trade Act of 1946.[90] These two bills became laws when President Truman signed them on April 30, 1946. In approving these laws, the President was reported to have said that these acts were "unprecedented" and that they were intended to serve as a notice to the Filipinos and to the world that "we are redeeming our promises to the heroic Philippine people."[91]

These two laws are complementary and their enactment gave to the United States Congress the happy privilege, according to Representative A. Willis Robertson of Virginia, of demonstrating to the world "that friendship with the United States does pay and that with us the payment of a debt of gratitude is a categorical imperative."[92] He described the Philippine Rehabilitation Act as an "act of justice implemented by generosity" while he characterized the Philippine Trade Act as an "act of justice implemented by an enlightened self-interest."[93] He supported the thesis of former Assistant Secretary of State Francis B. Sayre that the success of American ideas of individual liberty and democratic way of life in the Philippines would mean also "our success in furthering American ideas and ideals throughout the strategic East."[94]

The enactment of the Philippine Rehabilitation and Trade Acts of 1946 is unprecedented in the legislative history of the United States. Never before has the United States Congress been called upon to enact laws in anticipation of a situation such as provided for in these two measures. When they were being considered, the halls of Congress were pervaded by an atmosphere of cordiality and perfect harmony. Wanton destruction by the enemy of lives and properties in the Phil-

[90] *Public, No. 370* and *Public, No. 371* (79th Cong., 2nd Sess.).

[91] *New York Times*, May 1, 1946, p. 9.

[92] *Cong. Record*, 79th Cong., 2nd Sess., p. 2824.

[93] *Ibid.*

[94] *Ibid.*, p. 2825.

For Mr. Sayre's article entitled "Freedom Comes to the Philippines" see *Atlantic Monthly*, March 1945. See also his article entitled "Nationhood Comes to the Philippines" in *Think*, July 1946.

ippines as an object lesson to the Filipinos because of their unflinching loyalty to the United States, was offered as the main reason for the unprecedented action of the Congress in giving to the Philippines trade concessions the like of which were never extended to any country before. On the other hand, the metamorphosis of the trade bill in the House Committee on Ways and Means would seem to indicate that that harmonious atmosphere was made possible only after the knotty question involving domestic interests had been successfully ironed out in Committee hearings.[95]

In explaining why it took long for the Committee on Ways and Means to get out the Philippine trade bill, Representative Robert L. Doughton of North Carolina, chairman of the committee, explained the difficulties of the committee. According to him, it was "difficult to establish a policy which we considered would be fair to the Government of the United States and the government of the Philippine Islands" as well as "to draft the bill that would carry out the purposes and intent of those who are interested in the legislation."[96] Continuing, he pointed out that the concessions given to the Philippines were not only unique but liberal as well. He maintained, however, that assurance must likewise be required from the Philippines that American interests in the Islands must be preserved and protected.[97]

The salient points of the Philippine Trade Act of April 30, 1946, which are germane to the present study, may now be summarized. This law differs from all previous laws in that the economic relations with the independent Philippines were to be on a basis extending 28 years after independence.

Since the economic advantages involved provisions, on the part of the United States, normally found in a tariff act, and also other provisions determining the application to Philippine products of internal taxes, and on the part of the Philippines of similar provisions, it was necessary that the arrangement be incorporated into the statutes of the two countries. There were also immigration questions involved, which again are subjects on which national legislatures are very particular. It was therefore thought necessary by the United States Congress that the advantages to be given the Philippines should be incor-

[95] See *Hearings* before the Committee on Ways and Means of the House of Representatives, 79th Cong., 1st Sess., on H.R. 4185, H.R. 4676, H.R. 5185; held on October 15-17, November 14-15, 1945; February 15, and March 15, 1946.

[96] *Cong. Record*, 79th Cong., 2nd Sess., p. 2821.

[97] *Ibid.*

porated in an act and the advantages to be given to the United States by the Philippines be enacted into law by the Philippine Legislature. However, after July 4, 1946, the Philippines would be an independent country so that an agreement between the two governments would be necessary which would incorporate the obligations on the part of each government, both to include in its laws the requirements of the arrangement and with the provisions for the ending of the arrangement if either country did not keep its promise. To meet this situation Congress expressly authorized the President to make an executive agreement with the government of the Philippines under which each country would agree to maintain the advantages provided for the other in the act and to enact all legislation necessary for this purpose. The President could enter into the agreement only after it was accepted as law by the Philippine Congress, and that body had enacted the legislation necessary to make effective the obligations of the Philippine government. One of the obligations of the Philippines would require an amendment to the Constitution, so the President may make the agreement but terminate it if he finds that the amendment is not put through within a reasonable time. The act provides further that the advantages given to the Philippines would cease to have effect as laws of the United States on the termination of the agreement.

In order that the agreement should not be a strait jacket for the long period involved, it was provided that the agreement may be terminated by either party on not less than five years' notice, and it may be terminated on not less than six months' notice if either President "determines and proclaims" that the other country has adopted or applied measures or practices operating to nullify or impair the rights and obligations provided for in the agreement.

The trade advantages given to the Philippines were substantially a continuation of the quotas in the Tydings-McDuffie Act as amended. From July 4, 1946 to and including July 3, 1954, the following products of the Islands were to be admitted free of duty into the United States within their respective absolute annual quotas.

1. Sugar, 850,000 long tons, not more than 50,000 long tons of which may be refined sugar, that is, direct-consumption sugar as defined in the Sugar Act of 1937.

2. Cordage, defined to include yarns, twine (including binding twines), cords, cordage, rope, and cable, tarred or untarred, wholly or in chief value of manila (abaca) or other hard fiber, 6,000,000 pounds.

3. Rice, including rice meal, flour, polish, and bran, 1,040,000 pounds.
4. Cigars (exclusive of cigarettes, cheroots of all kinds, and paper cigars and cigarettes, including wrappers), a total of 200,000,000 cigars.
5. Scrap tobacco, stemmed and unstemmed filler tobacco, 6,500,000 pounds.
6. Coconut oil, 200,000 long tons.
7. Buttons of pearl or shell, 850,000 gross.

Beginning July 4, 1954 to July 3, 1974 inclusive, however, the above products will be classified as follows: (1) Those whose absolute quotas will be maintained but which will be subject to a graduated tariff. For the period of July 4, 1954 to and including December 31, 1954, the duty will be five percent of the lowest United States duty extended to any foreign country (now Cuba); for the calendar year 1955, the rate will be ten percent of such duty; for the calendar years 1956 to and including 1972, the duty will be increased annually by an additional five percent of the United States duty; and for the period of January 1, 1973 to July 3, 1974 the duty will be one hundred percent of the United States duty. Sugar, cordage, and rice belong to this classification; (2) those whose duty free quotas will be reduced annually by ten percent of their original respective quotas. It was provided, however, that articles under this classification may be entered in the United States in excess of their duty free quotas in any year—but within the limits of the absolute quota provided for each article—upon payment of the United States duty, the lowest rate of ordinary customs duty accorded a like article from any foreign country. Cigars, scrap tobacco, coconut oil, and buttons of pearls or shell belong to this classification.

As one of its obligations, the Philippine government must agree to enact and keep in effect laws necessary to make the allotment of the quotas among producers on the basis fixed in the act by the United States Congress.

Important for the coconut industry which is a mainstay for the small farmers in the Islands, is the obligation that the United States shall not decrease the two cents a pound preference under the processing tax[98] extended to the Philippine coconut oil derived from Philippine copra, except that the President of the United States, after conference with the President of the Philippines, may suspend the application of this tax on copra and coconut oil coming from foreign coun-

[98] Section 2470 Internal Revenue Code.

tries during any period, if supplies for these products from the Philippines are not adequate to meet the needs of the United States. As a result of this preference, practically all coconut oil and copra entering the United States has come from the Philippines.

Certain key words used in the law were defined by Congress. "Persons" includes natural persons, partnerships, corporations, and associations; "Philippine article" means a natural product of the Philippines, if manufactured, that should not contain foreign materials from any foreign country (except the United States) the aggregate value of which should exceed twenty percent of the total value of the manufactured product; "United States article" was given the same definition as that of "Philippine article"; "Ordinary customs duty" means a customs duty based on the article as such but which does include special duties such as countervailing duties, anti-dumping duties, etc.; "United States duty" is defined to mean the rate of ordinary customs duty which would be applicable to a like article if imported from that foreign country entitled to the lowest rate of ordinary customs duty (that country is now Cuba); and "Philippine duty" is defined in the same way as the "United States duty."

What was expected of the Philippines was specifically set forth in title III of the law, both as a possession of the United States until July 4, 1946, and as an independent country. From April 30, 1946—the date of the enactment of the law—to and including July 3, 1946, the Philippines is bound by the provisions of the law as a possession of the United States. However, beginning July 4, 1946 to July 3, 1954 inclusive, products of the United States which qualify as "United States article" will be admitted into the Philippines free of ordinary customs duty. From July 4, 1954 to and including July 3, 1974, however, these products of the United States entering the Philippines will be subject to a graduated tariff duty. From July 4, 1954 to December 31, 1954 inclusive, the duty will be equivalent to five percent of the ordinary customs duty of the Islands. From January 1, 1955 to and including December 31, 1972, the tax will be gradually increased by five percent for each succeeding calendar year. For the period beginning January 1, 1973 to and including July 3, 1974, the duty will be one hundred percent of the ordinary customs duty of the Philippines.

An important advantage to the United States is contained in section 341 which provides that "the disposition, exploitation, development, and utilization of all agricultural, timber, and mineral lands of the public domain, waters, minerals, coal, petroleum and other mineral oils, all forces and sources of potential energy, and other natural resources of the Philippines, and the operation of public utilities shall, if open to any person, be open to citizens of the United States and to all forms of business enterprise owned or controlled, directly or indirectly, by United States citizens." The Constitution of the Philippines will have to be amended before this provision can be put into effect.[99]

It is stipulated in the act that the value of the Philippine currency in relation to the United States dollar shall not be changed, the convertibility of the peso in the United States shall not be suspended, and the transfer of funds from the Philippines to the United States shall not be restricted. Only by agreement with the President of the United States could any of these provisions be modified.

There are also certain trade obligations which each country has to accept. To prevent discrimination through internal taxation, each country agrees that internal taxes can not be laid on products of the other in excess of similar taxes levied on like articles produced at home or imported from another country, whichever is the lower. Certain minor exceptions are made by the United States as to specified articles.

Furthermore, both countries will agree not to discriminate, in any manner, against the products of either country in favor of like products of a third country. Nor will either collect export taxes on the products imported by each from either country. Articles imported into either country for the official use of each government or any department or agency thereof will be free.

It is also provided that manila hemp (abaca) fiber not dressed or manufactured in any manner exported to the United States should be tax free in either country. And Philippine products, which do not qualify as "Philippine articles" when imported into the United States, should be levied a tax equal to that imposed on like products of foreign countries other than Cuba.

To assure the protection of domestic production in case of need, it was provided further that if after January 1, 1948, and after an investigation, it was found that Philippine products—other than those placed on quota basis—were coming or likely to come into substantial competition with similar domestic products, the President of the United States shall provide for these products annual quotas as well as their

[99] According to press dispatches from the Philippines, the Philippine Congress has approved this measure subject to a national plebiscite on March 11, 1947.—*New York Times*, October 10, 1946, p. 12.

allocation. However, the quota established for any of these products shall not be less than the amount determined by the President of the United States as the total amount of such class of Philippine product during the 12-month period preceding the start of the investigation.

As a precaution, the United States Congress required as part of the agreement a provision that if the President of the United States determines and proclaims, after consultation with the President of the Philippines, that the Philippine Republic or any of its political subdivisions or the Philippine Government are in any manner discriminating against United States citizens or any form of United States business enterprise, then the United States shall have the right to suspend the effectiveness of the whole or any portion of the executive agreement. Upon proclamation of the President of the United States, after consultation with the President of the Philippines, this suspension may be ended when the discrimination has ceased. On the other hand, if the President of the United States finds out that the discrimination has not ended after a time determined by him to be reasonable, the United States shall have the right to terminate the executive agreement upon not less than six months' notice.

There were also limited advantages assured to immigrant citizens of each country. Citizens of the Philippines who had actually resided in the United States for a continuous period of three years during the forty-two months ending November 30, 1941, were given non-quota status, if entering the United States for residence between July 4, 1946 to July 3, 1951, and a similar non-quota status was assured to United States citizens entering the Philippines under similar conditions. The Philippines will further admit, without regard to Philippine legal limitation, United States citizens in number and for a period to be fixed in an agreement between the two countries.

It must be observed that in prescribing for the above obligations and privileges for each country, the United States Congress thus sets forth under what conditions it would agree to bind itself. If the President of the United States could enter into an executive agreement with the President of the Philippines under the stipulations set forth by Congress, the President of the United States will then proclaim it and set the date for the taking effect of the agreement. Only until then would Congress agree to be bound by the executive agreement, and the provisions set forth in the trade act become parts of the laws of both countries.

Comparing the above provisions of the law with those which the bill (H.R.5856) provided when approved by the House of Representatives, the provisions of the law are, by far, more liberal. For instance, the law restored the original quota of Philippine sugar entering the United States. It is felt that the eight-year period during which Philippine sugar—as well as cordage and rice—could enter the United States free of ordinary customs duty, would give the Philippine producers and manufacturers of these products sufficient time to readjust their industries. It might be noted that the duty to be collected on Philippine sugar exported to the United States from July 4, 1954 through December 31, 1972 will actually be lower than those levied on Cuban sugar. For instance, from July 4, through December 31, 1954 the duty on Philippine sugar will be five percent of the Cuban duty, which is three quarters of a cent per pound. On the other hand, sugar from other foreign countries, when imported into the United States, pays a duty of 1.875 cents a pound. In the meantime, technological progress and development in the Islands will, it may be hoped, more than offset whatever drawbacks Philippine products may have in so far as production costs and other allied handicaps are concerned.[100]

General appraisal of the provisions of the Philippine Trade Act should be made conjointly with the general provisions of the Philippine Rehabilitation Act. Under this law, Congress provides for the payment of $400,000,000 for war damages to private properties in the Islands. In addition, Congress is to appropriate the sum of $120,000,000 to be allocated from time to time by the President of the United States as a manifestation of good will to the Filipino people for repair and rebuilding of public buildings, public roads, port and harbor facilities, and public health service. Such additional sums shall be appropriated also from time to time to carry out certain training research and survey programs which were provided for in the law aside from an authorization to transfer to the Philippines surplus property of the United States not exceeding $100,000,000 in fair value.[101]

Borrowing the words of Senator La Follette, some of the provisions of the Philippine Trade Act "are unduly harsh" and "go beyond the point to which we should go" in forcing the Government of the Philip-

[100] For an excellent statement of the basis for the provisions of the act and analysis of its terms see *House Reports No. 1821* to accompany H.R. 5856 (79th Cong., 2nd Sess.).

[101] *Public, No. 370* (79th Cong., 2nd Sess.); For a detailed discussion on these points see *House Report No. 1921* to accompany S. 1610 (79th Cong., 2nd Sess.).

Title VI of this Act provides that payment of claims for war damage in excess of $500 must await the conclusion of the executive agreement between the two countries provided for in the Trade Act.

pines to conform to them. But the Senator pointed out also that "time has become of the essence in this matter," and that "the best service which those who wish to be friendly to the Filipino people can render is to speedily enact this measure."[102]

While some of the provisions of the Philippine Trade Act would seem to be "unduly harsh" in view of the state of Philippine economy, on the whole the law will aid in bringing about stability in the Philippines. Generally, the Filipino people, in their abiding faith in the American people, read in the provisions of the Philippine Trade and Rehabilitation Acts of 1946 manifestations of good will. Commissioner Carlos P. Romulo even went further to say that these laws would mark the dawn of a new era in the Islands and enable the Filipino people "to enter into the unfolding day of opportunity and confidence."[103] How true this prophecy will be only time can tell.

Undoubtedly, the executive agreement[104] between the United States and the Philippines will be an internationally binding instrument. It contains within itself the conditions for its modification or its revocation in a specified manner in the event of a failure to carry out the conditions by either country. It has also a certain flexibility in that either country can denounce it on five years' notice. Either legislature might of course pass a statute amending the acts which make effective the agreement, but this they might do in respect to provisions of a treaty requiring legislation. Such action, however, would be a breach of the agreement and would entitle the other party to denounce it. However, the best guarantee that there shall be no such modification on the part of the United States is that Congress itself, after careful committee deliberations and hearings of all interested parties, believed that the United States should make the concessions, so that Congress in modifying the act would be going back on its own decision and not only on an agreement or treaty negotiated by the governments of the two countries. The Philippine Congress is most unlikely not to carry out its part of the agreement, since the advantages which it gains are fundamental to Philippine economy.

The United States Congress expressed its intent that no changes in the trade relations fixed in the act should be made under the statute permitting the President to make trade agreements with foreign gov-

[102] *Cong. Record*, 79th Cong., 2nd Sess., pp. 3611-3612.

[103] *Ibid.*, p. 2913.

[104] See Professor Edwin M. Burchard's observations on Treaties and Executive Agreements in the *American Political Science Review*, August 1946, Volume XL, No. 4, pp. 729-739.

ernments. Under section 509 of the Philippine Trade Act, the Government of the United States took occasion to give notice to third countries that the benefits granted by this law, and by the executive agreement "to the Philippines, Philippine articles or products, and Philippine citizens, shall not, by reason of any provision of any existing treaty or agreement with any third country, be extended to such country or its products, citizens, or subjects."[105]

It is imperative that the Philippines be given reasonable opportunity to survive the hard days of adjustment that immediately lie ahead. The maintenance of a sound public school system, good sanitation and public health, modern roads and transportation and communication systems, and the developing ability of self-government and civic responsibility among the Filipinos, must be provided for.[106] These are some of the bulwarks of democracy which no country which professes to be democratic can afford to neglect. Without the sustaining assurance of American aid during these trying days of adjustment, it would seem doubtful that a democratic way of life predicated on human liberty and the conservation of individual personality, can successfully thrive in those Islands.

Meanwhile, whether responsible leadership can arise in the Philippines from the ennervating influences of petty partisanship and be equal to the heavy demands of a badly shattered national economy, is the supreme question of the day. A tremendous responsibility is placed on the shoulders of President Manuel A. Roxas. It is the fervent hope and prayer of every Filipino that he will prove equal to the task. However, to translate his capacity into concrete action he will need the wholehearted support of his countrymen and the Philippine Congress. Will he receive their unfettered cooperation in putting on an even keel the listing Philippine ship of state? While it can be safely

[105] For copies of the notes released by the State Department received from some foreign Governments having commercial agreement with the United States embodying the principle of the most-favored-nation clause, and agreeing to waive their rights, during a number of years, to the advantages accorded by the United States to the Republic of the Philippines, see The Department of State *Bulletin*, May 5, 1946, Vol. XIV, No. 357, p. 773; June 16, 1946, Vol. XIV, No. 363, p. 1049; July 7, 1946, Vol. XV, No. 366, p. 38; July 28, 1946, Vol. XV, No. 369, p. 174; August 4, 1946, Vol. XV, No. 370, p. 235; September 1, 1946, Vol. XV, No. 374, p. 431; September 8, 1946, Vol. XV, No. 375, p. 463; September 29, 1946, Vol. XV, No. 378, p. 596.

[106] For an illuminating account on education, modern health, and public welfare program in the Philippines, see Joseph Ralston Hayden. *The Philippines a study in national development,* (New York, 1942), chapters XVIII-XXII, XXIV-XXVII, inclusive.

assumed that the American people will continue to be sympathetic to the general welfare of the Filipino people and remain interested in maintaining their independence, it behooves the Filipinos to help themselves individually and collectively as a nation. No self-respecting people will remain indifferent to the general welfare of their country. On the answers to these questions rests the hope of the survival of the Philippines as a truly independent country, and the flowering of a democratic way of life, predicated on the sanctity of human rights and human values, in that great part of the world loosely called the Far East.

6: Conclusion

SINCE THE INCEPTION of the American régime in the Philippines, American authorities in the Islands have systematically encouraged Philippine agricultural development, for, without it the general progress of the country would have been retarded. It was urged, therefore, that Philippine products should be admitted free of duty into the United States. But, failing this, the American authorities in the Philippines, joined by the sugar and tobacco interests of the Islands, have urged Congress to give Philippine products lower tariff rates than those charged on similar goods coming into the United States from foreign areas.

There were two reasons why from 1899 to 1909 a liberal treatment in the form of tariff reduction was not extended to Philippine sugar and tobacco entering the United States.

First, American sugar and tobacco interests were apprehensive that a liberal reduction of the tariff rates on these products might be followed by an intensive development of Philippine sugar and tobacco, which would develop serious competition with the American domestic industries. It was in recognition of this possibility that the American sugar and tobacco interests joined hands with those well-meaning Americans who opposed the establishment in the Islands of a plantation system to the end that a limitation on agricultural land grants was written in the Organic Act of July 1, 1902.

Second, the equality provision of Article IV of the Treaty of Paris providing for an equality of treatment between American and Spanish ships and merchandise in the Philippine Islands for a period of ten years caused apprehension on the part of American interests. As a consequence of this equality provision it was feared that the Islands might be transformed into a backdoor for competing products to enter into the United States on a favored basis as Philippine products.

Exporters of American goods felt that American products should be favored in Philippine markets.

The decision in the famous Insular Cases made it possible for Congress to satisfy these two interests in so far as the Philippine Islands was concerned. Thus, in the Act of March 8, 1902, Congress, by means of tariff classification, favored American products in the Philippine market while extending only a twenty-five percent reduction of the regular tariff rates to Philippine sugar and tobacco entering the United States. Although the Act of March 8, 1902, was amended twice in order to give more advantage to American products on similar foreign products entering the Philippines, the tariff rates on Philippine sugar and tobacco were continued.

When the equality provisions of the Treaty of Paris lapsed in 1909, a provision was inserted in the general tariff bill allowing the limited free entry into the United States of Philippine sugar and tobacco. However, should the annual quota given to these products be exceeded, this surplus when exported to the United States was to pay the regular tariff rates. Furthermore, manufactured products from the Islands were allowed free entry into the United States provided they did not contain foreign material to the value of more than twenty percent of the total value of the manufactured products. In consideration for this privilege, it was provided that American products be allowed unlimited free entry into the Philippines. Then too, the export taxes levied upon Philippine exports imported direct to the United States were removed.

In 1913 a new tariff act was enacted. Under this law, the quota limitations imposed upon Philippine products entering the United States were repealed, with the exception of the proviso regarding the twenty percent foreign-material content of manufactured products of the Islands imported into the United States. With the exception of this proviso therefore a complete free trade between the United States and the Philippines existed. This trade relation continued until May 1934 when the Jones-Costigan law was passed placing a quota on Philippine sugar that might be admitted into the United States duty free.

Previously, however, a Philippine independence act was passed by Congress. In this act the quota principle was revived. Philippine sugar, coconut oil, and cordage were given an annual quota limitation. However, the same act continued the unlimited free entry into the Philippines of American products.

In dealing with the Insular tariff Congress acted, in the main, in the interest of American producers while the American officials in the Philippines were insistent throughout on the interest of the Islands.

The position of the American-Philippine officials was illustrated by the Honorable William Howard Taft, who, as Governor of the Islands raised the claims of the Filipinos for a more liberal treatment, and who subsequently as Secretary of War and then as President, was instrumental in securing for the Filipinos the free entry into the United States of a fixed quota of the principal exports of the Philippines.

It is a notable fact that the American people as a whole was little interested in Philippine affairs. This was shown during the Congressional hearings on various Philippine bills which were presented.

It may be noted that as a result of the tariff advantage extended to Philippine products in the United States, agricultural production in the Philippines had been greatly helped.

A new phase in the relations of the two countries has come about since the independence of the Philippines. Congress, in the Philippine Trade and Rehabilitation Acts, has made provision to give the economy of the Islands time to adjust to its new status under independence and has secured to the United States important advantages in return. However, both acts stand in need of implementation before they can become generally effective. The coming into effect of the Trade Act hinges on the executive agreement between the United States and the Philippines. Similarly, the Rehabilitation Act needs implementation before it can become fully effective. Title VI of this act provides that payment of claims for war damage in excess of $500 must first await the conclusion of the executive agreement specifically provided for in the Trade Act.

Although these acts are of vital importance in the rehabilitation of Philippine economy, they are, at best, merely a start in the restoration of the economy of the Islands. It will take years before Philippine economy can be restored to its pre-war position.

Obviously, one of the greatest problems of the Government of the Republic of the Philippines, aside from the immediate necessity of preserving and maintaining peace and order, will be the winning of economic independence. The economy of the Islands must be geared to the realities of an independent life.

In the building up of a new and well-balanced national economy for the Philippines there must be required of the leaders of the country a high order of statesmanship. Meanwhile, Philippine and American statesmen have an obligation to deal with the problem of American-Philippine relations in such a way as to assure the continuance of good feeling between the two peoples, and the preservation of the Philippines as a real beach-head of democracy in the Far East.

Appendixes

APPENDIX I

Section V of the Payne-Aldrich Act of
August 5, 1909

(Quotation taken from *U. S. Statutes at Large vol.* 36 pp. 83-86)

That there shall be levied, collected, and paid upon all articles coming into the United States from the Philippine Islands the rates of duty which are required to be levied, collected and paid upon like articles imported from foreign countries: *Provided,* That, except as otherwise herein provided, all articles, the growth or product of or manufactured in the Philippine Islands or of the United States, or both, or which do not contain foreign materials to the value of more than twenty per centum of their total value, upon which no drawback of customs duties has been allowed therein, coming into the United States from the Philippine Islands shall hereafter be admitted free of duty, except rice, and except, in any fiscal year, sugar in excess of three hundred thousand gross tons, wrapper tobacco and filler tobacco when mixed or packed, with more than fifteen per centum of wrapper tobacco in excess of three hundred thousand pounds, filler tobacco in excess of one million pounds, and cigars in excess of one hundred and fifty million cigars, which quantities shall be ascertained by the Secretary of the Treasury under such rules and regulations as he shall prescribe; *And provided further,* That sugar, refined or unrefined, and tobacco, manufactured or unmanufactured, imported into the Philippine Islands from foreign countries, shall be dutiable at rates of import duty therein not less than the rates of import duty imposed upon sugar and tobacco in like form when imported into the United States: *And provided* further, That, under rules and regulations to be prescribed by the Secretary of the Treasury, preference in the right of free entry of sugar to be imported into the United States from the Philippine Islands, as provided herein, shall be given, first, to the producers of less than five hundred gross tons in any ficsal year, then to producers of the lowest output in excess of five hundred tons in any fiscal year: *Provided,* however, that in consideration of the exemptions aforesaid, all articles, the growth, product or manufacture of the United States, upon which no drawback of customs duties has been allowed therein, shall be admitted to the Philippine Islands from the United States free of duty: *And provided,* That the free admission, herein provided, of such articles, the growth, product or manufacture of the United States, into the Philippine Islands, or of the growth, product or manufacture, as hereinbefore defined, of the Philippine Islands into the United States, shall be conditioned upon the direct shipment thereof from the country of origin to the country of destination: *Provided,* that direct shipment shall include shipments in bond through foreign territory contiguous to the United States: *Provided,* however, that if such articles become unpacked while *en route* by accident, wreck, or other casualty, or so damaged as to necessitate their repacking, the same shall be admitted free of duty upon satisfactory proof that the unpacking occurred through accident or necessity and that the merchandise involved is the identical merchandise originally shipped from the United States or the Philippine Islands, as the case may be, and that its condition has not been changed except for such damage as may have been sustained: *And provided further*, that all articles, the growth, product, or manufacture, as hereinbefore defined, of the Philippine Islands, admitted into the ports of the United States free of duty under the provisions of this section and shipped as hereinbefore provided from said islands to the United States for use and consumption therein, shall be hereafter, exempt from the payment of any export duties imposed in the Philippine Islands: *And provided further*, that there shall be levied, collected, and paid, in the United States, upon articles, goods, wares, or merchandise coming into the United States from the Philippines, a tax equal to the internal-revenue tax imposed in the United States upon the like articles, goods, wares, or merchandise of domestic manufacture; such tax to be paid by internal-revenue stamp or stamps, to be provided by the Commissioner of Internal Revenue, and to be affixed in such manner and under such regulations as he, with the approval of the Secretary of the Treasury, shall prescribe; and such articles, goods, wares, or merchandise, shipped from said islands to the United States, shall be exempt from the payment of any tax imposed by the internal-revenue laws of the Philippine Islands: *And provided further*, that there shall be levied, collected, and paid in the Philippine Islands, upon articles, goods, wares, or merchandise going into the Philippine Islands from the United States, a tax equal to the internal-revenue tax imposed in the Philippine Islands upon the like articles, goods, wares, or merchandise of Philippine Islands manufacture; such tax to be paid by internal-revenue stamps or otherwise, as provided by the laws in the Philippine Islands, and such articles, goods, wares, or merchandise going into the Philippine Islands from the United States shall be exempt from the payment of any tax imposed by the internal-revenue laws of the United States: *And provided further*, that, in addition to the customs taxes imposed in the Philippine Islands, there shall be levied, collected, and paid therein upon articles, goods, wares, or merchandise, imported into the Philippine Islands from countries other than the United States, the internal-revenue tax imposed by the Philippine government on like articles manufactured and consumed in the Philippine Islands or shipped thereto, for consumption therein, from the United States: *And provided further*, that from and after the passage of this Act all internal-revenues collected in or for account of the Philippine Islands shall accrue intact to the general government thereof and be paid into the Insular Treasury, and shall only be allotted and paid out therefrom in accordance with future Acts of the Philippine Legislature, subject, however, to section seven of the Act of Congress approved July 1, 1902, entitled "An Act temporarily to provide for the administration of the affairs of the civil government in the Philippine Islands, and for other purposes": *And provided further*, that, until action by the Philippine Legislature, approved by Congress, internal revenues paid into the Insular treasury, as hereinbefore provided, shall be alloted and paid out by the Philippine Commission.

Section 4, paragraph C, of the Tariff Act of October 3, 1913

(Quotation taken from *U. S. Statutes at Large vol.* 38, Part I, pp. 192-193)

That there shall be levied, collected, and paid upon all articles coming into the United States from the Philippine Islands the rates of duty which are required to be levied, collected, and paid upon like articles imported from foreign countries: *Provided*, That all articles, the growth or product of or manufactured in the Philippine Islands or of the United States, or of both, or which do not contain foreign materials to the value of more than twenty per centum of their total value, upon which no drawback of customs duties has been allowed therein, coming into the United States from the Philippine Islands shall hereafter be admitted free of duty: *Provided, however*, That in consideration of the exemptions aforesaid, all articles, the growth, product, or manufacture of the United States, upon which no drawback of customs duties has been allowed therein, shall be admitted to the Philippine Islands from the United States free of duty: *And provided further*, That the free admission, herein provided, of such articles, the growth, product, or manufacture of the United States, into the Philippine Islands, or of the growth, product, or manufacture, as hereinbefore defined, of the Philippine Islands into the United States, shall be conditioned upon the direct shipment thereof, under a through bill of lading, from the country of origin to the country of destination: *Provided*, That direct shipment shall include shipments in bond through foreign territory contiguous to the United States: *Provided, however*, That if such articles become unpacked while *en route* by accident, wreck, or other casualty, or so damaged as to necessitate their repacking, the same shall be admitted free of duty upon satisfactory proof that the unpacking occurred through accident or necessity and that the merchandise involved is the identical merchandise originally shipped from the United States or the Philippine Islands, as the case may be, and that its condition has not been changed except for such damage as may have been sustained: *And provided*, That there shall be levied, collected, and paid, in the United States, upon articles, goods, wares, or merchandise coming into the United States from the Philippine Islands, a tax equal to the internal-revenue tax imposed in the United States upon the like articles, goods, wares, or merchandise of domestic manufacture; such tax to be paid by internal-revenue stamp or stamps to be provided by the Commissioner of Internal Revenue, and to be affixed in such manner and under such regulations as he, with the approval of the Secretary of the Treasury, shall prescribe; and such articles, goods, or merchandise, shipped from said islands to the United States, shall be exempt from the payment of any tax imposed by the internal-revenue laws of the Philippine Islands: *And provided further*, That there shall be levied, collected and paid in the Philippine Islands, upon articles, goods, wares, or merchandise going into the Philippine Islands from the United States, a tax equal to the internal-revenue tax imposed in the Philippine Islands upon the like articles, goods, wares, or merchandise of Philippine Islands manufacture; such tax to be paid by internal-revenue stamps or otherwise, as provided by the laws in the Philippine Islands; and such articles, goods, wares, or merchandise going into the Philippine Islands from the United States shall be exempt from the payment of any tax imposed by the internal-revenue laws of the United States: *And provided further*, That in addition to the customs taxes imposed in the Philippine Islands, there shall be levied, collected, and paid therein upon articles, goods, wares, or merchandise imported into the Philippine Islands from countries other than the United States, the internal-revenue tax imposed by the Philippine Government on like articles manufactured and consumed in the Philippine Islands or shipped thereto for consumption therein, from the United States: *And provided further*, That from and after the passage of this Act all internal revenues collected in or for account of the Philippine Islands shall accrue intact to the general government thereof and be paid into the insular treasury: *And provided further*, That section thirteen of "An Act to raise revenue for the Philippine Islands and for other purposes" approved August fifth, nineteen hundred and nine, is hereby repealed.

Section 2, Paragraph 9, and Sections 6 and 13 of the Tydings-McDuffie Act of March 24, 1934

(Quotation taken from *U. S. Statutes at Large, vol.* 48, Part I, pp. 457-464)

Sec. 2.—

(9) Acts affecting currency, coinage, imports, exports, and immigration shall not become law until approved by the President of the United States.

Sec. 6. After the date of the inauguration of the government of the Commonwealth of the Philippine Islands trade relations between the United States and the Philippine Islands shall be as now provided by law, subject to the following exceptions:

(a) There shall be levied, collected, and paid on all refined sugars in excess of fifty thousand long tons, and on unrefined sugars in excess of eight hundred thousand long tons, coming into the United States from the Philippine Islands in any calendar year, the same rates of duty which are required by the laws of the United States to be levied, collected, and paid upon like articles imported from foreign countries.

(b) There shall be levied, collected, and paid on all coconut oil coming into the United States from the Philippine Islands in any calendar year in excess of two hundred thousand long tons, the same rates of duty which are required by the laws of the United States to be levied, collected, and paid upon like articles imported from foreign countries.

(c) There shall be levied, collected, and paid on all yarn, twine, cord, cordage, rope and cable, tarred or untarred, wholly or in chief value of manila (abaca) or other hard fibers, coming into the United States from the Philippine Islands in any calendar year in excess of a collective total of three million pounds of all such articles hereinbefore enumerated, the same rates of duty which are required by the laws of the United States to be levied, collected, and paid upon like articles imported from foreign countries.

(d) In the event that in any year the limit in the case of any articles which may be exported to the United States free of duty shall be reached by the Philippine Islands, the amount or quantity of such articles produced or manufactured in the Philippine Islands thereafter that may be so exported to the United States free of duty shall be allocated, under export permits issued by the government of the Commonwealth of the Philippine Islands, to the producers or manufacturers of such articles proportionately on the basis of their exportation to the United States in the preceding year; except that in the case of unrefined sugar the amount thereof to be exported annually to the United States free of duty shall be allocated to the sugar-producing mills of the islands proportionately on the basis of their average annual production for the calendar years 1931, 1932, and 1933, and the amount of sugar from each mill which may be so exported shall be allocated in each year between the mill and the planters on the basis of the proportion of sugar to which the mill and the planters are respectively entitled. The government of the Philippine Islands is authorized to adopt the necessary laws and regulations for putting into effect the allocation hereinbefore provided.

(e) The government of the Commonwealth of the Philippine Islands shall impose and collect an export tax on all articles that may be exported to the United States from the Philippine Islands free of duty under the provisions of existing law as modified by the foregoing provisions of this section, including the articles enumerated in subdivisions (a), (b), and (c), within the limitations therein specified, as follows:

(1) During the sixth year after the inauguration of the new government the export tax shall be 5 per centum of the rates of duty which are required by the laws of the United States to be levied, collected, and paid on like articles imported from foreign countries;

(2) During the seventh year after the inauguration of the new government the export laws shall be 10 per centum of the rates of duty which are required by the laws of the United States to be levied, collected, and paid on like articles imported from foreign countries;

(3) During the eighth year after the inauguration of the new government the export tax shall be 15 per centum of the rates of duty which are required by the laws of the United States to be levied, collected, and paid on like articles imported from foreign countries;

(4) During the ninth year after the inauguration of the new government the export tax shall be 20 per centum of the rates of duty which are required by the laws of the United States to be levied, collected, and paid on like articles imported from foreign countries;

(5) After the expiration of the ninth year after the inauguration of the new government the export tax shall be 25 per centum of the rates of duty which are required by the laws of the United States to be levied, collected, and paid on like articles imported from foreign countries.

The government of the Commonwealth of the Philippine Islands shall place all funds received from such export taxes in a sinking fund, and such funds shall, in addition to other moneys available for that purpose, be applied solely to the payment of the principal and interest on the bonded indebtedness of the Philippine Islands, its Provinces, municipalities, and instrumentalities, until such indebtedness has been fully discharged.

When used in this section in a geographical sense, the term "United States" includes all Territories and possessions of the United States, except the Philippine Islands, the Virgin Islands, American Samoa, and the island of Guam.

Sec. 13. After the Philippine Islands have become a free and independent nation there shall be levied, collected, and paid upon all articles coming into the United States from the Philippine Islands the rates of duty which are required to be levied, collected, and paid upon like articles imported from other foreign countries: *Provided*, That at least one year prior to the date fixed in this Act for the independence of the Philippine Islands, there shall be held a conference of representatives of the Government of the United States and the government of the Commonwealth of the Philippine Islands, such representatives to be appointed by the President of the United States and the Chief Executive of the Commonwealth of the Philippine Islands, respectively, for the purpose of formulating recommendations as to future trade relations between the Government of the United States and the independent government of the Philippine Islands, the time, place, and manner of holding such conference to be determined by the President of the United States; but nothing in this proviso shall be construed to modify or affect in any way any provision of this Act relating to the procedure leading up to Philippine independence or the date upon which the Philippine Islands shall become independent.

APPENDIX II

TABLE No. 1.

Sugar Exports to All Countries

Years ended December 31	Sugar exported to all countries: Quantity (kilos)	Value (Pesos)	Average value per kilo	Per-cent of total ex-port	Sugar exported to the United States: Quantity (kilos)	Value (Pesos)	Per-cent of total value of sugar
1899	88,827,565	₱6,919,042	.8062	23	21,887,428	₱1,778,910	25.7
1900	65,190,951	4,794,288	.07354	10	2,153,477	186,944	3.9
1901	56,872,593	5,112,626	.08989	10	5,225,989	586,708	11.4
1902	98,596,473	6,692,300	.06787	12	5,120,133	400,000	5.9

Source: *Annual Report,* Insular Collector of Customs, 1927, Table No. 7, p. 76

TABLE No. 2.

Tobacco Exports to All Countries

Years ended December 31	Tobacco exports to all countries: Value (Pesos)	Percent of total exports	Tobacco exports to the United States: Value (Pesos)	Percent of total Value of
1899	₱3,862,506	13	₱ 6,810	.17
1900	4.522,464	10	11,338	.25
1901	5,263,882	11	984	.02
1902	3,925,248	7	52,544	1.33

Source: *Annual Report,* Insular Collector of Customs, 1927, p. 80

TABLE No. 3.

Copra Exports to All Countries

Years ended December 31	Total value of copra exported to all countries (value in pesos)	Value exported to the United States (value in pesos)	Percent of total value of copra
1902	₱5,403,450	₱18,114	0.3
1903	7,639,586	18,708	0.2
1904	3,962,244	12,850	0.3
1905	6,489,406	16,000	0.2

Source: *Annual Report,* Insular Collector of Customs, 1915, p. 18

TABLE No. 4.

Principal Imports of the Philippines and Countries of Origin for the Fiscal Years 1901 to 1908 Inclusive. Values Expressed in American Currency. Values in Cents Omitted. (Government Free Entries Excluded)

Articles and Country	1901	1902	1903	1904	1905	1906	1907	1908
Paper and manufacturers:								
All other countries	197,802	353,838	368,534	387,942	373,829	294,171	373,281	358,506
United States	77,192	280,192	134,701	102,864	141,232	115,912	135,473	167,928
Distilled spirits:								
All other countries	193,092	272,127	187,025	142,601	167,207	143,594	166,193	171,466
United States	218,767	238,131	120,656	84,977	102,499	55,931	52,774	68,760
Malt Liquors:								
All other countries	192,409	81,260	90,749	88,779	62,837	85,550	62,108	46,836
United States	855,326	466,257	397,382	221,632	215,895	139,932	79,730	43,756
Fish and fish products, including shell fish:								
All other countries	161,531	314,655	379,503	193,058	187,475	189,555	208,793	255,756
United States	8,416	56,278	52,983	38,942	56,325	73,361	86,121	138,904
Leather and manufactures of, including boots and shoes:								
All other countries	295,297	366,321	568,454	344,949	278,841	220,806	174,770	209,206
United States	38,086	83,610	118,332	147,586	214,326	240,414	304,364	462,756

Source: *Report*, Philippine Commission, 1908, Part II pp. 587-588

TABLE No. 4 *(Continued)*

Principal Imports of the Philippines and Countries of Origin for the Fiscal Years 1901 to 1908 Inclusive. Values Expressed in American Currency. Values in Cents Omitted. (Government Free Entries Excluded)

Articles and Country	1901	1902	1903	1904	1905	1906	1907	1908
Cotton goods:								
All other countries	$9,346,382	$6,798,091	$5,895,067	$4,642,688	$5,572,874	$6,363,533	$7,263,751	$7,325,915
United States	94,655	167,887	389,303	319,666	764,088	278,796	1,056,328	685,919
Rice:								
All other countries	5,490,958	6,578,481	10,061,323	11,548,814	7,456,738	4,375,500	3,662,493	5,861,256
United States	— —	— —	— —	— —	— —	— —	— —	— —
Iron and steel and manufactures:								
All other countries	1,573,991	1,656,222	1,436,771	1,591,776	1,591,776	1,498,736	1,680,656	1,362,594
United States	287,957	431,888	465,720	821,160	821,160	1,147,387	864,336	802,313
Flour:								
All other countries	145,006	43,298	41,659	9,852	113,604	337,958	518,903	537,335
United States	356,193	642,672	686,291	833,056	613,987	446,076	370,271	507,235
Illuminating oils:								
All other countries	428,601	284,327	326,981	238,916	349,385	86,086	238,748	186,567
United States	22,748	213,312	325,576	246,519	443,512	272,231	551,699	619,545
Opium:								
All other countries	619,338	819,625	721,551	770,596	850,381	440,464	513,241	143,670
United States	— —	— —	— —	— —	— —	— —	46	— —

TABLE No. 5.

Principal Exports of the Philippines, and Countries of Destination, for the Fiscal Years 1901 to 1908 Inclusive. Values Expressed in American Currency. Values in Cents Omitted.

Articles and country	1901	1902	1903	1904	1905	1906	1907	1908
Hemp:								
All other countries	12,050,243	8,579,857	9,387,263	11,163,369	9,191,726	8,278,543	9,758,217	9,627,808
United States	2,402,867	7,261,459	12,314,312	10,631,591	12,954,515	11,168,226	11,326,864	7,684,000
Sugar:								
All other countries	2,199,586	2,468,078	2,620,002	2,314,363	2,358,539	4,603,761	3,700,386	3,627,969
United States	93,472	293,354	1,335,826	354,144	2,618,487	260,104	234,074	2,036,697
Copra:								
All other countries	2,648,855	1,001,649	4,463,506	2,517,788	2,080,927	4,043,115	3,945,107	5,233,115
United States	4,450	7	9,173	9,231	14,425	— —	108,086	228,565
Tobacco and manufactures of:								
All other countries	2,212,701	2,492,852	1,835,628	2,011,430	1,989,218	2,358,887	3,102,911	2,692,376
United States	5,027	8,615	46,162	1,857	6,820	31,003	26,283	22,170

Source: *Report*, Philippine Commission, 1908, Part II pp. 587-588.

TABLE No. 6.

Relative Rank of Importing Countries

Importing countries	1902	1903	1904	1905	1906	1907	1908
United States	2	1	1	1	1	1	1
United Kingdom	1	2	2	2	2	2	2
Hongkong	3	3	3	3	3	3	4
China			6	4	6	5	6
France		4	4	5	4	4	3
Spain			8	6	5	6	5
British East Indies			5	7	7	7	7
Japan	4	5	7	8	8	10	11
Australia				9	10	9	9
Germany				10	9	8	8
Belgium							10

Note: Figures from 1902 to 1904 inclusive were taken from *Report*, Philippine Commission, 1904, Part III, p. 562; figures from 1905 to 1908 inclusive were taken also from *Ibid.*, 1908, Part II, p. 590.

TABLE No. 7.

Philippine Sugar Exports

Calendar years	Exported to the United States	Exported to other countries	Total
1895	59,615 tons	171,308 tons	230,923 tons
1896	98,624 "	131,289 "	229,913 "
1897	24,353 "	177,740 "	202,093 "
1898	27,997 "	149,698 "	177,695 "
1899	21,542 "	62,929 "	84,471 "
1900	2,120 "	62,041 "	64,161 "
1901	5,143 "	50,831 "	55,974 "
1902	5,039 "	91,999 "	97,038 "
1903	28,852 "	55,108 "	83,960 "
1904[a]	25,489 "	56,554 "	82,043 "

Note: Data for 1895 to 1899 compiled from official returns of the United States Agricultural Department; for 1899 to 1904 from official returns of the Insular Bureau.

[a] Ten months ending October 13, 1904.

TABLE No. 8.

Philippine Trade with the United States Compared with All Other Countries

	Years ended December 31	TRADE WITH THE UNITED STATES Percent of total imports	Percent of total exports	Percent of total trade
	1899	7	26	16
	1900	9	13	11
First Act of Congress	1901	12	18	15
	1902	12	40	25
	1903	11	40	25
	1904	17	40	28
	1905	19	44	32
	1906	17	36	27
End of Spanish equality;	1907	17	31	24
Payne-Aldrich Act	1908	17	32	25
	1909	21	42	32
	1910	40	42	41
	1911	40	44	42
Underwood-Simmons Act	1912	39	41	40
	1913	50	34	42
	1914	49	50	50
	1915	53	44	48
	1916	50	51	51
	1917	57	66	62
Jones Law	1918	60	66	63
	1919	64	50	57
	1920	62	70	66
	1921	64	57	61
	1922	60	67	63
	1923	57	70	65
	1924	56	72	65
	1925	58	73	66
	1926	60	73	67
	1927	62	75	69
	1928	62	75	69
	1929	63	76	70
	1930	64	79	72
	1931	63	80	72
	1932	65	87	77
Tydings-McDuffie Act	1933	65	86	75
	1934	65	83	75
	1935	64	80	72
	1936	61	79	71
	1937	58	80	71
Tydings-Kocialkowski Act	1938	68	77	72
	1939[1]	65	78	73
	1940[2]	74	75	75

Source: *Annual Report*, Insular Collector of Customs, 1941, p. 84.

Note: 1. From January to June 1939 only.
2. Fiscal year, July 1, 1939, to June 30, 1940.

TABLE No. 9.

Philippine Tobacco Exports.

Calendar years	Cigars, cigarettes cheroots, etc.		Leaf Tobacco				TOTAL	
			Philippine Exports		United States Imports			
	Philippine Exports	United States Imports	Quantity (Pounds)	Value	Quantity (Pounds)	Value	Philippine Exports	United States Imports
1899	$1,154,412	$2,340,124	14,050,310	$ 776,841	17,277,985	$11,789,539	$1,931,253	$14,129,663
1900	1,227,332	2,385,854	22,028,546	1,033,900	23,192,105	14,867,897	2,261,232	17,253,751
1901	1,883,456	2,589,903	17,391,595	784,485	28,017,550	16,190,526	2,667,941	18,780,429
1902	1,007,458	2,694,632	20,196,283	955,166	32,192,212	16,221,416	1,962,624	18,916,048
1903	992,616	3,142,051	19,249,094	954,259	32,997,923	17,272,682	1,946,875	20,414,733
1904	873,387[a]	3,945,677	16,443,430[a]	861,073[a]	30,602,306	16,658,223	1,734,460[a]	20,603,900

NOTE: Data as to Philippine exports compiled from official returns of the Bureau of Insular Affairs. Data as to United States imports compiled from official returns of the Department of Commerce and Labor. See also *Hearings* before the House Committee on Ways and Means, January 23-28, February 3, 1905, p. 148.

The apparent discrepancies between tables 5 and 9 could be ascribed to the fact that the former is for fiscal years beginning July 1 and ending on June 30 while the latter represents calendar years beginning January 1.

[a] Ten months ending October 31, 1904.

TABLE No. 10

Sugar Consumption in the United States

Calendar years	Total consumption	Domestic product	Deficit (importations)	Per capita consumption
1895	1,949,744 tons	377,306 tons	1,572,438 tons	63.4 pounds
1896	1,960,086 "	289,123 "	1,670,963 "	62.5 "
1897	2,070,978 "	355,371 "	1,715,607 "	64.8 "
1898	2,022,902 "	293,965 "	1,708,937 "	61.5 "
1899	2,078,068 "	233,426 "	1,844,642 "	62.5 "
1900	2,219,847 "	269,833 "	1,950,014 "	65.2 "
1901	2,372,316 "	815,335[a] "	1,556,981 "	68.7 "
1902	2,566,108 "	869,417[a] "	1,696,691 "	72.8 "
1903	2,549,643 "	1,010,877[a] "	1,538,766 "	71.1 "
1904	2,767,162 "	968,781[a] "	1,798,381 "	—— "

NOTE: Data compiled from official returns of the Department of Commerce and Labor and *Hearings* before the House Committee on Ways and Means, January 23-28, February 3, 1905, p. 142. [a] Includes Hawaiian and Puerto Rican sugar.

Bibliography

I. Primary Sources

Annual Report of the Bureau of Customs to the Secretary of Finance for the Fiscal Year Ended December 31, 1913 to 1941 Inclusive (Manila, Bureau of Printing).

Annual Report of the Governor-General of the Philippine Islands to the Secretary of War 1902 to 1934 Inclusive (Manila, Bureau of Printing).

Annual Report of the War Department for the Fiscal Year Ended June 30, 1899, 1900, 1901, 1904 (Washington: Government Printing Office).

Bulletin Number 14, 1898, of the United States Department of Agriculture, Section of Foreign Markets (Washington: Government Printing Office 1898).

Census of the Philippine Islands, 1903, 1918 (Manila, Bureau of Printing).

Congressional Record

57th Congress, 1st Session.
57th Congress, 2nd Session.
58th Congress, 3rd Session.
59th Congress, 1st Session.
60th Congress, 1st Session.
61st Congress, 1st Session.
63rd Congress, 1st Session.
63rd Congress, 2nd Session.
64th Congress, 1st Session.
70th Congress, 1st Session.
70th Congress, 2nd Session.
71st Congress, 1st Session.
71st Congress, 2nd Session.
72nd Congress, 1st Session.
72nd Congress, 2nd Session.
73rd Congress, 2nd Session.
74th Congress, 1st Session.
74th Congress, 2nd Session.
75th Congress, 1st Session.
76th Congress, 1st Session.
77th Congress, 1st Session.
78th Congress, 1st Session.
79th Congress, 1st Session.
79th Congress, 2nd Session.

Correspondence Relating to the War with Spain and Conditions Growing out of the Same, Including the Insurrection in the Philippine Islands, and the China Relief Expedition, between the Adjutant-General of the Army and Military Commanders, etc., from April 15, 1898, to *July* 30, 1902, in two volumes (Washington: Government Printing Office, 1902).

The Dingley Tariff, 1897, United States Treasury Department (Washington: Government Printing Office, 1897).

Hearings before the Senate Committee on the Philippines in relation to affairs in the Philippine Islands, in two parts, 1901-1902 (Washington: Government Printing Office, 1903).

Hearings before the Senate Committee on the Philippines on Senate bill (2259) providing for the extension of the American coastwise shipping laws to the Islands (58th Congress, 2nd Session).

Hearings before the Committee on Ways and Means of the House of Representatives on H. R. 17752 providing for the reduction of duties on Philippine products imported into the United States (58th Congress, 3rd Session).

Hearings before Secretary of War Taft and the Congressional Party which accompanied him to the Philippines held during the month of August 1905 on the question of Philippine tariff; the extension of the American coastwise shipping laws to the Islands; and the general economic conditions of the Archipelago (59th Congress, 1st Session).

Hearings before the Committee on Ways and Means of the House of Representatives on the reduction of duties on Philippine products imported into the United States—H. R. 3—(59th Congress, 1st Session).

Hearings before the Senate Committee on the Philippines on H. R. 3 (59th Congress, 1st Session).

Hearings before the Committee on Ways and Means of the House of Representatives on the Philippine tariff—H. R. 21449—(60th Congress, 1st Session).

Hearings before the Committee on Ways and Means of the House of Representatives on the Sugar and Tobacco schedules (E and F respectively) of the General Tariff, Volumes III and IV (60th Congress, 2nd Session).

Hearings before the Senate Committee on Finance on (H. R. 7456) the General Tariff bill, Volume V (67th Congress, 2nd Session).

Hearings before the Committee on Ways and Means of the House of Representatives on Tariff Readjustments, Volumes I, V, VI, X, XVI, (70th Congress, 2nd Session).

Hearings before the Senate Committee on Finance on (H. R. 2667) the General Tariff bill Volumes V, VI, VII, XVI, XVII (71st Congress, 1st Session).

Hearings before the Senate Committee on Territories and Insular Possessions on Philippine Independence. Parts I to VII inclusive (71st Congress, 2nd Session). (United States Government Printing Office, Washington, 1930.)

Hearings before the Committee on Insular Affairs of the House of Representatives on Philippine Independence (H. R. 7233), January 22, 23, 25, 26, 30 and February 1, 2, 6, 9, 10, 12, 1932 (United States Government Printing Office, Washington, 1932).

Hearings before the Senate Committee on Territories and Insular Possessions on Philippine Independence (S. 3377) February 11 and 13, 1932 (U. S. Government Printing Office, Washington, 1932).

Hearings before the Senate Committee on Territories and Insular Affairs on S. 1028 to amend the Act of March 24, 1934, held in Washington February 16 to March 15, 1939. (U. S. Government Printing Office, Washington, 1939).

Hearings before the Senate Committee on Territories and Insular Affairs on S. 1610.

Hearings before the Ways and Means Committee of the House of Representatives on the Trade Bills (H. R. 4185, H. R. 4676, H. R. 5185), to provide for future trade relations between the United States and the Philippine Islands, held in Washington, October 15-17, 19, November 14-15, 1945; February 15, and March 15, 1946 (U. S. Government Printing Office, Washington, 1946).

House Documents

No. 571, containing the petition of the Tobacco Worker's Guild of the Philippines urging the reduction of tariff duties on Philippine tobacco imported into the United States (58th Congress, 2nd Session).

No. 14, containing the Proposed Tariff Revision Law of 1909 for the Philippine Islands (61st Congress, 1st Session).

No. 524, containing a copy of the message of President Hoover vetoing the Hare-Hawes-Cutting bill (H. R. 7233) providing for Philippine independence and the copy of the bill (72nd Congress, 2nd Session).

No. 23, containing the General Tariff bill of 1929 (H. R. 2667) (7'st Congress, 1st Session).

H. R. Reports

No. 2907 to accompany H. R. 15702 providing for the reduction of tariff duties on Philippine products imported into the United States, ordered printed December 17, 1902 (57th Congress, 2nd Session).

No. 4600 to accompany H. R. 18965 to revise and amend the tariff laws of the Philippine Islands, ordered printed February 13, 1905 (58th Congress, 3rd Session).

No. 4867 to accompany H. R. 17752 to reduce the duties on Philippine products imported into the United States, ordered printed February 27, 1905 (58th Congress, 3rd Session).

No. 20 to accompany H. R. 3 to amend the Tariff Act of March 8, 1902, ordered printed December 20, 1905 (59th Congress, 1st Session).

No. 582 to accompany H. R. 13104 to revise and amend the tariff laws of the Philippine Islands, ordered printed January 25, 1906 (59th Congress, 1st Session).

No. 7 to accompany H. R. 9135 to revise and amend the tariff laws of the Philippine Islands, ordered printed May 10, 1909 (61st Congress, 1st Session).

No. 22, conference report, to accompany H. R. 9135, ordered printed July 31, 1909 (61st Congress, 1st Session).

No. 5 to accompany the general tariff bill, H. R. 3321, ordered printed April 22, 1913 (63rd Congress, 1st Session).

No. 86, conference report, to accompany H. R. 3321, ordered printed September 29, 1913 (63rd Congress, 1st Session).

No. 266 to accompany H. R. 11471 repealing the free-sugar provisions of the general tariff of 1913, ordered printed February 28, 1916 (64th Congress, 1st Session).

No. 499 to accompany Senate bill 381 declaring the purpose of the people of the United States as to the future political status of the Philippine Islands, etc., ordered printed April 6, 1916 (64th Congress, 1st Session).

No. 7 to accompany the general tariff bill, H. R. 2667, ordered printed May 9, 1929 (71st Congress, 1st Session).

No. 806 to accompany H. R. 7233 providing for the independence of the Philippine Islands, etc., ordered printed March 15, 1932 (72nd Congress, 1st Session).

No. 1811 conference report, to accompany H. R. 7233 ordered printed December 28, 1932 (72nd Congress, 2nd Session).

No. 968 to accompany H. R. 8573 providing for Philippine Independence and for other purposes, ordered printed March 13, 1934 (73rd Congress, 2nd Session).

No. 1058 to accompany H. R. 7096 to amend an act entitled "an act to provide for the complete independence of the Philippine Islands, etc." (76th Congress, 1st Session).

No. 1460 to accompany S. 1623 to suspend the export tax and the reduction of the quotas prescribed by section 6 of the act of March 24, 1934 (48 Stat. 456), as amended, etc. (77th Congress, 1st Session).

No. 1921 to accompany S. 1610 to provide for Philippine Rehabilitation, etc. (79th Congress, 2nd Session).

No. 1821 to accompany H. R. 5856 to provide for American Philippine Trade Relations, etc. (79th Congress, 2nd Session.)

Internal Revenue Code, chapter 21, section 2476.

Joint Preparatory Committee on Philippine Affairs, *Report* of May 20, 1938, Volume I.

Official Gazette of the Philippine Islands, etc., 1929-1935.

Papers Relating to the Foreign Relations of the United States, 1909, copy 2.

Proceedings of the Board of Officers to Revise the United States Customs Tariff and Regulations in the Philippine Islands, Convened at Manila, June 18, 1900 (Washington, Government Printing Office, 1900).

Report of the Military-Governor of the Philippine Islands on civil affairs to the Secretary of War, 1899 (Washington: Government Printing Office, 1900).

Report of the Philippine Commission, 1900-1915 (Manila, Bureau of Printing).

Report of the Schurman Commission to the President in 4 volumes (Washington: Government Printing Office, 1900).

Report of the Special Mission on investigation to the Philippines to the Secretary of War 1922 (Manila, Bureau of Printing, 1922).

Report of the Special Mission to the United States, 1938-1939, (Manila, Bureau of Printing 1939).

Report of the Technical Committee to the President of the Philippines, October, 1944, (Washington, 1944).

Root, Elihu, *The Military and Colonial Policy of the United States, Addresses and Reports* collected and edited by Robert Bacon and James Brown Scott (Cambridge, Harvard University Press, 1916).

Senate Documents

No. 62, Part I, 55th Congress, 3rd Session— containing the Treaty of Paris of December 10, 1898; the Protocols of the conferences at Paris; the Peace protocol of August 12, 1898, and correspondence; Correspondence between the Department of State and the Embassy of France at Washington, as representing the interests of Spain and other papers.

No. 25, 56th Congress, 1st Session—containing the Customs Tariff and Regulations for the Philippine Islands with the Tariff circulars modifying the same.

No. 134, 57th Congress, 1st Session—containing certain memoranda relating to the tariff between the United States and the Philippine Islands, printed January 21, 1902.

No. 171, 57th Congress, 1st Session—containing correspondence relating to the Philippine Customs Tariff, printed February 6, 1902.

No. 191, 58th Congress, 2nd Session—containing a copy of Governor Taft's address before the Union Reading College of Manila pointing out the advisability of tariff reduction on Philippine products imported into the United States.

No. 95, 59th Congress, 1st Session—containing the speech of Mr. Frye, President of the New England Tobacco Growers' Association delivered before the Association on January 10, 1906.

Nos. 180 and 217, 63rd Congress, 1st Session—containing the estimated revenue under the Underwood-Simmons Act.

Nos. 527 and 530, 64th Congress, 1st Session—Conference reports to accompany Senate bill 381.

No. 150, 71st Congress, 2nd Session—containing the memoranda of Secretary of War Hurley with that of the Chief of the Bureau of Insular Affairs relative to Philippine independence sent to Senator Bingham, chairman of the Senate Committee on Territories and Insular Possessions (United States Government Printing Office, Washington: 1930).

No. 57, 74th Congress, 1st Session—containing the report of a Congressional Committee sent to the Philippines pursuant to the request of the Philippine Legislature.

No. 101, 78th Congress, 1st Session—containing the message of the President dated October 6, 1943, recommending, among others, advancing the date of Philippine Independence and assuring for the Independent Philippines economic security wherever possible.

Senate Reports

No. 181, Parts I and II to accompany H. R. 5833 to raise revenue for the Insular government and for other purposes, ordered printed January 20, 1902 (57th Congress, 1st Session).

No. 2586 to accompany H. R. 15702 to revise and amend the tariff rates on Philippine products imported into the United States, ordered printed December 18, 1902 (57th Congress, 2nd Session).

No. 1178 to accompany H. R. 13104 to revise and amend the Philippine tariff laws, ordered printed February 20, 1906 (59th Congress, 1st Session).

No. 9 to accompany H. R. 9135 to revise and amend the tariff laws of the Philippines, ordered printed July 2, 1909 (61st Congress, 1st Session).

No. 80 to accompany the General Tariff bill H. R. 3321 to reduce tariff duties and to provide revenue for the Government, ordered printed July 18, 1913 (63rd Congress, 1st Session).

No. 18 to accompany Senate bill (381) to declare the purpose of the people of the United States as to the future political status of the Philippine Islands, ordered printed December 17, 1915 (64th Congress, 1st Session).

No. 37 to accompany the General Tariff bill H. R. 2667, ordered printed September 4, 1929 (71st Congress, 1st Session).

No. 781 Parts I and II to accompany Senate bill 3822 providing for the withdrawal of the sovereignty of the United States over the Philippine Islands, ordered printed May 29 (calendar day June 2), 1930 (71st Congress, 2nd Session).

No. 354 to accompany Senate bill 3377 providing for the independence of the Philippine Islands, ordered printed February 24 (calendar day, May 1) 1932, (72nd Congress, 1st Session).

No. 494 to accompany Senate bill 3055 providing for Philippine independence, ordered printed March 15 (calendar day March 19), 1934 (73rd Congress, 2nd Session).

No. 453 to accompany S. 2390 to amend an act entitled "an act to provide for the complete independence of the Philippine Islands, etc." (76th Congress, 1st Session).

No. 828 to accompany S. 1623 to suspend the export tax and the reduction of the quota prescribed by section 6 of the act of March 24, 1934 (48 Stat. 456), as amended, for a fixed period, etc. (77th Congress, 1st Session).

No. 755 to accompany S. 1610 to provide for Philippine rehabilitation (79th Congress, 1st Session).

No. 1145 to accompany H. R. 5856, to provide for American-Philippine Trade Relations, etc. (79th Congress, 2nd Session).

Statistical Bulletin Numbers 1-12 inclusive (1918-1929), devoted to the commercial and industrial development of the Philippine Islands, compiled from official returns and other sources, published by the Bureau of Commerce and Industry (Manila, Bureau of Printing).

Statistical Abstract of the United States (1913, 1936-1943) published by the Department of Commerce.

182 United States 1 (May 27, 1901).

183 United States 176 (December 21, 1901).

United States Statutes at Large

Army Appropriation Act for the year ending June 30, 1902 Vol. 31, chapter 803 (Act of March 2, 1901).

Public, No. 28, Vol. 32, Part I, Chapter 140 (Act of March 8, 1902).

Public, No. 235, Vol. 32, Part I, Chapter 1369 (Act of July 1, 1902).

Public, No. 114, Vol. 33, Part I, Chapter 1314 (Shipping Act of April 15, 1904).

Public, No. 141, Vol. 33, Part I, Chapter 1408 (Act of March 5, 1905).

Public, No. 27, Vol. 34, Part I, Chapter 509 (Act of February 26, 1906).

Public, No. 136, Vol. 34, Part I, Chapter 2071 (Shipping Act of April 30, 1906).

Public, No. 380, Vol. 34, Part I, Chapter 3912 (Act of June 30, 1906).

Public, No. 103, Vol. 35, Part I, Chapter 152 (Shipping Act of April 29, 1908).

Public, No. 5, Vol. 36, Part I, Chapter 6 (General Tariff Act of August 5, 1909).

Public, No. 7, Vol. 36, Part I, Chapter 8 (Philippine Tariff Act of August 5, 1909).

Public, No. 16, Vol. 38, Part I, Chapter 16 (General Tariff Act of October 3, 1913).

Public, No. 61, Vol. 39, Part I, Chapter 93 (Act of April 27, 1916).

Public, No. 240, Vol. 39, Part I, Chapter 416 (Act of August 29, 1916).

Public, No. 261, Vol. 41, Part I, Chapter 250 (Shipping Act of June 5, 1920).
Public, No. 213, Vol. 48, Chapter 263 (Jones-Costigan Sugar Act May 9, 1934).
Public, No. 311, (H. R. 7233), 72nd Congress, 2nd Session, (Hare-Hawes-Cutting Act, Jan. 17, 1933).
Public, No. 127, (H. R. 8573) 73rd Congress, 2nd Session, Part V, p. 5540. (Tydings-McDuffie Act, March 24, 1934).
Public, No. 137, (S. 2530) 74th Congress, 1st Session, Part IX, (Cordage Act of June 14, 1935).
Public, No. 414, (H. R. 7667) 75th Congress, 1st Session, Part VIII, (Sugar Act of 1937).
Public, No. 300, (H. R. 7096) 76th Congress, 1st Session, Part X, (Tydings-Kocialkowski Act, August 7, 1939).
Public, No. 367, (S. 1623) 77th Congress, 1st Session, Part IX, (Act of December 22, 1941).
Public, No. 370, (S. 1610) 79th Congress, 2nd Session, p. 4351, (Philippine Rehabilitation Act of 1946).
Public, No. 371, (H. R. 5856) 79th Congress, 2nd Session, p. 4429, (Philippine Trade Act of 1946).

United States Tariff Commission

Colonial Tariff Policies (Washington, Government Printing Office, 1922).
Comparison of Tariff Acts, a comparison by paragraphs of the dutiable schedules and the free list of the Tariff Act of 1922 with the corresponding provisions, respectively, of the Tariff Acts of 1909 and 1913 (Washington, Government Printing Office, 1922).
Comparison of Tariff Acts, a comparison by paragraphs of the dutiable schedules and the free list of the Tariff Act of 1930 with the corresponding provisions of the Tariff Act of 1922 (United States Government Printing Office, Washington, 1934).
United States-Philippine Tariff and Trade Relations Report No. 18, Second Series (Washington, Government Printing Office, 1931).

Magazines and Newspapers

The Century Magazine, August 1898, Vol. LVI. *New York Herald Tribune*, October 14, 16, 19, 1898.
Philippine Journal of Commerce published monthly by the Department of Agriculture and Commerce of the Philippine Islands.
Political Science Quarterly, Vols. XVI and XVII. *The Tribune*, Manila, July 30, 1933.

II. Secondary Sources

Beard, Charles A., *Contemporary American History* (Macmillan & Co., New York, 1921).
Chamberlain, F. C., *Our Philippine Problem* (Boston, 1913).
Conant, Charles A., *The United States in the Orient, the Nature of the Economic Problem* (Houghton, Mifflin & Co., Boston and New York, 1900).

Democratic Party, *Campaign Textbook,* 1900, 1904, 1908, 1912.

Elliott, Charles B., *The Philippines to the End of the Military Régime,* America Overseas (Bobbs-Merrill Co., Indianapolis, 1916).

The Philippines to the End of the Commission Government, a Study in Tropical Democracy (Bobbs-Merrill Co., Indianapolis, 1916).

Ellis, Lippert S., *The Tariff on Sugar* (Freeport, Illinois, 1933).

Forbes, William Cameron, *The Philippine Islands* in two volumes (Houghton, Mifflin & Co., Boston and New York, 1928).

Hayden, Joseph Ralston, *The Philippines A Study in National Development* (The Macmillan Company, New York, 1942).

Kirk, Grayson L., *Philippine Independence, Motives, Problems and Prospects* (Farrar & Rinehart Inc., New York, 1936).

Latané, John H. *America as a World Power* (Harper Brothers, New York & London, 1907).

Le Roy, James A., *The American in the Philippines, a History of the Conquest and First Years of Occupation with an Introductory Account of the Spanish Rule,* in two volumes (Houghton, Mifflin & Co., Boston and New York, 1914).

Malcolm, George A., *The Government of the Philippine Islands, Its Development and Fundamentals* (The Lawyers' Cooperative Publishing Co., Rochester, New York, 1916).

McClure, Wallace, *A New American Commercial Policy as Evidenced by Section 317 of the Tariff Act of 1922* (Studies in History, Economics and Public Law, Columbia University, 1924).

Morse, H. B., and MacNair, N. F., *Far Eastern International Relations* (Riverside Press, Cambridge, Massachusetts, 1931).

Olcott, Charles S., *Life of William McKinley,* in two volumes (Houghton, Mifflin & Co., Boston and New York, 1916).

Osias, C., and Baradi, M., *The Philippine Charter of Liberty* (French Printing Co., Baltimore, 1933).

Republican Party, *Campaign Textbook,* 1900, 1904, 1908, 1928. *Official Proceedings of the Twelfth Republican Convention held in the City of Philadelphia, June* 19-21, 1900.

Reyes, Jose S., *Legislative History of America's Economic Policy Toward the Philippine Islands* (Studies in History, Economics and Public Law, Columbia University, 1923).

Taft, Mrs. William H., *Recollections of Full Years* (Dodd, Mead & Co., New York, 1914).

Taussig, Frank W., *The Tariff History of the United States,* 8th edition (G. P. Putnam's Sons, New York and London, 1931).

Some Aspects of the Tariff Question, second edition (Harvard University Press, 1915).

Tugwell, Rexford G., *The Battle for Democracy* (Columbia University Press, New York, 1935).

Van Metre, Thurman W., *Economic History of the United States* (New York, 1931).

Wallace, Henry A., *New Frontiers* (New York 1934).

Wallace, Henry C., *Our Debt and Duty to the Farmer* (The Century Co., 1925).
Willis, H. Parker, *Our Philippine Problem* (New York, 1905).

Magazines, Newspapers and Pamphlets

Facts About Sugar, July 1927, Vol. XXII, Part II.
Recommendations Regarding the Future of the Philippines, by the Committee on the Philippines sponsored by the Foreign Policy Association and the World Peace Foundation, Foreign Policy Committee Reports No. 2, January, 1934.
Foreign Policy Association, *Foreign Policy Reports,* October 1, 1945.
New York Trust Co., *Index,* October 1935 Vol. XV, No. 16.
Lowry, Frank C., *Our High Tariff on Sugar and Its Affects,* a pamphlet.
New York Journal of Commerce, June 3, 1927, Vol. 135, Part I.
The New York Times, August 18, 1935, Sec. 3; May 1, 1946, p. 9.
The Philippine Research Bureau in Cooperation with The Royal Institute of International Affairs, *The Philippine Islands and the United States,* 1935, a pamphlet.
San Francisco Chamber of Commerce, *Comments on the Political and Economic Status of the Philippines,* 1930, a pamphlet.

Index

Bei Fragen zur Produktsicherheit wenden Sie sich bitte an:
If you have any questions regarding product safety,
please contact:

Walter de Gruyter GmbH
Genthiner Straße 13
10785 Berlin
productsafety@degruyterbrill.com